*How Managers
Make Things
        Happen*
Second Edition

HOW MANAGERS MAKE THINGS HAPPEN
Second Edition

George S. Odiorne

Prentice-Hall, Inc.
Englewood Cliffs, New Jersey

Prentice-Hall, Inc., *London*
Prentice-Hall of Australia, Pty. Ltd., *Sydney*
Prentice-Hall of Canada, Ltd., *Toronto*
Prentice-Hall of India Private Ltd., *New Delhi*
Prentice-Hall of Japan, Inc., *Tokyo*
Prentice-Hall of Southeast Asia, Pte. Ltd., *Singapore*
Whitehall Books, Ltd., Wellington, *New Zealand*

©1987 by

PRENTICE-HALL, INC.

All rights reserved. No part of this
book may be reproduced in any form or
by any means, without permission in
writing from the publisher.

10 9 8 7 6 5

Library of Congress Cataloging in Publication Data

Odiorne, George S.
 How managers make things happen.

 Includes index.
 1. Industrial management.   I. Title.
 HD31.O35 1982   658   81-12142
                              AACR2

ISBN 0-13-400557-0 {PBK}

Printed in the United States of America

A Word from the Author

A long-dead German General once issued a warning to his aides about picking people for key jobs in a military campaign. "Be careful," he warned, "about getting too many people who are stupid and energetic." "Such people," he advised, "will work very hard at making mistakes, and will cost you the war." Today we would hardly categorize people that way, but we still produce similar effects. We pick people with high motivation, then don't let them know in what direction the organization is headed. They accordingly don't know what is expected of them, can't tell how well they are doing while they are working, and never get rewarded for the right things.

All of which has much to do with people who make things happen. There are plenty of people who work very hard but never seem to get anywhere, who wonder why their diligence and hard work never seem to pay off.

The purpose of this book is to lay out, in readable and clear form, how you can become one of those people who make things happen. The basic ideas are simple to explain, but hard to do. They are hard to accomplish because the world is getting more overwhelmed by influences and people who spend their time preventing things from happening. Red tape, bureaucracy, and the staggering complexity of things all make it easier to follow the present ways than to change them. The change resisters of this world seem to be in charge, and the minority of people who can make a mark seem to be diminishing. In the late seventies, in fact, there was a chorus of pop sociology which informed the world that there was just no way that a lone person, stubborn, self-impelled and armed with some kind of special vision, could turn the world around. Team building, collaboration, and pulse-taking were the skills. Many veteran congressmen were said to have finally decided not to run because they could make no mark. All that was available to them, they declared, was to keep polling their constituents and voting the majority's will. In business, in nonprofit organizations, in universities, the pressure upon the single person, who knew the obstacles but chased a faint hope, seemed to be overwhelming to some. But there persisted a small group of people who took a sole idea and made it happen. Howard Jarvis, over seventy and laughed at by the entire political establishment, was able to generate a movement to curb the pervasive octopus of government. In areas of high technology, individual go-getters started new businesses which became sizeable corporate moneymakers, hiring thousands of workers and making their benefactors rich. From time to time, some special type of leader with a more compelling style of doing things took over a sick or dying firm and turned it around, making it prosperous once more.

While such apparent miracles didn't happen every day, they happened often enough to lead me to believe that it can be done by people who have the will and the skills to *make* it happen. At a more personal level, people take their lives, which have been messed up by individual errors, foolish mistakes, and catering to their own weaknesses, and shape themselves up into something more worthwhile. The original edition of this book was published by Prentice-Hall in 1961, and has been reprinted twenty times in the first edition, had seven more printings in paperback, and in dozens of foreign languages. Much of that original book has been outdated in examples, in research findings and in the size and complexity of the world in which the doer makes things happen. But the basic ideas that worked then, work now. The organization of this book is three steps: (1) You have to make up your mind that you do count for something, that the individual is not powerless and that you can, indeed, make things happen where you are. (2) You can't do this by yourself; you have to get others to act in your direction because they want to. (3) This means that you constantly work at building up some personal skills, applying the special skills of action to getting what others who don't get results seem to miss.

Many thanks are due to hundreds of thousands of managers who have been trained in this approach to managing, who sent me letters, or who talked to me at conferences, documenting how action-getting, compelling styles can work—and how they can fall on their faces. There are plenty of new ideas in this edition. There are more examples of successful firms, of new ways to live in the world of change resisters; there is a new look at growth for its own sake as a goal, at devising your goals into a two-part process, strategic and operational; ten new rules for finding areas for improvement, and dozens of others.

As you read, make notes of how you will apply this idea or that one to some actual problems which are stopping you from getting where you want to go. If you do, this book could actually change your behavior and help you join that small group of managers who make things happen.

George S. Odiorne
Amherst, Mass.

CONTENTS

A WORD FROM THE AUTHOR 5

Part I: GOOD MANAGERS MAKE THINGS HAPPEN

    Chapter 1: How Managers Make Things Happen 17

        Six reasons people become drifters instead of deciders, 18. The terrible effects of the activity trap on our lives, 20. The essence of making things happen, 22.

    Chapter 2: Management Means Deciding,
                Not Drifting 27

        Management is not a passive art, 28. The forces of inertia, 31. Profit requires action, 33. Making growth a company goal, 35. The manager and the world outside of business, 36.

    Chapter 3: Five Tests of Initiative 39

        Inner drive, 41. Pick the important things, 42. Tough-Mindedness, 43. Instilling a desire to excel, 46. Initiating intelligent action, 47.

Chapter 4: The Status Quo—It's Not Good Enough 51

The organization at rest is dying, 53. Ten rules for identifying business stagnation, 54. Why change is necessary, 57. The dynamics of management, 58. Why innovation gets top priority, 61. How innovation and control are related, 62. The dynamic basis for business action, 65.

Chapter 5: How to Identify What Needs Improvement .. 67

Rules for identifying areas for improvement, 68.

Chapter 6: Whipping Obstacles 77

Qualities of obstacle busters, 78. Various ways managers adjust to obstacles, 81. Good versus bad ways of obstacle licking, 84. Ends versus means in a free society, 88.

Chapter 7: The Information Revolution: How to Make a Decision 93

Decisions on familiar ground, 94. Making the momentous decisions, 96. Don't look back, 99. Why managers fear big decisions, 101. When to listen to others, 102. When to change a decision, 104.

PART II: GETTING OTHERS TO ACT

Chapter 8: Rigid Managers—New Ways of Making Them More Flexible 109

The rigid manufacturing boss, 111. The rigid engineer, 111. The rigid salesman, 112. The rigid cost accountant, 112. The rigid staff type, 113. Corrective action, 113. Goals can unfreeze behavior, 116.

Chapter 9: Using Behavior Modification to Change Poor Work Habits to Good Ones 117

Watch the work pattern, 118. Replace a bad habit with a good one, 119. Start the new employee right, 120. Show a reason for better habits, 120. Try the job yourself, 121. Set a good example, 122. Use team building, 122. Get participation, 123. Behavior modification is the key, 123.

Chapter 10: Getting and Using the Ideas of Others 125

How participative management works, 127. Learn to listen, 130. Some devices for springing others' ideas into action, 132. How democratic leadership works, 135.

Chapter 11: Using Competition to Spur the Organization 139

The basis of healthy competition, 141. Why people compete, 143. Using recognition as an action-getter, 144. Avoiding unhealthy competition, 145. Instilling the desire to win, 147.

Chapter 12: Coaching a Winning Management Team ... 151

Be systematic in coaching teams, 152. Teach basics first, 153. Condition the group, 153. Show interest, 153. Make changes carefully, 153. Picking and training good players, 154. Ten rules for good coaching, 156. Getting subordinate coaches to coach, 161.

Chapter 13: How to Use a Personal Staff ... 163

Your secretary can double your efficiency, 168. Train your administrative assistant to your work habits, 169. What assistants can do (and can't do), 171. Effective use of executive time, 174.

Chapter 14: Managing Cliques in the Organizations ... 177

Recognize that cliques exist, 179. Train managers in team building, 179. Catalog clique segments, 180. Study clique operating techniques, 181. Working through informal leaders, 182. Planning facilities, 184.

Chapter 15: The New Look in Effective Committees ... 185

When individual action is best, 187. Who should be on a committee, 189. Keeping committees under control, 191.

Contents

**Chapter 16: Harnessing Aggressiveness
in Management** 197

> The desire for mastery, 198. Three cures of excessive desire for mastery, 200. Desire for a good reputation, 201. What to do when desire for reputation leads to excess vanity, 203. The desire for wealth, 204. The cure for too much desire for worldly success, 206.

PART III: PERSONAL TECHNIQUES FOR ACTION-GETTING MANAGEMENT

Chapter 17: How to be a Lucky Executive 211

> Keeping abreast of latest trends, 213. Predicting the hot item of the future, 216. Planning for the unexpected, 217. Helping your windfall, 219. Moral courage and luckiness in leadership, 221.

Chapter 18: How to Keep and Use a Secret 223

> Handling the enjoined secret, 224. Being judicious with information, 226. When to give in order to get, 229. The hardest secret to keep, 231. Small talk, 232. Secrets versus good communication, 234. Integrity and secrecy in leadership, 235.

**Chapter 20: How to Pick a Fight and
Win in Business** 237

PART IV: CHECK AND CORRECT AS YOU ACT—THE IMPORTANCE OF REVIEW

Chapter 20: How to Conduct a Personal Inspection ... 245

> Watching for the important things on a visit, 247. Showmanship in personal visits, 250. The ethics of making inspections, 251. How to detect coverups during inspections, 253. The case for the leader being seen, 256.

Chapter 21: See It Big—Keep It Simple 259

> How to sift and screen information and opinion, 261. When over-simplification becomes falsehood, 261. Assessing detail against the overview, 262. On the importance of breadth of viewpoint, 263. Relating the organization to society, 264.

Chapter 22: The Gentle Art of Chewing Out a Subordinate 267

> A code for management discipline, 268. When to reprimand, 272. The seven deadly sins of reprimanding, 274. Reprimanding without losing the target's regard, 275. Discipline without loss of dignity to the subordinate, 278. The decline of the chewing-out, 279.

Index 281

Part I

GOOD MANAGERS MAKE THINGS HAPPEN

> "Suddenly Hopkins whirled and faced him. 'Somebody has to do the big jobs!' *he said passionately. 'This world was built by men like me! To really do a job you have to live it, body and soul! You people who just give half your mind to your work are riding on our backs.'*
> *'I know it,'* Tom said."
>
> SLOAN WILSON, *The Man in the Gray Flannel Suit*

1

HOW MANAGERS MAKE THINGS HAPPEN

> *"A system which has no goal or purpose transcending it makes man its appendix."*
>
> ERICH FROMM

"My life is pretty routine. I get up in the morning and get ready. I go to work and plug away at the same routines, go home and do much of the same things I did last week." This statement, which could be traced to millions of people, was actually said to me by a middle manager in a large firm. It could just as easily have been said by a secretary, an engineer, or a teacher. It is, sadly enough, all too typical of the average person who works, including many managers.

The world seems to be peopled more by drifters than deciders, by people who watch what goes on and go along, than by those who compel things to happen. Yet, they would admit that they admire the small group of people who seem to make things happen. They read about enterprising people with awe, and secretly envy those who start a business and become rich, or run for office and get elected. They stand in awe, as well, of the apparent lucky few who seem to have an impact on life, and master their world for some period of time. They often don't consider that they, too, could join that group of people who decide rather than drift. Even though a desire for mastery is normal in humans, few attain it; and, in the eighties, it seems that more and more people are feeling powerless in the face of a complex world full of impersonal forces which surround us.

This book aims at helping you achieve that sense of mastery, at least more of it than you feel now. It's a heady and exhilarating sensation, and worth trying for. Even if you can't achieve it fully, it's worth working hard to attain.

Six reasons people become drifters instead of deciders:

There are six ways people fall into the drifting pattern of living. Let's look at how it happens to most of us:

1. **We fall into the activity trap.** This is an insidious trap which catches normal people. They start out aiming for something great, a noble goal, an exciting destination; but in an astonishingly short time, become so enmeshed in activity that they lose sight of the reason for the activity. The activity thus becomes an end in itself. This is the *Activity Trap*. The means has become the end. The goal is lost in a flurry of process. Soon the victims of the trap are looking back and wondering where their time and their lives went.

2. **We become creatures of habit.** It's impossible to escape the activity trap completely. Even the most attractive goal calls for doing something, and we get so busy doing things, a temporary lapse takes control and we forget why we are doing it. Habitual behavior becomes more important than the goal. As a temporary lapse, no harm is done. We snap back to our purposes. For many, however, what started as a temporary lapse becomes a habit. Many of the most important, life-saving, pleasurable things we do become habitual. William James called habit the "flywheel of civilization." That's true, for there are so many things we do habitually, which, if done consciously, would stop us in our tracks. The buttons we button daily, tying our shoes, and making an omelet, all get done without a moment of conscious thought, after awhile. Thus, habit saves us time and energy. Then the habit takes over and keeps us doing things we should have ceased doing or should have done differently. It owns us and we become an appendix to the system.

3. **Activity, when it persists, becomes procedure.** People working together need some predictability in the actions of others. They solve this need by devising procedures. John Gardner declares that "the last act of a dying civilization will be somebody writing a procedure." Procedures are standard ways of doing things, of following set patterns of behavior. This is an advanced form of the activity trap. Even if the procedure is no longer productive, we stick to it. We no longer think about goals and the reasons for the procedure. In many organizations, the procedures become counterproductive, and even harmful. Regardless, we press on, follow the procedure, and enforce it on others when they slip away from following it. "There's no reason for it, it's just procedure" describes how endless numbers of people go about their jobs, their studies, their lives.

4. **The activity trap can become a profession.** When people engage in complex clusters of activity, they need to study how to do it at great length. They attend colleges and universities, get degrees in engineering, accounting, data processing, or teaching second grade. Having studied these activities for many years, being certified professionals, they then cling tightly to the professional way of doing things, long after that way is no longer productive. An engineering department of my acquaintance has one wall covered with certificates showing that every member of the staff holds a "Professional Engineer" certificate from the state in which they operate. The question, "Is the reason for the certificates because you can't tell the people are professional by what they produce?" occurred to me. Never mind that I didn't actually ask that question of the chief engineer. He was proud of the certificates and degrees held by the staff, and any dips and rises in output might well be overlooked in his pride. The professionalism of many experts is the only reason they can imagine for not changing their behavior in necessary new directions.

5. **The activity trap eventually becomes tradition.** Proud professionals occasionally look back to see how they have been engaging in the specifics of their profession, and proudly announce that "doing thus thusly is a tradition around here." Many firms, colleges, and institutions spend a great deal of their time and energy preserving a past which has been labelled traditional. Tradition is a valuable social force, by which we change our

behavior to fit a common activity of the past, and which we use as a guideline to try to force others to stick to that activity. History buffs who buy fancy colonial dress uniforms and march around like colonial armies are solemn respecters of tradition. So are people who tell subordinates in their company "Flour milling is an ancient and honorable profession," thereby resisting the needed changes, and losing factories and divisions which could make them productive.

6. **Finally, activity becomes a religion,** and people who insist upon doing wholly new things or making changes in existing patterns are heretics who must be punished. "Do it my way" becomes more important than "Produce a good result." Most wars and political battles are rooted in traditions and quasi-religious beliefs, which keep us stuck in a rut.

THE TERRIBLE EFFECTS OF THE ACTIVITY TRAP ON OUR LIVES

If all this were nothing more than an interesting and perhaps amusing observation of human foibles, it would be worthy of only momentary attention. But the effects of the activity trap on our lives on this planet are serious and often damaging. While there are certainly benefits from activity—we couldn't live without it—there are also high costs to human life, social structure, and business success, from being obsessed with activity alone—without results.

What are some of these damaging effects?

• The activity trap turns us into performance pygmies. When we become obsessed with activity for its own sake, we occupy our time with things that have little or no yield. In the process, we are taking the place of exciting, worthy, challenging or noble things which could be occupying us. The time spent—frittered away—in some triviality could have been used designing a new organization, inventing a life-saving potion, or beating out a competitor to a new market. It takes no longer to do the right things than the wrong, the useful rather than the damaging.

• When we get caught in the activity trap, we tend to fall out of phase with what the organization and our boss expects. Research shows that activity-centered employees are often not doing many things the boss fervently wishes would be done. Further, he or she is, at the same time, doing some things the boss wishes would be forgotten and stopped.

- The boss can't possibly give big raises, promotions, and higher responsibility to people who are enmeshed in the activity trap. They aren't being responsive to the dynamic needs of the firm, won't change when times change, and won't meet new needs. They are too busy meeting old needs that no longer exist. In one corporate giant, they found that an entire generation of middle managers was spending its time resisting new affirmative action laws, and grumbling about tougher safety standards, instead of tackling the problems brought about by the new laws. Granted that some of the laws were not all that useful. Nonetheless, the company was committed to obeying them. Yet, their managers persisted in hanging onto the attitudes of the 1950s, when the calendar read 1980s. It took some early retirements to solve the problem, and a lot of good-intentioned people were put out to pasture because they couldn't get out of the activity trap.
- The organization suffers when too many of its people are busily engaged in activity for its own sake, with no concern for goals, aims and purposes. One of my research projects, over the years, has shown that the average manager and subordinate, left to their own devices, focus upon activity for its own sake, and managers will fail to agree with the subordinates on the subordinate's job content at a level of thirty percent. Imagine the effect on company efficiency! Thirty percent of the things people are doing consist of activity that isn't related to what the boss wants done, cares about, or would like to see. Small wonder people caught in the activity trap cost money. Thirty cents out of every wage and salary dollar is wasted in activity which has no yield or low yield.
- People's capacity shrinks when they get trapped in fruitless activity, especially when they don't realize its fruitlessness, or perhaps how damaging it can be to the organization. The quality control manager acts as if the entire organization were put together so that he could shut it down. The production manager produces high volume without concern for quality, effect on the environment, or cost. The controller keeps books that nobody reads, but they are very professional. The sales manager presses for sales volume from which no profit could possibly result. These are but a few of the effects of the activity trap. People soon become identified as shelf-sitters. "Old Joe doesn't have the potential for promotion. After all, he is all wrapped up in his speciality." So goes the performance appraisal of old Joe, and it's true only because Joe is so enmeshed in activity, he can't see the reasons for the activity.

• When times change and we don't, we become misfits. The activity trap bids us not to change, and makes us misfits in our work.

What's the antidote to this terrible state of affairs?

THE ESSENCE OF MAKING THINGS HAPPEN

The job of management can pretty completely be enclosed in a *management cycle.* That's illustrated in the following diagram.

1. You start with *a goal and a plan for getting there.*
2. You activate things, *take action,* move things along.
3. You review and,
4. Feedback the results, either in a short term feedback to control things, or you change future plans in the long run.

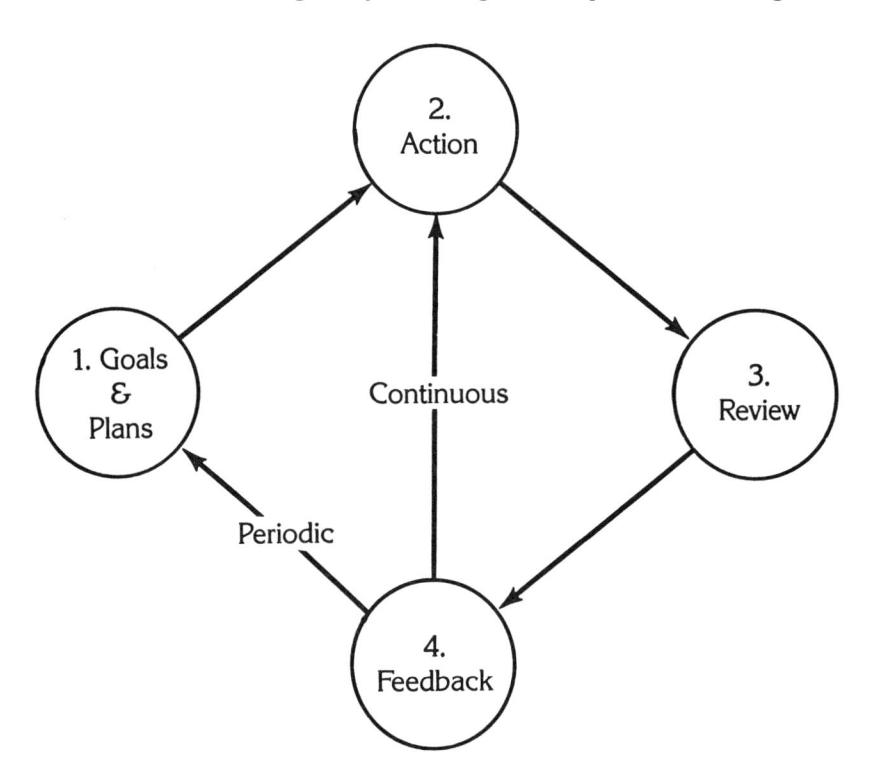

```
                    2.
                  Action
                   ↑  ↘
                 ↗      ↘
       1. Goals         3.
          &     Continuous  Review
        Plans            ↙
           ↖           ↙
             Periodic
                  4.
              Feedback
```

Let's look at each of these elements in a little more detail, for they explain the basic idea of this book.

1. **Goals and plans** are the first stage of the management cycle. This book isn't about goals and plans especially. Rather, it deals with the middle stage of the cycle: taking action. There are many books on goal-setting, plus a rash of them on planning and control.

The whole idea of the very popular system known as Management by Objectives is that you should set goals and review against them. This is all very true and unexceptionable. If you don't know where you are going, any road will get you there. If you aim for nothing, that's probably what you'll hit. Furthermore, you should have both strategic (long-run) and operational (short-run) goals and plans.

But goals alone, without action, are pointless and academic.

2. **Taking action toward the goals.** The great omission in many elegant managerial systems is the idea of making things happen. You can't be satisfied with the status quo. You need to keep your eye on the goals while you work, find deviations and note what needs improvement to get you back on track. When an obstacle occurs, you need to exercise special obstacle-busting skills. All of this means that you must be a self-starter and exercise maximum initiative in overcoming your deviations. There are five tests of initiatives proposed which you can test yourself against to improve your own self-starting talents.

It's not enough, however, that in taking action you should be a one-person gang. It's the essence of management as Larry Appley, long-time president of American Management Association, said: that "managers get results through other people." You must get others to act, as well as doing things yourself. Furthermore, you need to obtain and use their ideas as well as your own. If they are rigid, you need to break them out of their rigidities and their activity traps as they appear. This means changing bad work habits to good ones, it means dealing with the little clusters of people who form cliques that prevent you from getting to the goal; all of which makes you a coach of other people, both as individuals and as teams. As you rise in rank and responsibility, you may also have a small group of personal assistants and a staff (secretaries, assistants and the like) that can double your action-getting competence if you use them well.

It's a good idea to spur action in the organization through using committees creatively and constructively, and by getting a sense of healthy and not destructive competition going in the organization. There will be times when you must take a tough line and chew out a subordinate; and furthermore, do it in such a way that you won't tear the organization apart, but rather will strengthen its performance. This means making the organization aggressive in tackling its objectives, without being aggressive in ways that make individuals tear each other to shreds. The ideal is to have an organization which is aggressive toward competitors, markets and problems, but not toward other departments, groups or divisions in the same firm.

There are some personal techniques for action-getting management as well. You need to learn how much luck counts and how to make your own breaks through preparation and advance study. Information is vital in making things happen. You need to learn how to keep a secret and when to keep it—or release it. Being a tough battler, on occasion, may win the day in getting the goal achieved.

Finally, an essence of managerial action and making things happen is decision-making; in small decisions of a momentary and short-term nature, and in big decisions, the full effect of which can't possibly be known for years to come.

3. **Review and feedback to improve action.** The purpose of this book is to show you how a manager makes things happen. In short, the middle element of the Management cycle is the main thrust of the book, and its techniques are the topics of the various chapters that follow. Yet it would be remiss not to also watch the third and fourth parts of the cycle, review and feedback.

While you are taking action and making things happen, you need a steady stream of information on how well the results are coming out. Are you attaining your goals? Are the standards being met? Were the plans soundly conceived? Will you get where you aim for, on time and within cost? Was the design proper? Was the route the right one? All of this should be fed back to the manager in action, periodically and also continuously. That's the role of feedback.

While review and feedback are absolutely essential and should never be overlooked in seeing the proper place of action, the purpose of this book is to show *how a manager makes things happen,* takes action, does the job, runs the plant, sells the goods, moves the work force, executes the program, and gets the job done. That's what the rest of this book is about, but don't lose sight of the three elements; for, making things happen is important only when we avoid the activity trap and keep a steady stream of delivered goals, achieved dreams and realized ideals.

2

MANAGEMENT MEANS DECIDING, NOT DRIFTING

> *"People, it has been said, can be placed in three classes: the few who make things happen, the many who watch things happen, and the overwhelming majority who have no idea what has happened."*
>
> NICHOLAS MURRAY BUTLER

Harry and George were managers in the data processing department of a large eastern bank. They were bucking like crazy for the top job—vice president of the whole EDP department. Both had MBA's from good schools and a dozen or more years of experience in the field. The odds-makers around the water cooler who were handicapping the race had placed George in the front position. For one thing, he was better looking, wore his clothes better, was more personable, and frankly was more popular with the troops. Harry was less personable, and was often known to kick tail when things went wrong. George would be more likely to call a problem-solving conference. Both of them knew the business from top to bottom. Harry got the job. Why? The decision was easy for the top management: *Harry made things happen and George did not.*

This story is going to happen again and again during the eighties. It's not style but results that make the difference. Not just results for today or this week, but for next year and the year after. The high costs of failure won't allow management to pick people for their classy looks, or even for their repertory of fancy administrative practices. When Harry said that he would get a program completed and debugged by a certain date, you could bet your life on it. When George was squeezed hard enough, he sometimes made promises, but you could lay odds that his program wouldn't be completed when he said it would, or within six weeks, or maybe six months of that date. George always had reasons. The reasons were always very, very logical. It would break your heart to hear them. You would drown in your own tears at his bad luck.

The big difference, however, was that where George had reasons, year in and year out; Harry, who didn't make as classy a showing, had results, year in and year out. You could count on him.

Now what was the difference between them?

The important differences aren't in style, or procedures, or even skills, although all of them may help. Nobody would be foolish enough to suggest that skills, procedures, good administration, and a pleasing personality or popularity are bad. Thus, there are two major points from the story of Harry and George.

1. People who make things happen focus their efforts on results rather than on activity.
2. Good managers make things happen; good administrators just follow "proper procedures," whether or not they relate to the purposes of the organization.

MANAGEMENT IS NOT A PASSIVE ART

Being a manager means making things happen, which makes the manager an activist, not a passive presider over events. Unlike the ceremonial functionary who throws out the first ball at the start of the season and then sits back and watches the game, the manager is calling the plays, changing the players, and yanking pitchers and sending them to the showers when their arms go sour. This calls for some skills, some tools and some procedures, its true: but it's not the tools and skills that make the manager excel. It's the use of those skills and tools that produce a promised result.

It would be foolish to knock the skills and tools managers use. The manager who knows accounting, financial analysis, PERT,

MBO, data processing and all of the others has a favorable position over the amateur who doesn't have them. Many a start-up firm has gone broke despite high promise and potential because the chief person didn't know what every successful manager knows. Studying management is a good idea. Management is a body of knowledge and a field of study which is taught in schools of business. People write papers, take tests, prove that they have mastered the literature of the field, and can solve case studies in management. All of which is fine, except that it doesn't make you a manager; it makes you a graduate of a school. The final exam isn't on the last day of class, but starts with the first day on the job.

> There is no single tool, technique, system, body of knowledge, method, procedure, or device which will make you a good manager simply because you have mastered it.

Such things are necessary but not sufficient. You need them, but there is something more. That's what this book is about: the ways managers make things happen.

1. As a manager, you will have a lot of regular, routine, ongoing, repetitive kinds of work. Every level of manager has such boring stuff. The President of the United States has to sign numerous copies of things, attend routine dinners and functions, and keep the routines of state flowing. The presidents of the largest firms get involved in paperwork. John DeLorean, the feisty Vice President of General Motors during the seventies, declared that he quit his highly-paid job, in large part because of the endless amount of paper he was obliged to read and pass along. He preferred the more exciting tasks of designing, making and selling new cars. Everyone gets trapped in routines, but being a good manager of routine business doesn't make you a good manager.

2. As a manager you get problems. They rush in your door, often heralded by alarms and screams of pain or anger. The people who have the problems may be subordinates, government regulators, customers, or the law. Managers are problem-solvers, but that isn't all. The successful manager isn't merely a problem-solver.

3. The essence of the managerial job is to do both the above jobs and keep the decks cleared for the highest level of management; that which separates the stars from the hacks, the managers who make things happen, from the ones who watch what is happening and respond. Some managers are more *managed* than

managing. The manager who makes things happen is innovating, creating change, moving things, improving, growing, amending, building, and compelling things to happen. The third category is what this book is aimed at.

The first step in being such an activist is goal-setting. The manager is mainly a goal-setter. Every other act of management flows out of this. The goals-setter as a manager envisions things which should happen, and thinks through some ways in which these goals can be attained. At this stage few, if any, people might even agree that the goal is worthy or attainable. They may see such visions as pipe dreams, or the maunderings of a nut of some kind.

The good manager often seems to find goals where others saw nothing. More than a mere problem-solver or administrator, this manager has a mental image of what could be that doesn't now exist. It might be a new firm or a new plant, hiring thousands of people and changing the way millions of customers live their lives. It may be a small firm which its owner has visions of making into a large one. It may be an inventor with an idea to start a successful firm, or it may be general manager of a division, with ideas that could double its size. It might even be a clergyman administering a church who pictures doubling his congregation, or a club president who pictures dozens of new areas of member's service, and growth in membership size.

The vision and the goal itself aren't the end but the first step. Next comes the conversion of the goal into an action plan, covering every aspect of financing, technical, legal, cultural, and marketing, to get to the goal. Next, and perhaps hardest, is to enlist talents even better than those of the idea creator, to make the parts of the dream come true. Before long, the manager's goals are the peoples' goals. A full-scale movement starts rolling, and people are as involved in the original goal as if they had thought of it themselves. They internalize—like eating and digesting—the goal, and become ego-involved in its success. During the battle to accomplish the goal, the manager is there to help, to encourage, to cheer on. The manager keeps the employees pointed toward the objective, sets examples and shows the way.

Now he may do this by good administrative methods, it's true. Being a good manager *doesn't preclude* being a good administrator. It merely implies that he's not a passive administrator who's more concerned with a "clean desk" or proper decor for his office because he's been told that's how administrators' offices should look. Nor is he overly obsessed with procedures for control and review. The dominant trait of the manager who makes things happen is that he's *goal oriented.* It means further that he's actively and intelligently seeking his goal. He's doing more than presiding over a group of people; he's leading them somewhere. Furthermore, while he's doing that, the chances are that he's hatching even more ambitious objectives beyond that one.

When young Bill Marriott took over as chief executive of the Marriot chain of restaurants and hotels, the company was a $60 million firm. His father, Willard Marriott, Sr., had built it from nothing between 1924 and 1964. Yet young Bill brought new skills and high motivation, and grew it into a billion dollar firm in the next fifteen years.

The IBM story of active movement is equally, if not more, impressive. At a meeting of its top management team at Williamsburg in 1956, Tom Watson, Jr., the newly elected president, announced the goal of the company as growing from annual sales of $734 million in 1957, to $1.5 billion by 1962, with an increase of some forty thousand employees in the process.

By 1978, when Tom Watson, Jr. retired, the corporation was at $20 billion in sales and growing rapidly. His father had taken over a small, struggling firm known as CTR Office Machines Company in 1914, with sales at $1.5 million and grew it to an international giant. Not resting, Thomas Watson, Jr. grew an impressive giant, which his father would never have imagined in his wildest dream.

Stanford's studies also showed that those companies which have growth patterns have been led by management of great moral courage in making decisions in favor of growth, and stuck with them to make the growth occur.

> **To summarize this point:** action-getting management means more than hustlers in management positions. It means the intelligent choice of good goals, among the most prominent being the goal of company growth.

The Forces of Inertia

More often than fighting competitors or actual opposition from those who have different objectives, the manager who makes things happen finds himself fighting a force called organizational inertia. This inertia takes many forms.

The first is the natural tendency of inertia within the manager himself. The tendency to coast along, or to look back "and see how far I've come," overtakes some managers and they turn into administrators. The truly action-oriented manager seldom spends much time walking around his accomplishments, admiring what he's done in the past. He's too often engrossed in getting things moving toward the next higher goal.

Even when he hasn't this inward desire to taper off his efforts, the action-getter finds that he has the heavy responsibility for spurring others to overcome their own inertia. This demands that he have several important capacities. He's got to be able to move projects and people off dead center and get them rolling toward his goals. He's got to generate enthusiasm for these goals so that people adopt them as their own, with the result that they generate enthusiasm on their own part for getting there. He must further instill a desire to excell and do the job fully and without mistakes or faltering. To do this demands several traits in the action-getting manager, which he must assiduously cultivate at the risk of failure.

1. He's going to have to maintain optimism if he's going to overcome inertia. Most managers who make things happen have ego drives that push them on personally, and unbounded optimism and confidence that others will ultimately see his vision of what's to be accomplished, despite repeated defeats and failures.

2. He needs a sound knowledge of people to compel them to produce and create. He needs to know what incentives are required to get action from others and to have some artistry in using them.

3. He needs a certain callousness in demanding high standards of performance from others who are helping him. The manager with an overdeveloped sense of sympathy and understanding of failure will usually "usurp all of the dirty jobs for himself, while others stand about and marvel at his performance," as David Moore puts it.

One of the greatest wellsprings of inertia in an organization is its *size*. The big organization develops built-in inertias, simply because it's so big. Kenneth Boulding of Michigan University compares the giant corporation to a dinosaur, and warns that unless the big organizations overcome the inertia and ineptness which overtook the dinosaur, they might suffer the same fate. *Power* alone isn't enough to survive. It requires the ability to move with agility and vigor, and to handle a variety of problems, both big and small, which confront the big organization.

A number of things occur when an organization grows in size. The first effect is that communications between the top and bottom, and between the various members, becomes difficult. This means that the left hand sometimes does things that duplicate or conflict with what the right hand is doing.

Another effect of bigness is that the personal touch between the owners and the employees is lost; or, in the case of a publicly-owned organization such as a manufacturing corporation, between the management and its staff and employees. Since it's this personal touch which is often at the heart of getting action in an organization, the top man finds he is limited greatly when he has a great organization to run and must accordingly organize to overcome the effects of too much bigness.

Because the organization is big, it requires more rule of law (called procedures and policies) in order to govern it. These are perfectly sound things to install, but they are part of that body of knowledge called *administration,* and, at the same time that they make it possible for managers to function at all, they aren't by any means a guarantee of movement and growth. That happens when the manager in favor of action, makes his personal impact on the organization.

> **To sum up this point:** There's nothing about an administrative procedure which will overcome inertia. It takes an action-getting manager to make things happen.

Profit Requires Action

Being a successful manager in a commercial and industrial enterprise means being a profit-minded one. Conversely, it's the profit-minded manager at any level who stands the best chance of moving upward. This is more than simple avarice, or single-minded love of money for itself. It's largely because profit is a universal standard for measurement that is easily grasped by managers and is quite clearly understood by those who judge his performance.

It's entirely possible that someday a more commonly held standard will come along, for example—service; but it must always meet the standard which profit has become—immediate, easy to calculate, universally accepted.

Even doing things ethically requires that the company be profitable before it can be the kind of corporate citizen it would like to be. Often it is the pressure of financial loss which presses people into cutting ethical corners. Further, the search of gain has universal appeal. As Nobel prize-winning economist Milton Friedman has noted "none of the early immigrants who came to this country came here to go broke—or lose money. They hoped to better themselves."

Profit, for all the criticisms leveled against it, is the best available instrument and standard of managerial success and organizational performance. With adaptations it applies to any organization, even in Soviet Russia.

We hear a great deal of pious foolishness written and said about profit. At the annual congress of industry of the NAM each winter, solemn and quite pompous words are uttered in defense of this mysterious lubricant which causes the wheels of industry to turn. To some it becomes a divinely inspired instrument which it becomes sacrilegious to damn. This, of course, is not the point here.

There's still another error which is perpetrated by accountants when we think of profit. It's widely held fiction that profit is something exact and precise which comes without deviation or man-made influence out of the impersonal exactitude known as "the books" of the company. This, of course, is nearly as fallacious as the assumption of its divine nature. All of the ingredients which come out at the end of the year under the over-all label of "profit" are quite flexible and under the control of individual decisions made by managers or administrators.

Such things as expenditures for research, training, public relations, personnel management, and so on, are all drains on the immediate profit in the current accounting period. You'll note that all of these are the results of the decision of management to spend money out of current income in order to assure the future growth and stability of the company.

> Profit, then, is more than an accounting term. It's a positive creation and standard for measuring effectiveness of management action and decision-making.

Making Growth a Company Goal

From these examples and many others which are similar, a few dominant trends seem to emerge. One of these is that *company growth* is one present-day goal which seems to spur executive action and make things happen. This has some important implications for the company which wants to grow. It also has a great deal of relevance to the budding manager—or the one who's arrived—who has talents for making things happen and seeks ample opportunity to demonstrate his prowess along these lines.

Studies by the Stanford Research Institute of several hundred companies with records of growth show that there are several traits common to most of them. For one thing, they are oriented to growth industries. Not only are the managements of these companies alert to where opportunities lie; they are also not averse to dropping lines which are shrinking in market importance and future opportunity. Growth, and management action to accomplish it, are less likely to be found in the hay and grain business, or horse shoe manufacturing than in electronics, missiles, atomic energy, pharmaceuticals or chemicals. Far too many companies fail to grow, the Stanford studies show, because the managements of these companies have a sentimental attachment to products or processes which were once growing and profitable, but which time has now proven outmoded.

Let's illustrate this. A large company begins by having some kind of trade advantage—either a patent right to exclusive manufacture of a product, or a dominant position in a market due to aggressive salesmanship. Theoretically, each company has such a special advantage which keeps it alive in the face of competition.

Yet companies go bankrupt. One study of the 100 largest firms in the United States in 1927 shows that only 50 percent of them still exist. In its early days, the National Cash Register Company used to maintain an exhibit of machines produced by companies which had attempted to enter the adding machine business and had gone broke in the process. Oswald Knauth, former treasurer of Macy's store, once said that "almost all trade advantages can be duplicated." Except for certain patent arrangements or exclusive access to raw materials, there are few advantages which a company can acquire that will preclude the necessity of managers who continue to discover and build up advantages for their own firm through personal leadership. These include actions which will build up its internal and external position, and the development of people, trade connections and experience which results in profit.

The world of automatic competition which Adam Smith depicted, with the functioning of "natural laws" arranging the levels of profits of the respective firms, was never really a picture of life. Profit is the result almost wholly of the *actions of managers* who exercise initiative and leadership of a dynamic nature, and of the people who respond to this leadership to carry through toward the goals of the organization.

There is probably no company in business today which couldn't be out of business through lack of profit inside of ten years if its management attempted to conduct its affairs simply through mechanical application of administrative practice, at the expense of the more vital, personal, and human application of individual leadership.

THE MANAGER AND THE WORLD OUTSIDE OF BUSINESS

This individual leadership, which produces action and results, isn't limited to the four walls or administrative boundaries of the firm. Profit, survival, and growth of the firm today—and in the future—will demand that managers be able to make things happen in circumstances in which a lot of the important variables won't be under their jurisdiction. Let's look at a few of them:

- The company which isn't attuned to public opinion is taking undue risks with its future.
- Government actions have a vital part in business policy.
- What's happening abroad is sufficiently close to business decisions today that they must be part of the action-getting manager's calculations.

One of the paradoxes of our time is that the model manager, who is sometimes identified as the "result-getter" and the hustler within the business, is so engrossed with day-to-day decisions inside the firm that he doesn't take time to watch these key developments outside.

However comfortable it might be for such an executive to concentrate on the places where his efforts seem to show immediate results, it's highly improbable that he can continue to do so with continued success. It's a further paradox that, when confronted with such outside problems as international trade, tariffs, cold war, inflation, and government control, he often throws up his hands in despair.

> The new action-getting manager must be one who can make his force and result-getting talents felt on both internal and external matters to the company.

3

FIVE TESTS OF INITIATIVE

"No sooner said than done—so acts your man of worth."

QUINTUS

One hot summer evening in Hamilton, New York, a group of executives attending the AMA management course at Colgate University were having a bull session.

"What's the biggest mistake you ever made in management?" somebody threw out to the group. There were a variety of responses. One fellow had missed a big order because he forgot to follow up. Another had picked the wrong man for a job and lived to regret it. Still another had recommended the purchase of a patent right which had resulted in a great fiasco for his company. One manager, a general manager for an appliance company, struck a responsive chord.

"The biggest mistake I've made was every instance where I should have done something and didn't. All the errors I regret seem to center around missed opportunities which I could have taken but didn't, because I decided too late to do it."

Many others chimed in as example after example followed of projects that were half done, or opportunities that were missed because of that initial step which wasn't taken, or not taken in time.

This process of moving quickly to get things into action is sometimes called initiative. It's compounded of a variety of properties and skills, which the action-getting manager seems to have; that his less effective competitor lacks.

A study of the qualities that go into making up these executives who make things move, shows five basic qualities. These are major characteristics and are compounded of a lot of little habits and skills which these people may have been born with, but most often they acquired them early in their careers.

The connection between the performance of individual firms and the attitudes of the general public at large are not vague or amorphous. A study by Professor Arie Reichel of New York University shows that people who find satisfaction in their job are more apt to be satisfied with the system. People with great confidence in the corporate form of organization are people who also say that they like their job. People who have little confidence and trust in the corporation report that they dislike their job, feel powerless in influencing things where they work, and don't understand their own job's purposes.

Where the job itself is seen as meaningless and dead-ended, the worker, whether a machine operator, professional, or middle manager, will feel a loss of confidence and trust in the entire social system. Such powerless people are the basis of increased government regulation, more government control of business operations, higher and more confiscatory taxes, and more government bureaucracy to restrain business as it goes about its affairs. Trapped in a job where purposes are not defined, people don't know what is expected of them, they don't know what their authority is, they don't know how well they are doing in their work, and they don't see achievements related to rewards. Thus, they flow through the "Three A's"; from anger to apathy, and finally to alienation.

Thus, external affairs, government regulation, and lack of the proper climate in which the firm can do business are directly related to the skill and artfulness with which the management directs the affairs of the firm. The first step for the firm, in dealing effectively with external affairs, is to run a good business which makes a profit and fulfills the needs of all of its employees as human beings.

- Initiative begins with inner drive which less effective managers lack.

- Initiative means sorting out the vital from the trivial, and driving for the vital goals.
- Initiative means that its possessor is tough-minded.
- The action-getting manager instills a desire to excel in other members of the organization, and releases their initiative as well as having it himself.
- The result-getter initiates intelligent action, not just random activity.

Only a few of these qualities are innate or natural. The rest are acquired and can be taught to others. Managers need to either have them or develop them if they are to cope with two major forces that are pressing in management today: the larger size of companies and the wide range of problems a manager must cope with to keep abreast.

As companies get larger, they run into what Kenneth E. Boulding has called the "scale barrier." This invisible threshold, a little like the sound barrier in flying, seems to stop programs from moving along, plans from being carried through, or the word from getting down from the top. As a result of this invisible wall, which takes the form of procedures, regulations, and plain inertia, a lot of solid administrators in top spots get stuck on dead center when it comes to results. Staffs get so tied up in clearing every decision and writing memos that they don't quite connect fast enough to capitalize on profit opportunities.

Let's look at each and see how those who make things happen overcome this obstacle, and how we can learn to be like them.

INNER DRIVE

Some people with this trait are endowed with an over-active thyroid or an abundance of animal energy, but this isn't always the case. The big difference isn't mainly physiological. It's a habit of vigorous and positive approaches to everything, of restless unhappiness with things as they are, and a roving eye toward the possibility of improvement.

The doer has developed the talent for picking a single goal out of the millions available, and mustering all his other talents, knowledge, powers of persuasion, and leadership to reach it.

The doer may pause while choosing a plan or mapping strategy, but, once it's selected, all energies concentrate in a controlled form of organizational fury. More than simple activity, it is directed energy focused by an intelligent and well-disciplined mind.

Building or training this inner drive isn't done through pep talks. It's a matter of coaching to peak personal effectiveness in daily work habits. When that level is reached, the next step is to give big challenges, which test and prove those skills.

PICK THE IMPORTANT THINGS

In terms of skills which a manager can develop in order to function as a result-getter, one of the key abilities is to pick out the important things for action. The doer's desk gets piled with the same assortment of trivia as yours and mine, and gets as many requests for time. The doer is invited to as many meetings and has as many opportunities to dawdle as the next person.

The first step in becoming an action-getter is to learn how to wade through the underbrush to find the really important things and do them first. This means that we have mastered several difficult steps along the way. Scan the whole range of things that are pressing and quickly evaluate the importance of each. One executive I know, for example, gets ten requests for speaking engagements monthly. Rather than turn them all down or accept them all, he measures the effect they might have on his other goals.

He might, for example, pick one with a small group of investment analysts if he's planning to go to the security markets soon. He might talk to an education group if his company is about to launch a recruiting campaign in the colleges. If community relations is a problem, he may accept chairmanship of a fund-raising drive. He may address a group of professional men if his company has market interests among them.

His power of purposeful selection tells him which meetings to miss, which conferences not to attend, which visitor not to see, and which letter to pass on to somebody else to answer.

He knows that everything he could do is not equally important. Because he knows this, he digs for the vital things. He looks for bottlenecks that will hold up a lot of other projects and breaks them. He puts the vital few things at the top of his list and pushes the many trivial ones to the bottom.

He's profit-minded and he pounces upon things that might increase profits through immediate action, and will prevent loss if done without delay. He then uses this priority list to shuffle his schedule so that the essential gets done now and lower-priority items get done later.

The good user of time is quick to spot a trend that requires some action. Relations with a big customer are sliding? Don't wait to see what happens next. Start an immediate action program to get things corrected so that the cause of the discontent won't recur, then go to the customer and explain what's happened. Go to the top person in the customer's company—at least as high as you need to go to set things right. As one executive put it:

> "I find it better to deal with the chief of the tribe than with one of the Indians."

The important point again isn't that we must have a natural whirlwind to start with. Everybody has capacities which he may or may not be using. Focused energy gets more done than general or diffused energy.

TOUGH-MINDEDNESS

Despite a concern with meeting the needs of others and meeting the basic needs of people, the action-getter has developed a tough-mindedness. For one thing, as Chris Argyris has put it, the action-getter has "a high tolerance for frustration," and plugs through all sorts of red tape when he has to without blowing his top. The tough-minded manager frequently endures the delays and runarounds of committees and clearances with Spartan endurance. Being patient, where such patience is the only possible way of getting the final pay-off, is part of being tough-minded.

This patience isn't submissiveness, however, and when the time for patience is past and more direct action is called for, the action-minded manager is willing to be ruthless. When the choice is between maintaining old relationships and getting the job done, be ready to decide in favor of the job. Stepping on people's corns isn't first choice, but do it firmly if the occasion demands.

One executive found that his plan for a marketing campaign violated certain canons of taste and preferences belonging to his boss's wife. Wiser heads and politic minds advised him to drop it and choose another. After weighing all the factors, he finally went ahead. When the results were outstandingly successful, his boss confided in him that, despite some troublesome moments at home, he was personally pleased that the executive had decided to go ahead with the program.

This tough-mindedness sometimes looks a little like inflexibility. Once it is decided what action is best, the tough-minded manager sticks to it no matter how the weather blows. This is partly constitutional doggedness, but it occurs mostly because vacillation will be worse than picking a specific tack and holding on. Pressures for change are inevitable, no matter what course is set. It is part of the price for making headway.

Action-minded managers are probably tough-minded in their relations with people, willing to stick by their people through their honest mistakes—or to chop off heads as the need arises. They are made of tough stuff and will work hard and take heavy blows as a price of making a living and contributing to the success of the business.

A good manager will urge on a worker who is working at less than his best abilities. He is liberal with recognition for good work, and equally liberal with a reverse kind of recognition for the people who aren't performing up to their capacities. People over their heads in their jobs find this action-minded boss a fearsome figure, one who will certainly drive them to perform things they hadn't thought possible, or face up to the fact that they have no great future in the organization until they do.

Good managers are tough-minded, and willing to pay the prices for personal success. Long hours, hard work, and killer travel schedules are often a way of life. They concentrate on their jobs with the singleness of purpose that reduces other things to a lesser role. This doesn't mean being inhuman or a dull grind, for pleasure and recreation are often found only in work. As one such executive put it:

"I think people in positions like mine have found a secret weapon which really isn't a secret at all—we don't quit. As I look back over forty years and see the fellows who didn't go as far as I did, I think it's probably because they took a good look at the price you pay in family life and so forth, and decided to settle for less. I can't say they're wrong, it's just that they didn't make the same decision I did. They were willing to let themselves be outworked. Add a little luck to that, and it's a secret formula."

How do you get all of these qualities? First, they aren't learned in a course. They are learned in tough situations. This becomes a matter of assignment of people to places where they take pressure. Ford, General Mills and other companies now believe that the best place to start a young trainee of great promise is on the job where he or she will develop calluses that make him or her a tough, resourceful manager at 45.

In developing managers who make things happen, the major emphasis, it would seem, should be on careful selection of people who are willing to pay the price—people with hides thick enough and frames sufficiently durable that they can learn by being tossed against problems bigger than themselves.

Although conferences and courses can help, most observers agree that major emphasis should be on systematic coaching and carefully-planned job assignments. In essence, a program to produce a manager who makes things happen must instill some habits. The ingredients in this program will vary to meet the needs of the person, but they will include:

- Early identification of the people who have the native equipment. This isn't much different from what we're doing at present.
- Assignments that give these three major opportunities for development:

1. Tough problems to solve and big jobs to do where the trainee can see the results of good—or poor—performance early.

2. Assignment under an action-getting manager. One action-getter can strike off several copies of himself. If several go-getters are assigned to an action-getting manager, they'll strike sparks off one another, too. Healthy competition is a good force for bringing out the "will-do" factors, and it causes people to bring out their best abilities.

3. Work for the manager to help coach and guide these people. Once you've got an action-getter in a spot where he or she

can develop his or her own talents, get out of the way and let him or her move.

INSTILLING A DESIRE TO EXCEL

The action-getter can use the initiative latent in subordinates. Nobody in the company, especially the boss, has all the good ideas. He or she builds a climate in which a good idea will get itself into application without a great deal of clearance and approvals all up and down the line.

In one large company, a staff department was sagging badly because of the bottleneck at the top of the department. The staff, whose job was to develop new ideas for use in line departments, was in a state of near standstill. A close check by an executive found that every new idea or plan which was developed in the organization was being sent in memo form to the man at the top. After doing all of the necessary preparation and careful scrutiny of it for possible points of criticism, it was common practice for everyone to then type "first draft" at the top of the first page before sending it to the boss for approval and checking. Since the boss inevitably found things in these recommendations which should be changed around, no completed staff work was ever done in the department.

When this procedure was pointed out, the boss began to route the "first draft" papers back with the note:

"Don't send me first drafts, I want your considered judgment and recommendations for action."

After several came over with only half the work done (the expectation of the originator being that changes would be forthcoming), the department head wrote:

"If this is your best judgment—let's go ahead and issue it *over my signature.*"

The result was an immediate and drastic improvement in the volume and quality of work in the department. The boss soon learned whose work could be relied upon, and whose would need some improving through coaching.

All this implies that the action-getter is more than a self-appointed genius who swings his or her weight around to get people scurrying. Bosses get employees to initiate by making certain that they are ready and able to start things in motion. Bosses listen patiently, asking questions, probing deeply into half-formed ideas to help the initiator develop them more fully. They also make it worthwhile for a man to excel in the job by paying dividends to people who move quickly and skillfully in their jobs.

When you see a half-baked idea, don't kill it summarily, but listen to hear the whole story. If it's off the beam, explain carefully to the originator why it can't be used. If it's good, give the initiator sincere credit for having thought of it and put it into application.

Create a climate in which people are scrambling hard for new ideas and better ways of doing things. Make it plain that you are tolerant of mistakes, and won't hand a worker his or her head for the first or even the second one. The organization which is initiating ideas will have to make some errors in judgment. Don't be afraid to generate and try out a few of your own, know that an occasional mistake won't cost your scalp.

This desire to excel—so difficult to achieve—lies under the whole idea of initiation. It presumes that ideas and excellence grow out of making each person responsible for the results in his own area. Decentralized companies such as General Motors, Prudential Insurance, Ford, Du Pont, and ITT, with their great records of growth, have generally found that this desire to excel in every level of the organization is what keeps them out in front.

The interesting part of such growth is that it hasn't, in many cases, decreased the agility and vigor with which the organization tackles its problems, nor its speed in solving them. The small company which is dominated by one person is often slower than the corporate giant. This anomaly grows out of the place where initiative rests.

> As a rule, initiative in an organization should be pushed down to the lowest possible level where decision can be made, through instilling a desire to excel at every level.

INITIATING INTELLIGENT ACTION

Simply getting the ball in motion isn't enough. It requires *intelligent* action if the best results are to be achieved. This requires two things:

- **a goal** which is realistic and attainable; at the same time, it's hard enough to attain that it challenges people.
- **a plan** which spells out, in an orderly fashion, how the organization will arrive there.

This requires more than simply getting things into motion. It means movement toward the objective. Managers who have "initiative" or the ability to start moving, based on emotional drives or instinct, won't be as successful in the long run as the one who acts upon reflection and conscious planning. A lot of initiative is based on such instincts and reflexes, which sometimes leads to self-cancelling or inconsistent action.

There's a metal working plant in the east where the top man has created a climate of reflex and instinct that isn't paying off. Every time there is a production stoppage, everyone in sight rushes to the spot and, as one of the workers put it, "all hell busts loose." Mechanics work under pressure, and do a slipshod job. Supervisors get rattled and bawl out operators and mechanics. Inspectors and supervisors tangle with angry words if the shut-down is for quality.

The best kinds of initiative are those which are based on experience, and pre-planned procedures. *Pressure* alone isn't properly showing initiative.

Another key ingredient in intelligent action is taking initiative that will carry the unit or department toward the larger plan for the whole company. A plan which makes one department look good at the expense of another, or adds to another department's cost, isn't good initiative.

The following case illustrates the crafty type of initiative which doesn't do the overall organization any good.

> "The dominant theme of Soviet railway transport policy," writes one expert in the jargon so dear to experts, "has been that of maximizing the volume of services provided while devoting the minimum possible resources to them. As freight traffic manager on the Vladivostok section of the Trans-Siberian Railway, Comrade Vorobiev was a man with a mission to fill, and the imagination to overcome obstacles. His job was to move a specified tonnage of freight. But what if there was not enough freight to move?" The latest issue of *Gudok,* the Soviet railway journal tells how Comrade Vorobiev met his problem.

Traffic manager Vorobiev's line was in grave danger of falling behind its monthly norm in tank car loadings. Desperate for something to transport, and finding no petroleum, alcohol, milk or other useful liquid available, Comrade Vorobiev gazed about him, cast his eye upon the liquid in a nearby river, and quick as a flash filled 50 of his cars with water and sent them rattling off from Voroshilov. At a siding of the Trans-Siberian line the water froze solid in the cars and it took a month for workmen to chip it out with pickaxes. But no matter—Vorobiev had made his quota.

4

THE STATUS QUO—
IT'S NOT GOOD ENOUGH!

> "The new American—the child of incalculable coal power, chemical power, electrical power, and radiating energy, as well as new forces not yet determined—must be a sort of God compared with any former creature of nature."
>
> HENRY ADAMS (1904)

All of the cards are stacked in favor of the person who can make things happen in management. Unlike the stagnant societies where caste and custom, tradition and religion militate against change at a most fundamental level, in the United States, one is rewarded amply for the ability to get things done. Here's why:

• The American Economy is tied inextricably, for the foreseeable future, to being a growth economy. It's part of our culture, and energy shortages notwithstanding, we are on an upward growth merry-go-round. The firm which gets off will be left behind or bought out.

• The fruits of research and development continue to make it likely that today's products, methods and systems won't be around tomorrow.

• Most major companies today are spending substantial sums each year on product research and development, market development and human resource development to produce growth. The firm which doesn't keep abreast of the leaders will end up only working for them.

The name of the game, then, is change. Not blind growth, just getting bigger to get bigger; but selective, intelligent choices are among the alternatives. Better people, better products at lower costs, being tough about abandoning losers, are all part of the pressures of the market to "get off the dime" of maintaining the status quo.

An expanding population and a more productive labor force call for three supporting forces to expand accordingly: more employment opportunities, higher levels of investment, and increased consumption.

This growth pattern of the economy is not an automatic process. It is the result of conscious planning and effort, and hard work from many people. The leadership in this growth will be required in many places, including corporations, unions and in the government.

This economic climate for growth poses some special problems for the manager. If the economy grows at a steady rate and everyone else is moving ahead with expansion and growth, the individual manager can do no less if he or she keeps hold of today's relative position. Let's see how this works out for the individual company.

Productivity per worker. This is one of the key areas where management must continually improve its performance if it's going to keep abreast of the economy. It's most unfashionable—or perhaps unpatriotic—not to do so. The pinch in *not* increasing productivity is that the competition is probably doing so. This means they will be producing products at a lower cost, and possibly gaining sufficient edge to take over pieces of the market your company now holds.

New capital investment. The company which trims its sails in investing in new and better plants and equipment may find itself noncompetitive with the companies which have not done so. Since the obvious and apparent pattern is one of great capital investment—mainly from plowed back earnings—the company which won't, or can't because of low profit, keep its capital investment up to its competitors will find itself in a competitive bind within a relatively short period of time.

Research and development. New products and improvements of present products are part of the growth pattern of successful companies. Take the case of the large consumer products company which trimmed its expense for research on products for three years, in the face of some slight market and profit reversals. During this lull in research on its product, one of its competitors pressed ahead and made a breakthrough in product quality and design. With the improved product in hand, it poured great sums into marketing the new style and captured more than thirty percent of its one-time dominant competitor's customers. Although the first firm immediately accelerated its development program to catch up, it was too late, and it will require several years and plenty of grief before it can regain its position.

Cost reduction. The need for constant attention to rising costs, and the development of better and more economical ways of doing things, points to the cost reduction job of the management. Fat is becoming more and more unhealthy, and the pressure of inflation demands more aggressive and intelligent control over expenses, and positive management action to reduce them.

THE ORGANIZATION AT REST IS DYING

All this proves simply that the company which hopes to survive in today's economy must grow or it will fall behind and probably fail, or be merged with. There are some very real evidences that this will happen—and in fact has happened.

One of the dramatic stories which illustrates this is that of the Ford Motor Company. During the latter years of Old Henry's life, the company, which had once set the pace for the industry, was losing money at an appalling rate. The methods of modern management and innovation had passed the older management by, and in its resistance to change was draining away its lifeblood. Henry Ford II, recently out of Yale and with limited experience in the firm, was thrust into the top position. By hiring away such men as Del Harder from the E. W. Bliss Company and Ernest Breech of Bendix

Aviation, he reversed the trend and led Ford back into a strong position among the top three.

The strong electronics firms are those which turned quickly to TV, missiles, and other growth products after the war, when the radio business was threatened with obliteration. Motorola Company is an excellent example of how one firm can be big and adjust to changes in the economy and markets, and use this dexterity in managerial decision-making to gain market position.

One of the great dangers which any manager can face, at whatever level, is the acceptance of the infallibility of past methods. This is especially true following a period of some success. The empty and decaying textile mills of Lowell, Lawrence, and Manchester, along the Merrimack River in New England, stand as monuments to managements who thought they could live forever on the fruits of dead men's ideas.

Stanford Research Institute's study of why companies grow demonstrated that the expanding companies usually build on a hard core of successful past operations. From this we can conclude that they haven't broken completely with the past, and their future relates to their past in this way. There's a lesson here for the manager in any business, at any level.

> Survival for the company or any part of it means that the management is building on past accomplishments to make it grow.

TEN RULES FOR IDENTIFYING BUSINESS STAGNATION

During the depression of the thirties, many economists developed a theory of "secular stagnation" which they declared had overtaken our economy. They declared that the end of the frontier, the leveling off of population, and the inability of the economy to grow further for these reasons, meant that greater government investment and intervention to provide jobs for all was indicated.

Since the end of World War II, we've heard little of such theories. For one thing, the population has risen steadily, and the frontier which was the American west has been supplanted by the frontier of research. Through new products, processes and methods, new employment and investment opportunities have been created with the result that both investment and employment opportunities have been at peak levels.

Yet this specter of stagnation is always just ahead of us in individual companies or their departments. Despite the economic forces which make for vitality and growth, there still remains the overbearing necessity for managerial action to make the growth occur. What indicators could we find that the danger point of stagnation is setting upon an organization?

Usually the stagnant organization has ten key characteristics:

1. Its officials are out of touch with broad trends. Often the organization at rest is headed by officials who have become inbred within their own company and see little significance in what the economy or their competitors are doing. Often, this state occurs when some slight technical difference from most other companies in the business seems to exist. The phrase "our company is different" is often the first sign of decadence in management, since it indicates a general unwillingness to keep abreast of new ideas.

2. Unwillingness to experiment. The management which hesitates overly long in accepting new methods or relinquishing old ones may be headed for oblivion.

3. It never looks beyond its own markets. When they run into hard times with product marketing, their only reaction is to mine deeper in the same vein, rather than seek new fields for utilizing their products—or their organization—to recoup losses.

4. It demands great conformity from its people. The organization which doesn't allow at least a few mavericks who will question and probe present methods and programs will probably stagnate shortly if it hasn't already done so.

5. It neither rewards merit nor punishes failure. The organization which operates with a "civil service" mentality, without paying for performance alone, is on the verge of stagnation.

6. Managers and staff do little self-development. One of the benchmarks of the stagnant organization is the managerial staff which makes little or no effort of its own accord to learn new methods, study new techniques, discuss ways of improving, or show any evidence of a thirst for better ways of operating.

7. It is inbred. One certain evidence of stagnation in an organization is its isolation from new ideas, new people and fresh viewpoints. Such a company seldom permits its people to attend professional meetings, permits little exchange of information with other companies and abhors consultants. The overall climate is one of smugness, self-satisfaction, and self-congratulation.

8. It is overly-obsessed with immediate profit. A company which is unwilling to invest certain portions of its present income in enlargement and developmental activity such as personnel, public relations, management development, scientific research, marketing research, or long range investment in tangibles soon begins to show organizational hardening of the arteries.

9. It attracts passive and dependent people. One of the surest identification marks of the organization which is on the road to stagnation, if not already overtaken by the dull gray look of mediocrity, is an overabundance of passive and dependent people. These are people who are frightened of the boss, who seek security rather than opportunity, whose principal trait is obeisance, not only to orders, but to what they *think* the boss would want. Such a climate soon repels the vital and energetic employee of ideas and ambitions, and he or she seeks out a livelier and more fertile climate.

10. The stagnant company is a boring place to work. Ruled by seniority, privilege, and low turnover, it has a dull, colorless and nearly lifeless passivity about it. There is little fire which comes with innovation, change, and the conflict and confusion which comes with growing pains, but which also are signs of life and energy. Often it's a humorless place, in which the officials take themselves seriously, treating restlessness and desire for change as discordant influences which must be put down.

Often, the organization which is afflicted with these symptoms can be identified simply by walking through it. There is little of the hustle and burgeoning activity which seems to surround the organization on the move. In some cases it's apparent by the appearance of its managers, who are dull people, and occasionally by its decor, which is outmoded and plain. There's little of the stormy, husky or brawling nature of the broad-shouldered organization. It's seldom coarse, strong or cunning in its dealings. Pale and dissatisfied, it stands ready to fall before the company which is young in nature and willing to build and break and rebuild again in the battles of the marketplace.

Alan Harrington, in his book *Life in the Crystal Palace*, describes it this way:

> I think that our new species may be distinguished from other American working people in at least one way; by an absence of nervousness. We are not worried about our jobs, about the future, about ... much of anything.

The corporation about which he wrote subsequently went out of business!

WHY CHANGE IS NECESSARY

However restful the stagnant organization may appear, the disruptive and sometimes exciting world of change is the route to survival for the well-managed company. The favorite cliche of executive speeches, "the organization which is not growing will die," is less fully understood than it might be. In this instance, there is some logical evidence which points to the validity of this oft repeated homily. Some of the major reasons for this imperative need for change in a business organization might look like this:

Costs have reached such a scope in most firms that near herculean efforts are required to keep them from running the firm to the wall, if the firm is careless about them. The secular—and constant—upward trend of costs, through rising labor costs, rising material costs and the higher costs of government has the only hope of holding inflationary forces under control through the vigorous and active leadership of management. It's perfectly true that this pressure was suspended in large part, for many years, in its more serious forms, through the simple mechanism of shifting the incidence of costs on to the consumer through price increases. However, this circularity in economic management inevitably has its bad consequences in inflation, which devalues fixed incomes and did, in fact, create substantial consumer resistance to further price rises. Thus the only remaining alternative for managements in the face of such pressures—sometimes identified as the "cost-price squeeze"—is to cut other costs in the face of rising labor costs.

Such improvements can only be brought about through better organization, which is to say, changes in traditional and past methods of organizing work. This extends to methods, equipment, rules of work, and procedures. Without such changes in the individual firm, loss of profit and inevitable economic disaster are the only alternatives. In the economy at large, the unthinkable alternative of runaway inflation would ensue.

Competition of a new order in the economy requires that the firm which would survive make constant change a way of life for itself, in all of its methods of doing business. This is most often gradual change, conducted along orderly lines, but is often disruptive in its scope. The newer patterns of lower tariffs has meant that foreign goods may enter the domestic market freely, with their frequent labor-cost advantages, and less often their material-cost advantages. This too implies that substantial change for cost reduction, through better organization and methods, must be a matter of unremitting concern to domestic managers.

Not long ago, I visited a manufacturer of supplies for the automobile industry, in the Detroit area. He has recently developed a process of producing a product which cut labor costs from $.34 a yard to $.08 a yard. For the time being, he told me, he was going to continue to sell his product at competitor's prices, until he could finance enough of the new equipment to produce enough to take over a dominant share of the market for this particular product. It was then his intention, he said, to cut his price in half, and grab a much bigger piece of the total market.

"Won't this irritate your competitors?" I asked.

"Irritate 'em, Hell!" this owner replied, "I'm going to wipe them out!"

This surging competitive rambunctiousness for lower costs and higher quality is not only characteristic of our economy; it is the most cogent reason imaginable for adopting change as the customary way of life for the modern firm.

THE DYNAMICS OF MANAGEMENT

This changing world puts demands upon the skills and practices of management, which promise to create a whole new breed of people in charge of our business enterprises. We've alluded to some of the ways in which this new management leadership is different from the "model administrator." The significant differences lie in this desire and ability to bring about change and improvement, and to force innovation into the position of being a primary skill of the manager.

Perhaps the first step in the changing fashion of management will be the decline of those powers which we sometimes ascribe to administrators known as *control* and *veto power*. Study the functioning of the typical administrator in the traditional sense and you'll find that much time and effort are designed to accomplish *review* and *control*. Actions by subordinates or other managers are channeled in such a way that they must feed through the filter of the "exception principle." Exceptions, and in some cases routine actions by subordinates, are structured to feed through the mechanism which measures them, stopping them in mid-flight for the purpose of being assessed by the administrator. Those actions which have conformed to the pre-determined pattern of the administrative directive and procedural instruction are permitted to pass on. Those which vary in the slightest are either altered or rejected to be returned to its originator for retouching. However laudable this may be, in terms of preventing some backward slipping in the organization, it is essentially a provost marshal's approach to management and does nothing more than maintain the status quo.

> Controls tell what has happened or is happening. They don't make things happen by themselves.

It may seem reckless and irresponsible to suggest that such controls are not always worth all of the time and effort which goes into their design and operation. Yet, as a major preoccupier of management time, they have several basic defects which make them unsuitable in an economic environment where change is so sorely needed and improvement becomes the pressing requirement for growth—and survival. More, there's some doubt in many quarters about the necessity of arming the organization for controlling things when the controls themselves are more costly than the potential losses which could occur from errors in procedure.

Take the case of the firm which found that audits and detailed reviews of expense accounts took the full time of three people. This was in addition to the time of messengers, typists and the managers themselves in making the detailed corrections which were demanded when an error occurred. A study of the records showed that the total savings, over a two year period, from this tight administrative control was $125.50. It was decided that two of the clerks could be eliminated, and the time of the remaining one used in simply posting and issuing checks from the statements as received. In other words, the controls over possible padding of checks (which went on, in fact, but this review couldn't catch them) was greatly in excess of any savings that might grow out of the controls.

In many instances, such control measures are passed to a computer which performs the calculations, sorts the data and compares it against pre-fed standards and announces the results. Even here there is some question as to whether the computer's time might not have been used more profitably than in exercising *overcontrol* of negligible expenses.

Diametrically opposed in philosophy to this static form of control and administrative practice, which serves to maintain the status quo, is the dynamic concept of *action* being the primary requirement of the manager.

A recent example, which I saw in a manufacturing plant, occurred when a new plant manager took over. As he walked around the plant he struck up conversations with the several foremen in charge of departments. As he went into one department, he noted that the housekeeping was nearly perfect. The machines were painted, the floor clean, and over the bulletin board was a plant safety award for the best departmental accident record. His assistant informed him that this department was managed by Jim C., who was by far the best foreman in the plant. In production, quality, housekeeping, safety, spoilage, yield, maintenance, and grievances, he stood far above the rest. The plant manager sought out this paragon and introduced himself.

"Jim, I understand that you run the best department in the plant."

"Could be."

"What is your accident frequency and severity rate per million employees?"

"Damned if I know."

"Well, what is the hourly average from your machines for the past month and the past six months?"

> "Beats the hell outa me."
> "And your spoilage rate per thousand pieces for the year to date?" The foreman shrugged indifferently.
> "Look Mr. X.," he said, "I'm so damn busy running this place well I don't have time to keep score."

Obviously we might want a little more knowledge of the "score" from a manager than Jim C. professed. Certainly, if Jim is going to move upward, he's going to have to learn to use records. The point, however, is that we might also legitimately wish that more of the others, who probably knew their statistics cold, could have Jim's attitude of attention to fundamentals—which was getting things done first and counting the figures afterward.

> No manager ever produced anything by merely watching a figure; management dynamics emphasizes the doing first, and the administrative totalling-up second.

WHY INNOVATION GETS TOP PRIORITY

Change can be of two sorts. It can be simply the change which comes about because the people running the business can't make up their minds on the best way, and keep flitting from one method to another without making real progress. Or, the other type is change which is rooted in *innovation*. This innovation is the process of infusing new and better products, methods, and processes into the concern to do the job better, faster and cheaper. Bell and Howell reports that 65 percent of the company's sales are in products which weren't even in existence five years ago. Rather than resting on their laurels, they continue to press for even greater advantage through new products. Some growth firms now account for 80 percent of their sales with products that didn't exist ten years ago.

Planning ahead for profits, calls for dynamic, imaginative thinking. Innovation is the lifeblood of any growth business. I don't mean just those ideas that come out of the professional "idea men" in research and development. I mean the innovation in methods that happens when every manager, every staff person and every employee is taking a cold, critical look at the present methods of doing things with a view to finding a better way.

A Princeton University group studied innovation and concluded several things about the companies in which it occurs. For one thing, it has a way of changing the personnel make-up of the organization. There usually is more highly-talented, trained professional, technical and managerial manpower when innovation hits an organization. This new concentration of highly-talented manpower, because it's been attracted or assembled in a climate of innovation, in turn creates more innovation, which attracts more highly-trained people.

From this we can conclude that building a strong organization, which has the talent to grow and get action for corporate growth, is centered around innovation.

This high priority on innovation isn't limited solely to the research laboratory or the scientist. Those responsible for evaluating suggestions for technical work must have a clear understanding of the company's field of commercial interest. Researchers must also have a clear understanding of the company's manufacturing facilities and financial resources. Finally, innovation through research must be geared to the ability of the sales organization to sell and service a new product or process.

> Innovation, then, is a force for improvement through infusing new ideas and products into the organization as a whole, which must be a top priority if a company is to grow.

HOW INNOVATION AND CONTROL ARE RELATED

One of the mysterious features about improvements in management methods and organization is the phenomena which we may call the "backsliding" characteristics of innovation and improvement over time.

Take the case of the typical sales contest. The sales and marketing managers dream up a wonderful plan to boost sales through a giant promotional campaign. In order to cash in on it, they announce a contest for salesmen. The winner and his or her spouse will get a free trip to Paris at company expense. Hundreds of other valuable prizes are announced for regional and local winners. Meetings are held and posters are tacked to the sales office wall. A monster rally is held, and the president himself makes a speech to the entire sales organization via closed-circuit TV.

The Status Quo—It's Not Good Enough

During the weeks that follow, the pressure and hoopla continue unabated, and the red line on the thermometer chart on the sales manager's wall goes up and up until the top is blown off. Salesman Jones is finally announced as the winner, and he and his wife have their picture taken as they stand at the foot of the ramp to the great jet that will whisk them away to Paris for two weeks with all expenses paid.

The following month no charts are kept, and it's a good thing! Sales have fallen well below the peak of the contest. In fact, it is somewhat below the monthly average before the contest began and even the same month for the last five years.

What happened?

Here the sales manager and his team developed (innovated, you might say) a new idea, and carried it off beautifully, but the slump wiped out the gains from the campaign.

An investigation shows that Salesman Jones can well afford to take time off for the trip to Paris, because if he were out covering his territory, he probably wouldn't get any orders from any of his regular customers anyhow. Their stocks and warehouses are piled high with several months' supply ahead, and until the stuff has moved off the shelf, they'll be saying "no thanks" to Jones when he calls. Knowing that the contest was a temporary figure to beat, the canny Jones has used pressure and persuasion to get them to stock up during the contest. Taken on a national scope, the contest proves to be a real headache to management and productive of little by way of new and permanent business.

> Good innovation has built-in snubbers which are designed to prevent any sliding backward after temporary gains. It's not a campaign!

This implies some controls, and really pinpoints the place where controls enter the picture, preventing losses and backsliding from the newly won positions.

The kinds of controls which were mentioned earlier, in the example of the manufacturing manager who watched his records and ran his department with a view to score-keeping, do, then, have an important part to play once the organization has reached a new plateau. Organizations on the move seldom take time to dig defensive positions in the middle of their bayonet charge. Once they've achieved their first objectives, however, and are pausing to reload their guns before jumping off again, it's wise strategy to post sentries and outposts to prevent loss of the things already accomplished. In management, these are the establishment of sensitive control reports and sensing systems to report promptly the first signs of sliding back.

Management consultant Joseph Juran[1] summarizes this difference in this way:

> *To establish control to maintain the status quo.* Management establishes norms about which performance will fluctuate under normal operating conditions. If actual performance keeps within the range of expected variation, then the situation is under control. Observing performance and checking and correcting variations of results which fall outside the norm is part of routine management control, with maintenance of the status quo.
>
> *Diagnostics for Breakthrough.* In order to raise the general levels of performance, it takes more than simple control. This requires some special "diagnostics," as Juran puts it, to bring about new and different methods or techniques which will innovate and improve upon existing standards.
>
> Once such a breakthrough is established, it then becomes time to re-establish control to maintain the *new status quo* at the better level of performance while the next breakthrough is being planned.

Using this viewpoint, let's look again at our sales contest and see just what happened.

First, the objective of the breakthrough was clearly defined. The real purpose management had in mind in running a sales contest wasn't just to give sales a temporary spurt. (Although this might possibly be a sales contest objective—to clear the shelves of old stock in preparation for a new item.) Its goal was to raise the general level of sales for the company, permanently, it was fondly hoped by the planners.

Secondly, the entire incentive plan was aimed at causing salesman Jones to speed up rather than do anything different. The purpose of the contest was to take customers away from competitors and to keep them once taken. It also hoped to spur the

---

[1]Speech, University of Michigan, August 1960.

salesman to finding new customers, and to break into markets which had previously not been hit.

Yet the contest merely whipped up enthusiasm for *more*, and with the wonderful reward for selling more so dramatically spelled out, the salespeople went out to sell more in the easiest way, thereby winning themselves a free prize.

Building controls into the contest might have been accomplished in several ways:

1. Make only new sales qualify for the prize. That is, sales to customers who were buying from competitors exclusively have extra value over sales of more products to old customers.

2. Tie the awards to sales of new products to customers who had never bought them before.

3. Run the contest over a longer period of time, such as six months or a year. This wouldn't arouse the fervid enthusiasm of a one- or two-month campaign, it's true; but the raising of general levels of sales would have probably been more permanent.

4. More importantly than any of these, the contest might have been prefaced by some careful diagnosis of markets and sales patterns, and the incentives tied to breakthroughs into new and untapped markets, with no incentives for repeat sales or extra "pushing" of goods to old customers as advance stock.

5. It might have been supplemented by additional incentives for "business held for six months." These and several other steps, which smart sales managers all know, might be considered as practical techniques ensuring innovation by building in controls to maintain the new levels.

Campaigns which are based on pressure and pep talks that have as their objective the speeding up of efforts are always destined to be followed by a let-down.

> Genuine innovation, based on careful diagnosis, has built-in controls to maintain the new levels of performance and prevent sliding back after installation.

THE DYNAMIC BASIS FOR BUSINESS ACTION

Our economy and social system is geared for change and improvement. Each year new models of automobiles, clocks, radios, TV sets, computers, refrigerators, and Miami hotels pop onto the market. The very air seems to create a climate of innovation and change. In such an atmosphere, the company which fails to be agile and is not prepared to leap to better positions is often left behind. Despite the fact that stagnant organizations are characterized by certain traits and even certain physical characteristics, it's not easy for a company to recognize that it's falling behind merely because it's standing still. This knowledge only has pertinence and meaning when it falls into the hands of a manager who can make things happen that will alleviate the situation.

Such managers have two major characteristics. The first is that they are action-oriented and are willing to put aside their preoccupation with score-keeping when they are in the middle of the contest, and concentrate upon getting things moving and keeping them headed in the right direction. This means that they not only stimulate innovation from the top, but also gear the whole organization to accept innovation and create new things themselves. Yet innovation and moving forward requires that the action-getter have supplementary skill in building sufficient controls to prevent loss of the momentum and backward movement, in order to consolidate the gains.

This double objective of getting action for innovation and improvement, and holding onto them are the minimum requirements of the leader in management positions.

5

HOW TO IDENTIFY WHAT NEEDS IMPROVEMENT

> *"As any industrial society advances it becomes increasingly dependent upon the brains and much less upon the brawn of its working forces."*
>
> S. E. HILL AND F. HARBISON

It's said that management expert Frederick Taylor was able to size up the quality of management in any company by simply walking through the plant. Self-trained to look for key indicators of ineffectiveness and inefficiency, the "father of scientific management" probably possessed critical facilities which most of us don't possess. It's also true that his sojourns through the factory were made on an earlier day when the entire scope of the business would be encompassed in a single visit or through a single set of indicators.

Probably the latter day appraiser of a firm would start in a different spot in his study. In the large and complex business firm of today, we'd start somewhere removed from the plant gate, and track a different course in identifying possible areas for improvement.

The chances are we'd begin with a look at the attitudes of management itself. Stagnation in an organization begins with the management and extends outward in peripheral rings to its finances, its plants, its marketing plans, its research, the quantity and sagacity of its staff work, and its community relations.

The manager who makes things happen knows how to identify the areas where improvement is needed. The fact that things have been done a certain way in the past isn't justification for doing it the same way in the future. The improver's eye is trained to look at jobs critically, assured before beginning that there is a better way of doing it, a newer system or procedure, or a sharpening of old practices which can be applied. The improver has a restless desire to see things done better and easier, and knows that even the best method can be improved if brains and energy are applied to doing it.

The improver is not particularly impressed by triumphs of the past, but fixes a cold eye on the problems ahead; pictures new markets to be captured; new products to be developed, tested and marketed; and new processes to produce these products at higher quality and lower costs.

For the management with such an attitude of constant improvement, the problem isn't primarily one of technique, but first of identifying what particular job, product or project should come first. This requires some techniques for spotting what needs improvement.

RULES FOR IDENTIFYING AREAS FOR IMPROVEMENT

Setting these priorities requires some standards for picking targets for improvement. Studies of managers with records of accomplishment in making things happen would tend to show that they usually have intelligence to discriminate between the many types of activities and focus on those that would produce the greatest gains.

Here are ten rules for finding these areas for improvement that will get the manager into most of the key areas where improvement efforts will pay off soonest and with the greatest results:

1. Fix your eye on costs. Whether the organization is a company which is in business for profit, or is an institution operating with a budget such as a government agency, school or hospital, the good effect of starting with cost reduction is immense. Cost has the quality of being a universal measuring instrument that responds to improvement, in most instances, by going down. This doesn't mean that a narrow attention to pennies and elimination of necessary services is an indicator of good management. It doesn't mean, for example, that you cut away income-producing activity in order to save the money which produces the income. It means you try to spend your cost dollars in such a way that they are producing more service or more income for each dollar spent.

> For example, you don't want to be like the one ice cream company which reacted to a decline in sales by firing its salesmen and eliminating most of its advertising. It means that you take a look at what you are spending and act aggressively to see how it can be used to produce more—or to see how the same volume of service can be produced at less cost.

One paper company during a recession attacked the problem of cost reduction by asking every factory employee to suggest savings which would be allocated to advertising and marketing to boost sales and preserve their jobs. The results were a great improvement. Not only did the factory people cut their own costs, but the marketing and advertising staff, knowing that their expenses were coming from pennies squeezed out of operations, worked harder to make them more productive.

The organization, which is flourishing and is blessed with a rising sales curve and rising profits, may find that excess expenses are less important than getting the goods out and meeting deadlines and schedules. In such periods, it's the professional who is able to capitalize on the favorable situation and cut costs.

2. Is it a bottleneck? One of the key indicators that management action is needed is if one thing is causing delays which holds up several other things. These vital spots comprise a fertile field for improvement, since they pay larger dividends in releasing the productive efforts of other machines, processes or people who have been held up by the offending spot.

3. Is it taking too much time? One management man found, after some study of his personal time, that he was spending an inordinate amount of his time on the phone calling and checking travel reservations. By passing this chore to his secretary, he was freed for more productive work. The principle here can apply on a wider scale as well. The things which are taking up too much of anyone's time are probably costing more than they should, and are a fertile area for improvement.

4. Has it drifted imperceptibly in the wrong direction? One large sales organization found that it had stopped its growth in customers and number of orders from old customers. In checking on the reasons for this declining rate of growth, the sales manager discovered that *service* to the customer had slipped in the haste of gathering orders, and a distinct advantage which the company had held in the beginning was sliding away in the urge to get big. By concentrating on reestablishing the quality of service rendered her customers, she was able to start the trend upward once more.

This is all too often true in the organization which starts out with an original leverage in quality or styling, but as it succeeds, it lets this original feature go by the board. Such drifting toward the worse can happen without any drastic event to point it up, and when discovered it can be a source of big dividends in improvement.

One eastern bakery began with homemade pies which tasted just like ones mother used to make, and found itself swamped with orders. As they expanded and went into regional distribution, they hired more bakers and bought more equipment. Without anyone noticing it, their pies began to look and taste more and more like everyone else's. One day, the woman, who had started the company with her own recipe and was now a director, walked into the board room with two pies. One she had purchased from a company distributor; the other she had just baked in her own oven from her original recipe. Taking out a knife and some plates, she served a small piece of each to the officers of the firm. The point became immediately obvious, and a drastic revision in bakery processes took place to get more of the home-baked quality back into the product. As a result, this company rose to the top in sales.

5. Have outside conditions changed? Often the world changes and the company stands still, with the result that the company which was pioneering when it began is now left far behind. Henry Ford pioneered in the manufacture of automobiles, which you could "get in any color as long as it was black." This was exactly what the situation called for in his day. Yet, after World War II, this very policy threatened the company with extinction.

Many companies today have expanded into international operations in an attempt to capture foreign markets. Those companies which continue only to sell their domestic customers often find themselves faced with the statistic of a relatively shrinking market for their products.

Unionization has changed wages, hours and conditions of work in the manufacturing industry and in many professional service industries. The change in labor markets from one of labor surplus in the thirties to a later labor shortage, the expansion of the population, the move to suburbia, the decentralization of industry into smaller units of more manageable size, the shortening of the work week for many occupations, an energy shortage rather than a surplus, foreign competition and inflation all are typical of the drastic outside changes which have their impact on business.

One food company, for example, has capitalized on the new leisure and higher incomes of people to enter the gourmet food business in order to capitalize on such a development. Keeping abreast of the gamut of social, political, economic, and habitual patterns of consumers is essential in identifying areas for improvement or innovation.

6. Is it being done the same old way? In the light of the dynamic nature of business, it becomes a fairly safe conclusion that if a job or process is being done the same old way it was done ten or fifteen years ago—or even last year—it may be ripe for improvement. The facts of innovation and change are that competition in new ideas is increasing, and once they've been introduced, it's often too late to catch up. Therefore, the only safe course is to assume that the other fellow is improving his methods and products, and that doing it the same way, year after year, is courting disaster.

7. Good Strategies Come Before Good Operations! Cost reduction is a solid way of keeping competitive on a day-to-day operational basis. But there is a higher level of profit improvement which must acompany efficient operations. Those are the general directions in which the firm is going, sometimes known as strategic goals. Strategic goals are those that answer the question, "Are we doing the right things?" and should come ahead of asking, "Are we doing things right?" Strategies are the multi-year targets and goals which change the character and direction of the business. Good strategic management is usually the responsibility of the officers and perhaps the directors of the firm. It consists of doing a regular review of the company's position and laying out answers to four key questions:

    a. **Where are we now as an organization?** What are our strengths, weaknesses, problems? What threats hang over us? To what risks are we exposed? What are the best long-run opportunities for us, in the light of all of the answers to the foregoing questions.

    b. **Trends:** What major trends affect us? If we didn't do anything differently than we are doing right now, where would we be in one year? Two years? Five to ten years? Do we like the answers to this, and if not, what should be done about it?

    c. **Missions?** What business are we in? What are we in business for? What would be some suitable indicators of success?

    d. **Strategies:** What would be the best strategy? What options are there? For each option, what would the contribution to our mission be? What would each one cost?

Such strategic thinking and long-run goal-setting, coupled with tight operational and cost control, will provide both innovation and control.

8. **Watch Inputs and Outputs, Not Just Costs.** While it's important to watch costs, it's also important to watch what is being produced. Mr. Frank Cary, long time president of IBM, is reported to have worn a button on his lapel from time to time, as he toured his plants and laboratories, which declared "Add value not costs." This whole idea is based upon a systems approach to managing. A business, so goes this approach, can be described as three major elements:

inputs ⟹ activities ⟹ outputs

The **inputs** are the resources, money, labor, capital, and the like which are put-in (hence in-put).

Activities are the process, the work, the effort, the professional processes that convert materials into more useful and salable products or services.

Outputs are the end products, which should be more valuable at the end than the resources consumed in their production. Hence, value-added means the added worth resulting from the whole process of operating the organization.

Too many managers get stuck on one element of what must be a three-element system. They worry exclusively about expenses (the "bean counter" mentality) or about working hard (they get enmeshed in the activity trap) or they become output fanatics. The best managers are those who see all three elements all of the time, and keep their people working to maximize value-added.

9. Getting Commitment by Goal-Setting. Making a general identification of inputs and outputs doesn't do the whole job, however. What's needed in every organization is a system in which every manager and subordinate sits down regularly and hammers out the goals of the subordinate's job. The loftiest strategy and the noblest dream are worthless until some responsible person makes a commitment—usually to somebody else whose opinion is important—to make that goal happen. This is the system known as *Management by Objectives.* In a majority of today's Fortune 500 corporations, as well as thousands of smaller firms, hospitals, government agencies, and volunteer groups, the power of managing by commitment is being tapped by this relatively simple concept.

> The manager sits down with his subordinates at least annually, and jointly they work out a set of objectives which are: (1) organizational improvement, (2) profit improvement, and (3) personal development for the manager. The subordinate and boss hammer out these objectives for the organization under the manager's jurisdiction, and each retains a copy of the written objectives for the period ahead. At the end of six months, and again at the end of a year, these are reviewed. This comprises the performance review for the manager, and is couched wholly in the terms of his or her accomplishments against the goals the subordinate and boss have agreed upon.
>
> Within such a framework, each manager is made aware of the need for identifying specific things

that need improving (including his own personal skills and abilities) and in collaboration with the boss, puts him- or herself on record as identifying the areas that need betterment.

This procedure for identifying change is supplemented by the boss asking the subordinate, "What can I do, do differently or refrain from doing that will help you meet these objectives?" This serves to identify the needed improvement in the subordinate-boss relationship required to accomplish the job and get the improvement into effect.

10. Outside Conditions Impinging Upon Business Need Managing. Such a procedure as management by objectives works admirably in identifying areas for improvement within the cost structure of the firm. It must always take into account the outside forces which are impinging upon the business. Since these outside effects often have a greater effect than internal inefficiencies, they too require clear identification. Unless they are identified before it is too late, they may be insoluble problems for management. Let's look at some of the major ones:

a. The community. Businesses operate inside the institutional environment of a community. The "community" may be local, regional, national, or global. It draws its employees from the surrounding labor markets, pays taxes and obtains services from local, county, state, and federal governments. It also is restricted and bound by the federal government which, under the Constitution, serves to maintain commerce between the states and in world trade. This puts the government squarely into business in the form of regulation, service and advice. Many companies, such as General Electric, have standard forms of "business climate" surveys, which cover such things as the general economic health of the community, its educational system, its roads and transportation systems, its churches, the availability of airports, and hundreds of other details of community characteristics. These are not forces which are immutable but they can be improved through intelligent business interest and attention to their role as citizens of the community in which they function.

Permitting executives to take part in civic and community activities, to hold offices in associations and organizations, to lead civic betterment campaigns, or to go to Washington to hold public positions, are often a result of identifying problems which exist in the community that need good men's efforts for solution.

   b. *The corporate image.* As often as not, this overseeing attention to community affairs grows out of habit or imitation among the majority of those who participate. Occasionally it takes the form of justification of the corporate activities— "creating a favorable image" in the eyes of the public upon which the firm depends for its survival.

   Let us assume that the executive image is widely accepted and is an unflattering one—that the executive is pictured as a heartless rascal, a greedy grubber after power and wealth, concerned more with things than human needs, more with profits than with persons. Consider then, how the legislator in Congress, or in state or local government, will respond to proposed legislation in such areas as tax policy or restrictions upon corporate growth: what will his actions be toward proposed acts to restrain this executive in his control of economic affairs in the marketplace?

   The inevitable result must be greater constraint upon the decision-making power of the executive. The important point to be made here is that restraints upon the behavior of companies and corporations will hardly be based on the behavior of executives.

   Images and opinions of business which have an all too immediate impact upon their success will be built up piece by piece from the selected images of executives. The image of the American in business is hardly attributable to that godless, soulless entity— the corporation, but to the individual decisions of managers.

   Take the case of the large company in the midwest which announced to the newspapers that it would move all of its plants to another state if a certain rather trivial piece of legislation were enacted by the state legislature. Actually, this bit of bluff was the personal statement of its president, issued as the voice of the company. One legislator remarked that the company must indeed be rather whimsical and erratic in its big decisions if it would spend countless millions in moving, as well as sacrificing the jobs of thousands of its employees, in order to have its way in the state capitol.

   Perhaps the more fundamental fact is that images are seldom based on press releases, or upon publicity campaigns, but upon solid works and accomplishments in betterment of the community and nation. Such actions must inevitably be taken personally by important officials in both personal and official capacities.

In a free society, the corporation and its managers may be unable to survive where too many of them operate on the assumption that they live on an island populated only by other profit seekers. Making things happen in management also requires that executive action be diverted to work with voluntary and civic associations, and the maintenance of quality institutions outside the firm.

6

WHIPPING OBSTACLES

"The world is cluttered up with unfinished business in the form of projects that might have been successful, if only at the tide point someone's patience had turned to active impatience."

ROBERT UPDEGRAFF

When Ethicon Inc., a subsidiary company of Johnson and Johnson, decided to expand its suture manufacturing and selling operations into a new market, they called in Richard Sellers, a promising young salesman. The new area, they explained, was in Canada, and if he wanted the job he could be manager of the new subsidiary. Sellers leaped at the chance. Arriving in Montreal, he found that he had neither plant, warehouse, nor any employees. On his first night there he was alone in a hotel room, and in his suitcase and sample bag he held the whole Canadian subsidiary of the firm! Ethicon's plants in New Jersey stood ready to supply his orders if he got any, and its management stood ready to back him if he could prove he was there to stay—and grow.

Within two years, he had a national sales force selling across the dominion, was selling from his own well-stocked warehouse, and had created, out of his own energy and drive, a whole company which today is incorporated as J&J Canada. Beginning with the thing he could do best—which was selling—he visited doctors and hospitals and cracked a foreign market, in some cases cutting across habits and language barriers that would have stopped lesser men in their tracks. His ability to overcome obstacles led him to the presidency and chairmanship of the parent company before he was forty, and ultimately to vice chairmanship of the parent company of Johnson and Johnson.

Such ability to overcome obstacles is more than a random collection of techniques and routines. It's part of an attitude toward obstacles which prods the obstacle-solver onward to accomplishment of his goals where others with less satisfactory attitudes will fail.

This attitude is the nucleus of actions which prove successful in overcoming obstacles and is far more important than the steps themselves, since the steps are created out of whole cloth in order to accomplish the goal.

QUALITIES OF OBSTACLE BUSTERS

1. A strong goal orientation. The person who will probably have the greatest success in overcoming obstacles has established some clear cut goals and is determined to achieve them. The fact that this goal entails the same red tape, difficulties and suggestions for delay that have stopped others, doesn't faze him or her in the least. All of these blocks diminish in importance in the bright light of the goal. The goal itself is the motivator.

2. A callousness to defeats. The good obstacle-hurdler normally has a built-in optimism that makes such things as inertia, opposition, confusion, timidity, and ignorance mere details to be brushed aside or otherwise managed.

3. Decisiveness. The most pernicious trait a manager can have when faced with obstacles is indecisiveness. Very often this is explained away as a need for mature consideration of the situation, but actually indecision is the result of the mind slipping away into inappropriate or trivial matters. Ordering a new desk or settling a squabble between two secretaries is much more intriguing than writing the order or picking up the telephone to announce the decision. The obstacle-hurdler makes moves decisively and the sooner the better. How can such ability be developed?

4. High Energy Levels. Managers who pursue goals with the greatest success usually do so with more vigor than others. This energetic approach alone will count for a great deal of their success at overcoming obstacles. Often, such people take time to keep themselves physically in shape to work longer hours or to maintain higher levels of intensity than other people. While it is true that there are flabby executives who do well, they appear to be a minority. During the seventies, jogging became a national craze, attracting many middle-aged and older executives. Fitness programs, reports professor Richard Pyle, have become widespread in American corporations, with health and fitness centers being found available to executives in over 300 of the largest corporations. Other firms, such as Coors brewing, Chase Manhattan, and others, send executives on wilderness trips under the "Outward Bound" program to physically upgrade them and hone their aggressive qualities. While much of the benefit from such programs shows up in cardiovascular fitness and a diminished level of executive heart attacks, it also produces a habit pattern of vigor and energy in attacking obstacles.

5. A Striving for Perfection. People who are chronic and persistent achievers seldom rest on their laurels and gloat over their triumphs, but rather have a drive for improvement which is absent in others less goal-driven. They apparently would agree with Andrew Carnegie who once said "all's perfect, we're getting better." This has been described by David McClelland of Harvard as "achievement motivation." This kind of motivation, he suggests, is characteristic of leaders in advanced countries and is absent in leaders in underdeveloped nations. It consists of strong goals, a language of success which they speak constantly, the development of success-breeding systems of work, and well-developed teamwork.

The qualities become instruments which seem to characterize obstacle-busters and are highly personalized skills in doing things. Occasionally these are closely allied to the actor's, and include dress, mannerisms, and poise under stress. Yet many less successful managers who have graduated from the right ivy-league school affect the same manners without having any of the same qualities. More frequently than Brooks Brothers' attire and the other outward accoutrements of success, the quality of *earthiness* in fundamental things appears.

6. Good Memory Skills. A variation of this is the immense ability to carry details in his head, or a carefully cultivated memory for names and faces. In the early stages of a man's career, he will use this facility to amass a great array of names and faces of all levels in the organization. He'll have a speaking acquaintance with as many of the great and successful as he can achieve, and by making sure that it covers a decent spread of those of more lowly station, he can avoid the reputation of being an apple polisher or boot licker. Then too, he'll want to make these acquaintances among the lesser ranks, especially among the promising ones, for they may, in turn, become important.

7. A Clear Picture of Reality. The executive conscience and sense of honesty is a commonly cited quality for a successful manager, which is perfectly sound for a manager to develop since it helps him overcome obstacles which he might otherwise fail to reduce. Simply put, it eliminates the necessity for maintaining a tangled fabric of distortions or misrepresentations which must be constructed in order to bolster up the first lie. The truth, however bad, is always preferable to the slight lie which looks more favorable since it requires nothing by way of extraneous and superfluous effort and psychic energy to recall in an instant. The manager who weaves a tangled web of half truths or whole untruths must constantly be vigilant to construct a perfect pattern to camouflage his deception. The honest manager may rely upon simple recall of actuality, and finds his mental processes freed for problem-solving and decision-making.

8. Using People Well. Equally vital among the qualities of the obstacle-breaker is that of using people without becoming sentimentally over-involved with their successes or failures. A survey of fifty company presidents by two graduate students at the School of Business at Michigan University showed that such things as fraternal connections and other sentimental ties rated last among these executive's considerations when picking men for positions of leadership.

All of these qualities, however, are subordinate to the manager's ability at problem-solving, of the lock-picking, maze-solving type. This is a function of his powers of adjustment to different and changing circumstances.

VARIOUS WAYS MANAGERS ADJUST TO OBSTACLES

Adjust he must if he is to overcome obstacles, for problem solving and overcoming difficulties is a process of adjustment that stems from the goals the man has, his urgency in wanting to reach them and his ingenuity in eliminating or neutralizing the things that block him from his goals. The process for every human looks something like this:

QUALITIES OF OBSTACLE BUSTERS

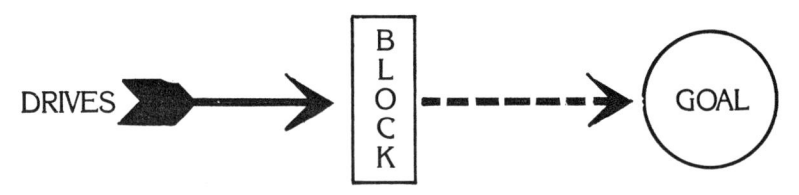

```
DRIVES ▶───▶  [BLOCK] ---▶ ( GOAL )
```

He's driven by the desire for worldly goods, for prestige, for reputation, for self-expression or one of the other multifarious goals that impel people into action. Yet in everyday affairs—including those of business—blocks occur. Two people want the same goal which is available to one only. Other people's cooperation is required, and they are reluctant or violently unwilling to offer such assistance. What happens when a goal-seeking man reaches the block is dependent upon his ability to adjust. These forms of adjustment take on a wide range of alternate forms.

Direct attack. Some people find that the normal reaction for them, when faced with an obstacle, is to lower their head and charge. When this pattern seems to work for them once, they'll try it again. They'll continue as long as it works, and will only try another attack when they finally run into a block that won't topple when it's hit. Since most people run into such an obstacle at one time or another in their life, most good obstacle-overcomers use direct attack along with *other* methods of arriving at their goal. Knowing when to attack and when to look for a better way is the first step in adjusting to blocks.

Substitute goals. Another form of adjustment is to replace the goal from which you're blocked with another which *can* be attained. In some cases this may be a goal which is just as satisfactory as the first one, or it may result in lowering the standards of what's expected. While this may be disappointing and even result in a loss of face, such adjustments are often required in business as elsewhere, and the important thing is that the manager not let the fact of having to change goals ruin his ability to adjust well in the future.

Trial and error. Still another way managers adjust to obstacles is to continue a wide range of trial and error responses, to overcome or otherwise get around the block. In one example, a general foreman in a large carton factory found that every time he made a suggestion for improvement to his plant manager, it was always found somehow to be lacking. If it were the type of suggestion which could be completely reversed, the plant manager seemed to automatically suggest that alternative.

One day, the general foreman went into the manager's office to discuss the layout of a new piece of packaging equipment. It was his idea that the machine should be bolted and suspended from the ceiling, thus saving floor space and leaving room for storage under the machine. Knowing that such a novel idea would immediately be pooh-poohed, he fastened upon a scheme.

"One thing is sure," he said, "we don't want to suspend that machine from the ceiling like I've seen some plants do."

"Oh no?" said the plant manager. He then proceeded to berate the general foreman for making such quick assumptions and spent several minutes selling him on his own idea, which, if it had been presented as a positive suggestion in the first place, would have been given the customary negative treatment.

Perhaps one of the greatest mistakes one can make in adjusting to obstacles is to rely too heavily upon a single response. Efficiency in adjusting to obstacles depends upon the ability of the individual manager to continue varying responses until success is achieved.

Skill in overcoming obstacles in management requires that the executive become a student of the arts of overcoming blocks to avoid being thwarted by them. For one thing, know something about the nature of the obstacle. Usually these obstacles to getting what we want are one of several types:

Environmental obstacles. Those are the blocks which are created by the material circumstances. For example, the manager of an international division may find that he or she is blocked by a shortage of skilled labor in the country, or that the union has a set policy of opposition to changes in work rules or methods. Perhaps certain materials or facilities are unavailable. Yet these environmental obstacles seldom are the heart of failure in obstacle hurdling.

More often some *personal* skill deficiency prevents attacking the problem properly. Such a defect may be a habit of giving up, or it may be a lack of skill, experience or training in the kind of behavior that the problem requires in order to be solved. In many instances, these personal defects are more imaginary than real, and can be either effectively ignored, or in the case of lack of training, can be overcome by hard work and practice. People of little ability are more apt to let an obstacle throw them than people of great ability. These abilities aren't necessarily ones with which the person is born, however; their lack implies a self-development program for the manager as an aid to obstacle-hurdling ability. Physical vitality and energy are often at the root of poor obstacle hurdling, and on more than one occasion, a physical checkup and corrective therapy has transformed a so-so performer into a successful action-getter.

Conflicts of motives are often important sources of delay and ineptness in obstacle hurdling and adjustment to blocks in a manager. These consist of situations in which we find ourselves between two desires which are mutually exclusive. The normal desire to live a full family life and the desire to move ahead in the organization, which requires that we give extensive time traveling away from home, are typical of such conflicts. Unfortunately the two conflicting urges cancel one another and leave the person bland or neutral. They create tensions which feed on one another, and result in vacillation and "neutral," nonproductive activity. A manager split over various alternatives which are opposed to one another, often vents this tension upon such harmless and useless jobs as cleaning out the files, or dropping into the office of another staff memeber to pass the time of day. While such actions solve the tensions, it doesn't get over the hurdles to succeed in the job.

Such words as "worry" and "indecisiveness" are apt labels for the situation in which the manager is torn between desire for the goal and fear of failure, or simple tension caused by the pressures of two strong motives pushing him from either direction.

G. S. Kennedy, former chairman at General Mills, has pointed out that decision-making at the higher levels of management is like walking a girder high above the street. The iron worker is able to walk the narrow girder forty flights up because he has overcome the "worry" or fear of falling. The top executive makes decisions which are no more difficult in terms of pure decision-making techniques than that of the foreman. It's simply the fear of failure and the enormity of effect if he does so that causes him to tighten up and grab for safety.

Much nonsense has been written about the techniques of decision-making, as though the failures in this vital area were a lack of understanding of the process. Far more often than inability to handle the data and arrive at the solution is the fear of failure and the conflict between wanting to get the decision made and that worry about making the wrong one. This puts decision-making as an obstacle-busting method into the area of adjustment, and only in part into the realm of techniques of collecting, sorting and analyzing data.

GOOD VERSUS BAD WAYS OF OBSTACLE LICKING

This worry and indecision is but one of the wrong ways of adjusting to obstacles. The range of bad adjustments is wide, and the correct ways are limited to those which relieve the tension of the individual and bring him to his goal.

> The satisfactory ways of adjusting are those which help the manager arrive at the goal within the framework of the ethical and value systems in which he works.

To a large extent then, the manager who is successful in overcoming obstacles is the one who successfully avoids those things which keep him or her from achieving it. For the preservation of our ego, it's possible to relieve tensions at levels lower than the goals which have been set. If this weren't true, then every person who didn't reach his goal in management—or a satisfactory substitute—would be "off balance" mentally. What are some of the less satisfactory forms of adjustment?

Adjustment by withdrawal. Although there are many occasions in life when the manager must recognize that discretion is the better part of valor, and must retreat from his or her stand, this can't be termed unsatisfactory. From the action-getting viewpoint, such withdrawals are merely regrouping for the next attack. Such retreats become unsatisfactory from the viewpoint of management action when the manager never returns to the attack but sits down before the block and vegetates. In some cases, we may become publicity-shy when publicity would be the best thing for the situation. In others, we become timid and respectful where boldness and brass are called for. Occasionally, we will plead more ignorance than we actually should, as justification for inaction. In some instances the withdrawal turns into a form of negativism such as that of the plant manager in the example above. In still others, we simply retreat before opposition or even a tough hurdle. In other situations, we engage in daydreaming about irrelevant things, which proves a successful substitute for action.

In a medium-sized company in the East, the president was often observed in various forms of withdrawal. The son of the founder, he withdrew into philosophizing about the nature of management theory, and spent an inordinate amount of his time in making philosophical speeches before various management and engineering groups about the theory and philosophy of management. When forced back to reality and the necessity of solving particular problems which were blocking the company, he lapsed into theory. Finally he settled into a highly watered-down version of "participative management" in which he covered his inability to make any decision, however trivial, under the guise of being "democratic." Far from using these instruments effectively, he used them as tools of withdrawal with disastrous results to the company.

Perhaps one of the more interesting forms of withdrawal which every normal person engages in at some time, and which managers do too, is fantasy. This is a form of daydream. Rightly oriented, these daydreams can become the plans for achievement, and are part of the goal-forming process for the manager. The manager who dreams of a new plant may have this fantasy become so firmly fixed that he or she exerts tremendous effort in order to achieve it in actuality. Such daydreams are a positive aid to the action-getter, and a good supply of unfulfilled daydreams keeps him or her alive and moving forward.

When daydreaming and fantasy are a form of substitute for actually accomplishing something which we wanted to do but couldn't reach because of some obstacle, then it's probably harmful. These daydreams often run into several forms in their undesirable aspects. The manager may fail and enjoy reveries of becoming the conquering hero, a great tycoon or a master builder of industrial empires.

If such daydreams are the hard schemes of an ambitious and practical climber, they may even come true. Where they are the daydreams of a manager who has just failed to carry off a deal, a merger or a sale, they're both useless and harmful. They waste time and dissipate energy. When a manager slips into the habit of fantasy of an undesirable kind, this only fritters away time, and instead of actually doing, planning and analyzing, which the situation demands, he or she floats away into a haze of imagined pleasures and accomplishments.

Adjustment by defensiveness. When a manager hits an obstacle, it's also a common thing to adjust by building up defenses against the real reasons for failure. If the results of hitting an obstacle have been especially painful, it may result in a resolve not to get caught so severely again, and we erect barriers to protect our sensitivities. One president of a small company, for example, led his firm into a new product line quite radically different from the traditional lines it had been in before. The effort fizzled badly, and for many years after that, nobody dared mention the product, which had been the focal point of the fiasco, in his presence. He often took personal affront if any slight reference to this product were made in normal conversation with him.

Evidences of this defensiveness are sometimes characterized by avoidance of certain topics or people. One executive who once received a slighting reference in a press release showed great abhorrence for all newspapermen and press relations after that. Another manifestation of defensiveness in managers is that they will seek out and be overly responsive to flattery. A company officer of my acquaintance, who had limited formal education, found that this limitation caused him some difficulty early in his career. By dint of great drive and native intelligence, he overcame this handicap and went on past many of his better-educated friends. Yet he never fully shook his defensiveness about this seeming defect, and was especially subject to any form of flattery which bolstered his reputation as a thinker, scholar or well-informed person in the arts and sciences.

For the manager to handle adjustments to obstacles by establishing defense mechanisms isn't usually a conscious process. Defense mechanisms are learned through trial and error, and often grow out of the fact that the manager isn't clearly aware of his or her own drives in the first place.

Adjustment by compensation. When the reasons for failure to overcome obstacles are rooted in some personal defect in the manager, the kind of adjustment, which results in overemphasis of a trait to overcome a feeling of deficiency in it, may occur. The supervisor who really feels inferior to many of his or her associates may affect a lordly and overbearing manner to compensate for his inward inadequacy. The president of one chemical company was a very short man, and compensated for it by talking tough and acting very roughly with his subordinates and equals. The staff specialist who has few abilities in management may develop uncommon knowledge and ability in one field and thereby acquire status and respect for it.

In some instances, individuals who have achieved little in their own careers may become "people builders" of younger persons of greater promise and endowments, finding satisfaction thereby. Unable to lick the obstacles which blocked him or her from success, he or she adjusts by arming and training others who seem to promise that they can do what he or she was unable to do. The obstacle is hence overcome, and the manager becomes instrumental in its demolition.

Other ways of adjusting. To describe these forms of adjustment doesn't necessarily imply that they are all necessarily bad. There are some forms of adjusting, however, which are usually unfortunate for the manager who uses them, since they arouse reaction against him or her which prevents success in future attempts at overcoming their obstacles. *Egocentrism* is such a form. Just as the defensive person may retreat from the press, the attention-getter may seek to get before the public on every occasion, and retain expensive retinues of press agents to "build up" a reputation. In its worst forms it turns into pathological lies or self-accusations. *Rationalization* is another form of adjustment to hitting an obstacle that stops a manager. Managers who fail will go to great lengths to give socially acceptable and rational explanations of failure. Blaming the tools, the bankers, the workmen, or luck are such rationalizations. Occasionally this becomes a system of projecting low motives to others, deprecating the goal which we really want or, more commonly, declaring that what we accomplished was "exactly what I had hoped for in the first place." Two danger signs in such adjustment are in seeing conspiracies among others as the cause of failure, and delusions. The latter two are fortunately uncommon, and are symptoms that the person may be in need of professional assistance in his adjustment problems.

ENDS VERSUS MEANS IN A FREE SOCIETY

All of this is, of course, couched in terms of the long-run *effectiveness* with which a manager adjusts to the obstacles in carrying the organization onward toward the goals set for it. These really are some standards by which the directors might appraise its officers' and executives' ability to get things done, for example. Or perhaps it might be a standard by which the vice president of manufacturing judges a plant manager's actions, or by which a general foreman evaluates the results and actions of foremen. But they aren't the only standards.

If we were to assume that reaching the goal were all that was required of a manager, then more direct attack and less of other forms of adjustment might be expected. Yet direct attack often leaves in its wake a series of bobbing heads shouting for succor. Under such circumstances, the captain of the ship may rightly ask whether or not such expenditures of good people who were unfortunate enough to comprise a block to the action-getting manager, weren't due more civilized treatment. In a more practical vein, the form of action-getting in management, which results in a tangled pile of bodies in the wake of the on-rushing hero, may be the cause of his or her ultimate downfall and be bad business for the firm. This concern for people, and the dignity of each person—even when one is an obstruction to the path of progress—is one of the underlying values of our society. Because it's much easier to uphold the individual dignity of people who lend us a helping hand than those who thwart us doesn't change the underlying ethic. The facts are that the end alone does not justify the means used in overcoming obstacles. This requires some further clarification of how managers become obstacle-busters, since the *means* must also be measured by several criteria which haven't a thing to do with the virtue of the goal or the sterling qualities of the manager who pursues them.

Ours is a materialistic society, and profit, for all the damnation which has been laid upon it by those not immediately charged with producing it, remains the primary goal of business. The production of great profit has never been damned even by its most vocal critics except as it bears upon the ways in which that profit is obtained. Marx decried profit and surplus, as being resultant of the exploitation of the worker. Government committees wield the public interest as a club, and seek to preserve the purchasing power of the public through investigations which would induce corporations to cut their prices, thereby enhancing this purchasing power. Large profits seem to automatically elicit accusations that somebody is being exploited in order that high profits be achieved. Despite the possibilities of such exposés and criticism, for the manager it's safe to assume that making higher profits his or her primary goal will please most of the masters whose approval is of greatest importance. This, I would suggest, is true for *most* managers.

The clear superiority of this goal for management over everything that follows it in rank order doesn't necessarily mean that the other considerations don't exist, or that they can be ignored. These considerations have to do with the judgments which outsiders will place upon the *means* of accomplishing this end. The manager who makes things happen thus is bound by certain criteria as to means by which he or she must adjust the obstacle-solving activities to survive. Survival, in this instance, means that he or she must circumvent the severe criticism of methods which will loudly resound in the ears of owners and judges, so that it might offset the wonderful effects of having accomplished what he or she set out to do.

A. A. Berle, with uncompromising clarity, makes such a charge to management in his book *Power Without Property,* when he points up that managers of modern corporations are wielding power without holding property rights to the vast resources they direct. The legitimacy—inchoate if not statutory—of the manager's role, he suggests, exists only because his management is efficient, and *because it takes into account the needs of workers, custom-*

ers, owners, and the public. Without the latter considerations, Berle suggests, the inchoate legitimacy of management rights is lost, and he implies that statutory and administrative power will be stripped away in time as a result.

Criticism of management methods, as it attempts to demolish the obstacles to profitable operation and corporate growth, takes a number of forms. These assume some importance since they automatically—in the eyes of the modern professional manager—become further restrictions upon methods of overcoming blocks to progress. To clearly understand these criteria, it's necessary that management identify them more clearly than being that of other classes of people, as Berle does. It means that the modern manager is constrained from violating certain value systems in which our business system must function if he is to avoid the reverberations from his or her own superiors. These value systems have several facets.

1. **Management gets action inside a human value system.** This human value system in America provides for the dignity of people regardless of race or sex, and respect for their rights to move freely and serve voluntarily in the marketplace. The use of tangible force is long outlawed. The use of naked economic coercion must be used sparingly in getting people into lines of conformity with management goals. A hint of behavior which conjures up the image of the corporation, with all its economic might, using its power to squelch the economically inferior individual, will always result in strong disapproval from the wider public and ultimately from the owners.

2. **Management gets action within a system of ethical values.** The "new Puritanism" of the seventies, growing out of the scandals, dishonest advertising, bribery, and conflicts of interest are but symptoms of an underlying set of ethical standards which existed all along. Management, the prevailing folklore holds, must be ethical and achieve its profits honestly and in a forthright manner. Integrity is a minimum requirement of the manager, and its absence results in retaliatory action by those whose ultimate power is in the political processes which govern all of the institutions and people.

3. **Management gets action within an institutional value system.** The role of free enterprise and private corporations is not

only circumscribed by law, but also by prevailing sentiments about it. Managers who hope to accomplish their goals as leaders in such organizations must recognize the role of other institutions—and respect it. The labor union, the government, the civic and social institution, the educational system, the church, and other institutions have status in the eyes of the public. The relationship of the corporation to them takes certain broad forms which are really expectations that the public at large charges them with. For the manager who attempts to overcome his personal obstacles, respect for these institutional values are, by and large, impossible to ignore.

Unfortunately, for the manager who wears blinders to these respective value systems, the ultimate power to control his own actions rests with government, and under the proddings of a populace dissatisfied with means of management, restrictions upon management can—and have been—imposed without compunction. Often these expectations go beyond simple disapproval of certain practices. They are enlarged to expectations of things that the firm should voluntarily do. It should actively support the national defense. It should pay taxes without evasion. More than this, it should contribute of its profits to educational institutions and of its managers' personal time and money to good causes. Such things are part and parcel of overcoming obstacles to business success.

7

THE INFORMATION REVOLUTION: HOW TO MAKE A DECISION

> *"There are divers kinds of decisiveness; there is that of temperament, and that of reason, and there is that which is compounded of both, and this last is best..."*
>
> HENRY TAYLOR (1836)

Recent literature on decision-making in management has laid great stress upon the rational aspects of decision-making. "Get the facts, weigh and decide, take action, and follow through," so went the famous course which was offered foremen by the hundreds of thousands during World War II. New decision-making courses, taught by playing management games, in which answers are produced from the bowels of a computer, or simply mathematical exercises to substitute "minimax" for intuition in decisions, are part of this new apparatus of decision-making.

None of these approaches, however laudable they may be from the viewpoint of improving rationality, attack the central block to decision-making which makes, or fails to make, things happen in an administrative situation. For the executive who gets things done, there are habits and patterns of behavior that make up the proper mix of fact-gathering and decision, in which reflexes move surely from facts to action without undue haste or the deliberation and delay which marks the indecisive person.

For most managers, this cycle of decision-making to get things done is a *compressed* running of the cycle of thought and decision, which has the appearance of elimination of certain key steps. Yet the manager who makes things happen makes more right decisions than wrong ones. It's this ability to compress time in adhering to the safest procedures for decision-making that mark the action-getting executive. What, then, is in this decision-making process that makes for both fast and good decisions? This should be followed by the logical question: once you know the process, how can you compress the time for decisions in order that each turn of events may be capitalized upon?
First, the cycle of decision-making:

- orientation to the situation
- identification of the key facts
- identification of the major problem or problems
- proposal of possible causes and identification of one
- the scanning of probable solutions
- the aggressive application of the solution
- checking whether it's right or wrong and trying again.

Let's look at each of these steps, find any pitfalls in them, and take some examples from actual cases in which executives made good decisions that paid off for their organization.

DECISIONS ON FAMILIAR GROUND

The experience of most managers is that they can make better decisions on familiar ground than on strange subjects or in strange environments. The sales manager of thirty years' experience, consciously or not, is basing such a decision upon complete familiarity with the situation, in which he or she operates. The veteran knows perfectly well, without consciously setting them out, all of the possible causes of the problem, and some of the pitfalls which befall the unwary. In a single instant, his or her mind feeds up into its consciousness a vast potpourri of experiences and strong impressions from over the years. Such decisions, made on familiar ground, are said to be rooted in the experience of the decision-maker, and often account for the speed, accuracy and brilliance of the decision. How then can a satisfactory decision be made when one is confronted with a new situation?

> When making decisions on unfamiliar ground, it's necessary to give oneself a complete orientation to the situation.

In other words, the substitute for long experience is an ability to master the facts and attitudes involved, in as short a time as possible. With such orientation to the situation, two things emerge for the less experienced person.

- Intuition and intelligence in problem solving give us some inkling of the probably satisfactory results or conditions in the situation.
- We identify the key facts that indicate what conditions should exist if the situation were ideal.
- From this orientation to the situation—perhaps from experience in similar situations—we begin to see several major gaps between what's right and what exists. These comprise the major problems which must be solved.

Take the case of the company which found itself with overloaded warehouses of product, yet orders were not being delivered because the right products were not on hand. A consultant brought into the situation quickly outlined the major facts as stated briefly above. He saw the problem as being one in which too many of the unnecessary items were being produced, while needed products were being shunted aside. He saw a variety of plausible causes for the trouble, and investigated each one carefully. Finally, he concluded that the problem lay in the lack of feedback from the production department to the scheduling section. Orders to run a certain quantity were not being followed, and since the schedule department received no reports of actual performance against schedules, it had no controls which would have prevented over-runs on certain orders at the expense of others.

The procedure here was one which might have been followed by an experienced hand who took the time to organize an approach to become completely familiar with the situation, identify the gap between actual and ideal, and direct action toward closing this gap. In this instance, the consultant set up a system of feeding back to the scheduling department actual results of production against scheduled amounts. With a few stiff warnings issued to the manufacturing supervisors when overruns or underruns occurred, the situation straightened itself out.

Everyone had a small piece of the situation, and it was only when the consultant entered the scene and familiarized himself with the entire picture that all of the facts were available in one place which could result in a decision that solved the difficulty.

MAKING THE MOMENTOUS DECISIONS

Such a situation as the production control problem which the consultant faced, however complex it may have seemed, was nevertheless less difficult than many in which managers must take part. Many important decisions are of a type which have no single best solution, and in which facts alone are insufficient basis upon which to choose one course of action.

> Many of the big decisions cannot be made on the basis of past experience.

This is because decision-making is something apart from problem solving. The kinds of decisions which are made on familiar ground are really tests of problem solving ability, rather than ability to make a decision on a course of action among several alternatives. In some instances, these decisions made on familiar ground are made under conditions where it is almost certain that the decision will produce a desired result—or at least a predictable one. In others there is risk of failure or loss. This risk, however, is minimized when the ground is more familiar, since many of the obvious risks have been allowed for and their possible effects circumvented.

Most big-business decisions which cause the executive to pause in the decision-making process are made under conditions that are neither familiar nor allow for prediction of risk. In fact, in many such decisions, there is downright *uncertainty,* not only about the situation and full facts, but about the possible outcomes of following any specific course of action.

How then, can the executive be one who makes things happen when faced with the possibility of failure, or even possible setbacks to the organization? Under such circumstances there are some basic approaches to decision-making which serve to make the big decisions more viable for the action-getter.

1. Assume that what's worked in the past will continue to work. In the face of uncertainty, it's better to assume that the things that have proven successful will continue to be the best—until there is some convincing evidence otherwise. Experimentation with untried methods and unproven people isn't to be done on a wholesale basis in the area of decision-making. If you have a solid performer who has done well in the past, he or she is apt to be the best bet for carrying the heavy jobs in the future. If one territory has always led the pack in volume and quality, you can assume that they'll continue to do so in the future—unless some strong evidence causes you to question that assumption.

2. Identify the things you know for sure. Even in every decision made in the face of uncertainty, there are some hard facts. These can be relied upon and should be identified, labelled clearly and fixed in mind. They shouldn't be confused with opinions, which are sometimes as firmly held as facts, but are less apt to be reliable.

3. Pinpoint the areas of decision-making which require pure reasoning. Once the facts are in hand and opinions labelled as such, the decision in the face of uncertainty should require clear marking off of the area, which can only be concluded from reason, logic, conceptual exercise, discursive logic, and intuition. These should then be defined in as clear and logical language as possible under the circumstances.

4. Try to find a theory that covers the subject at hand. Here you are seeking analogies, general precepts which have worked in the past and generalizations which probably will apply to the decision-making situation. Using the right principle voluntarily the first time, often pulls into the decision the accumulated experience of the past toward the correct decision in this case.

> In one large meat packing firm, the manager of research reported to the board of directors that irradiation of food by radioactive isotopes was making such progress that it warranted a substantial investment in research and development. He further predicted that, if the research were successful, the entire food business

would be revolutionized. The board was faced with the choice of allocating funds to this new idea or to an expanded program of conventional research on present methods of preparation and production of meat.

"The principle which I think we must follow," one director said, "is to prepare for changes, without sacrificing the present successful line of business."

Whether or not the board adopted his "principle" isn't relevant. More important, they were dealing with an intangible decision in the face of uncertainty, assuming that what worked in the past would continue to work, relying on certain things they knew for sure and the clear identification of the decision as one of "how fast" the innovation of food irradiation would come. The decision in this case was that food irradiation was possible but wasn't imminent within the next couple of years, and therefore the balance should be in favor of present products and a substantial increase in atomic irradiation of meat, but not predominantly so.

5. Don't underestimate force and action in affecting the decision. Often the decision is made on the basis of static facts and past experiences, which always works in favor of the conservative decision. This may sometimes overlook the effect of force and action upon the outcome of a decision. The decision that a certain course would be the best one may be self-fulfilling if it is turned into aggressive action with vigorous and forceful behavior, when attempting to prove that the solution was the best. In the face of uncertainty, it may be that any of several decisions will work; the one finally chosen as best will work if it is aggressively applied and made to work through force, energy and action by the organization.

> In other words, decisiveness itself is an important ingredient in decision-making under uncertainty.

The decisions which may be "wrong" often turn out well, and a satisfactory result is achieved if they are implemented with force and action. Of course, under these circumstances, nobody may ever know that the wrong decision was made.

> Take the case of the small ceramic company which was, by most standards, on the downgrade and ready for the receivers. The board decided to assume that it would succeed if it expanded and went even further into debt for a new kiln. The sales organization was

expanded and sharpened up for the expanded capacity. Through hard-driving effort and herculean energy they pulled it off, and within two years were well on their way to leading the industry in return on investment. The president reported that numerous bankers and more rational businessmen had advised him to get out with as much as he could recover, rather than sink more into the firm. Yet, because they decided to grow rather than fold up, and worked at improvement, the decision proved to be the correct one. Yet, without the force and action which went into implementing the decision, the wrongness of the decision could have proven perfectly accurate.

DON'T LOOK BACK

Under such circumstances, it would seem advisable for uncertain decision-makers, once they have made their decision, not to spend too much time looking back to see if they are too far from shore or are in danger of being caught. The very act of making a decision work requires a certain blindness to both the possibility of failure and the closeness of the wolf to the front door of the executive office. This coolness under fire, this willingness to take risks and accept uncertainty without lapsing into indecisiveness, lies behind the success stories of many individuals and firms.

Much of the success of the manager who makes things happen is obliviousness to the possibility of a wrong turn in the road.

Decision-making under conditions of uncertainty in business practically demands that the manager avoid vacillation. Having mapped out a strategy, taking the possible actions of competitors into account and exerting rationality to its utmost, we then need to put aside deliberations and the kinds of reflective, cogitative skills which we applied in the decision-making process and channel our energies into making the decision work. At this point, decision-making is done for the moment and aggressive leadership to get to the goal is in demand.

This cut-off point in decision-making may not be until after some experimenting has been done on a smaller scale to decide whether or not the proposal would work in the larger organization.

> "I always find one department or section where there's a progressive man at the top to try out a new idea," reports one general manager. "If it works there, with good leadership giving it a fair try, I can then put it into action in the rest of the organization."

This testing process that the general manager used offers some other safeguards to the decision-making process, too. In the hands of a good manager, the idea will have its flaws revealed, and minor alterations can be made. Or it might be that some major loophole, which was overlooked in the original planning, can indicate a major overhaul of the decision or even that it should be scrapped.

On the other hand, once the commitment is made, there's little advantage in constantly peering backward and wishing that things had been done differently.

> Take the case of the company which made a wrong decision in its capital budgeting. Admittedly it was working in an area with a few guideposts, but with more uncertainty than certainty. It followed all of the accepted practices of allocating its available capital against the demands upon it, yet found that once it was committed and the money borrowed and spent, it could have done much better. It seems that some new technical developments in their business had been just about on the verge of breaking forth, and they had underestimated this possibility. As a result, they were faced with a long haul, using equipment which would become more and more uncompetitive. The chairman of the finance committee of the board told the board this:
>
> > "It's going to cost us something to get out of this situation, but let's not cry over spilt milk. Let's ask everyone from top to bottom to pull as hard as they know how, to get the most out of what we've got, and we'll come out a lot better than if we mope about it."

To waste energy, and drive on ruminations about what might have happened if a better decision had been made in the beginning, is as destructive as making the wrong decision in the first place. More people fritter away their time and lapse into indecisiveness, playing the mental game of "if only I had done otherwise," rather than making foolish, hasty or ill-advised decisions.

Rationality alone won't make a decision work, however perfect in its structure and logic. Only leadership and force which result in action will do that.

WHY MANAGERS FEAR BIG DECISIONS

Putting an end to personal indecisiveness is more a matter of temperament than of rationality. Several distinct causes for this indecisiveness appear to be prevalent among poor decision-makers.

- **Lack of a clear-cut goal.** Where the manager isn't aware of what the central purpose of the organization is, or what his or her part in it is supposed to accomplish, he or she can't act freely. Fear of decision-making frequently started with a fear of failure, while, at the same time, no standards exist to indicate what failure—or success—consists of.
- **Insecurity in the management position.** The manager who doesn't feel that he or she is held in high regard by the boss, or is uncertain about whether he or she will hold that position if any mistake occurs, will probably be indecisive.
- **The manager is on strange ground.** Often the basis for being afraid to step up boldly to big decision lies in the strangeness of the environment. The dynamic executive from business who goes to Washington to accept a government job may become timid and wavering in behavior there amidst the strange world of politicians and government routines.
- **The manager doesn't know his or her authority.** The big decisions often go by the board when the manager isn't aware of them or wrongly feels unentitled to make such decisions.

    In one company, a general manager awaited word from the corporate office on whether he should add to his sales organization. Meanwhile, back in the corporate headquarters, top management watched his sales figures, anxiously wondering why they weren't rising. When he revealed that he needed more salesmen, he was informed: "For heaven's sake go hire them, that's your job."

- **Clinging to the status quo.** People have a tendency to cling tenaciously to what's been done and has worked before, and when the decision involves changing the present ways, however slight, there's a fear that the expected benefits may be offset by losses of what's presently in hand.

"My manager of manufacturing obviously isn't doing the job that I want done," said one division general manager. "But I can't just move in and fire him. First, I don't know that his understudy is even as good, and second, to bring in an outsider might be very disruptive and I'd be worse off than I am now."

Often indecisiveness is based upon the fact that things haven't yet gotten to the state where the person at the top can say: "I guess I'll do something because I couldn't be any worse off than I am now."

WHEN TO LISTEN TO OTHERS

Group-think is a term described by critics of modern group decision-making processes to imply that individual decisions are superior to the group decision-making processes. This is, of course, a half truth. There will be times when the manager must make decisions alone. On the other hand, there are times when retiring to the cell alone to reflect and decide would be a sheer waste of available talent and experience. What are some guides to the action-oriented manager for determining when to listen to others?

- **Listening is cheap.** The best rule to guide decision-making is that listening won't hurt anybody. Even when the aurally received material goes in one ear and out the other, it doesn't harm anything and helps the person who is talking. It always opens the possibility that something useful might be said.
- **When listening makes the program stronger.** There are some decisions that will depend upon support and teamwork for the execution. If listening to others' suggestions

adds impetus to the execution and gains acceptance for the final decision, it's worthwhile.

- **When it wins over hostile forces.** One of the best ways of gaining an ally is to ask an enemy for assistance and advice. Critics say things that make them part of the decision as it's finally made and will be identified with it.
- **When the decision to be made is already decided.** One firm had decided to go into defense work for up to 20 percent of its sales volume. Numerous suggestions were made, and arguments were given for and against going into defense work for several weeks after the decision was made. All were noted and the suggestors were seriously thanked.

  "It didn't hurt us to listen, and we got a lot of our people involved in what was going to happen. We couldn't make the announcement for several weeks, so freely listening was a way of keeping everyone happy. Actually, they almost all recommended that we do what we were going to do anyhow."

- **When the person talking is an expert.** At many stages in the decision-making process, careful listening to all ideas, especially from people who know some special facet, can improve the decision considerably.

What are some of the kinds of decisions in which listening to a group of others or to single experts is sound strategy? Product research, finance, marketing development, mergers and acquisitions; establishment of personnel policy, purchasing policy, public relations policy, and patent policy are ones in which most managers will want to involve more than their own thinking. The key seems to be that expert advice is desirable.

This kind of listening to others and group decision-making is probably less effective when rapid action is needed, when there aren't any experts on the subject matter at hand, or where the results of a bad decision don't seem to be very great. Some examples of these solo decisions might include: to buy or not to buy decisions, for purchasers; to ship or to scrap some off-quality work, for the vice president of manufacturing; or the granting of a credit rating by the credit manager. There's probably no need to get others' views on a decision where the matter is covered by policy and seems clear-cut in terms of precedents under the policy. The decision has already been made, and it's simply one of execution, which is more often a matter of individual action.

WHEN TO CHANGE A DECISION

The decisive manager is probably identified as a person who sticks to a course once chosen. This is a perfectly laudable trait, but it can backfire. Despite the necessity of applying force and action to a decision, there's bound to be an occasion when the use of further force is foolhardy and disastrous. This may be because the decision was wrong in the first place. How can a manager recognize the point to back off and change his or her mind?

First there are some guides on when not to change:

Don't change your mind merely because you're running into obstacles. These can't all be foreseen in detail, and the fact that they're tough ones may not mean your decision or choice of action was wrong. It's just the way the road is strewn.

Don't change your mind under the pressure of such difficulties if it's a problem in execution rather than in the propriety of the goal.

Don't try to redo all of your thinking in a hasty moment if your decision was made on the basis of carefully-developed study and analysis to begin with. You probably won't improve that rationality when you are under stress.

> Take the case of the personnel manager who decided to set up a program of meetings to communicate benefits to all employees. Surveys showed that the company wasn't receiving credit for all of the fringe benefits it was giving its employees. She decided to arrange a series of meetings, using supervisors to transmit this information.
>
> As the meetings progressed, she discovered that many of the supervisors who were supposed to be doing the communicating weren't doing a good job—in fact were probably doing more harm than good. Rather than scuttling the program or taking back the job from the supervisor, she quickly prepared a further

training session for the supervisors and had them practice and rehearse on each other before trying it on their employees. As a result, she had more than the success imagined possible.

Nevertheless there are times when it becomes obvious that the original decision was wrong, and the decision itself should be changed. What circumstances justify such a switch in plans?

Don't hesitate to change plans if some *important new facts* enter the scene. In one automobile company, there were numerous wildcat strikes at one of the accessory plants. The management decided to meet this problem head on, with firm supervisory actions, discharges where necessary, and a general stiffening of the discipline. The program was under way and meeting some rigid opposition from the union, when suddenly an upheaval in the union officers took place. A new crew moved in and took control. The officers of the new union came to management and asked a letting up of some of the pressure, assuring management that they, in turn, would put an end to the wildcats and slowdowns. The company quickly changed its decision to exert pressure upon the employees and, as a result, a complete turnaround in the problem occurred. No more slowdowns or unauthorized strikes occurred.

Don't hesitate to *strike while the iron is hot.* If new opportunities which can extend the benefits of the action appear, it's imperative that the decision and plan be amended to encompass the new opportunity. An aircraft company was in search of a director of research and, after some mulling over the problem, decided to go outside the firm to hire a top-flight person. After numerous contacts with possible candidates, they found one with a competitor who was interested and could also bring seven key associates. The decision to hire one outsider was quickly enlarged to include the entire group. As a result, their research program was jacked up to a higher level at a single step. The distinct advantage which a manager of action has in decision-making, over those who view administration in a more passive light, is the ability to alter the *cause-effect* nature of decisions. To view this entirely as a linear relationship which always prevails is to ignore the effects of aggressive action, force, and determined behavior on the part of the decision-maker to consummate the result of his or her decision. It would be a major mistake for the manager to see decision-making as a purely rational process. Where the manager has the capacity to make things happen, this latter quality in itself can make many otherwise diffident decisions take on the quality of vitality and life which is needed for their successful execution.

Part II

GETTING OTHERS TO ACT

"I believe the greatest assets of a business are its human assets, and that the improvement of their value is a matter of both material advantage and moral obligation."

CLARENCE FRANCIS

8

RIGID MANAGERS—NEW WAYS OF MAKING THEM MORE FLEXIBLE

> *"It is well for the world that in most of us, by the age of thirty, the character has set like plaster, and will never soften again."*
>
> WILLIAM JAMES

One of the toughest problems for the top manager is dealing with an important member of the management team who is too rigid.

This rigid man won't see anybody's viewpoint but his own, and often resents any suggestion that he should change. Much has been written and said about the person who resists change because of habit or insecurity, and who longs for the good old days. There's another type of rigid person in management, however, who's rigid for different reasons. Such inflexible people are overly oriented to their own department or specialty.

Within a specialty such as accounting, engineering, sales, or manufacturing, they may actually be progressive. Management's problem is that some of these people can't see anything but their own special division as having any real importance in the business.

This makes this person not only difficult to do business with but impossible to promote.

For the company's good, management needs to do something to break down this rigidity. Six ways of doing this have proved helpful when properly used:

- Job rotation
- Coaching and counseling
- Civic and community activities
- Management courses
- Psychological counseling
- Surrounding the employee

Rigid people weren't born that way. To some extent, the specialized nature of modern jobs forces people to adopt habit patterns that become rigid. Like automobile drivers who are perfect gentlemen when afoot but turn into raging maniacs at the wheel, the rigid men are often affable outside the job.

Although psychologists warn us against stereotyping everyone we meet, it's not too dangerous and is sometimes helpful to have some general guides to recognizing the rigid people in management. In most companies, they fall into five major types.

1. The manufacturing type
2. The engineering type
3. The sales type
4. The accounting-financial type
5. The staff type

Not everyone in these areas is the rigid type, of course, but it is easy to recognize those who are. It is even easy to overemphasize rigid behavior in the other person.

Everyone in manufacturing knows how rigid the controller is, and the sales people know how rigid manufacturing people can be.

It's tougher to face up to your own rigidity. Behaving in a certain way consistently is often a logical response to the situation in which the smart person finds him- or herself in the company. Most successful managers start out in some specialty and prove their mettle in it before being given a chance at more general management jobs. It's during this early apprenticeship that the rigidities creep in and sometimes never go away.

If you sometimes wonder if you may be getting too set in your ways, you might run a quiet check on yourself. If one of the following descriptions seems to fit you, you may want to consider ways, with or without company help, of breaking out of the pattern.

THE RIGID MANUFACTURING BOSS

You're rigid in this job if you have a deep conviction that you are the only real doer in the company; a two-fisted, tough-talking type who makes things happen. Presses bang, machines clatter, and people sweat at your bidding. Because of you, the stuff goes out the back door, and all's right with the world because you are tough.

Naturally, everyone not in manufacturing is a little bit befuddled. They don't get action. They fiddle around with nice words and pieces of paper.

You hit the ball, get action, crash through to the goal. Occasionally you discover you are correcting the same things over and over again, but that's because of some incompetent people the personnel department sent you. What's needed is harder drive, more demand for results; take no excuses, cut through delay. Your worst insult is to call somebody "impractical." *You're rigid if you can only think in terms of action.*

THE RIGID ENGINEER

You're the possessor of a wonderful instrument called the engineering mind, which has a monopoly on logic. You combine the knowledge of the scientist, mathematician, chemist or physicist with the ability to turn this logic into beautiful and practical objects. This engineering mind sees every subject more clearly, and defines the essence more succinctly than anyone who doesn't possess it. You can't stand anything but facts ... you are made ill by people who play politics, talk glibly and verbalize too freely, turning the business into a wind tunnel of hot air. Things and facts can be counted on. People and verbal abstractions can't, so it's best to go it by yourself, then you can be sure it's done right. You are underrated by your employer (who is living off your brain), by your spouse, and by society generally. *You're rigid if you stress things and ignore people.*

THE RIGID SALESMAN

People don't really understand you. They think you are a huckster, an extrovert, a back-slapper. Yours is really a creative job which is based upon the solid human instinct of wanting money.

You know that the dollar is the lubricant that makes the wheels turn. Being a hot salesman makes you free of discipline and company rules. Salesmanship is the basis of our civilization. Under this plan, everyone is either a customer or a salesman. If you are the customer, you can rough up people such as waiters, other salesmen, hotel managers, and taxi drivers, then patch their wounds with a buck, because anybody will jump for a price. Buyers are entitled to treat you the same way, of course. Things will always be better than they are now, and pep, drive and the discipline of the dollar are the keys to success, which is what everyone really wants. You'd crawl a mile over broken bottles to get a fat order. *You're rigid if you see satisfaction only in money.*

THE RIGID COST ACCOUNTANT

Every day you lay out on sheets of paper the essence of the business, and control it by changing figures in the columns. You sit at the eye of the storm, the nerve center of the company, and watch for signs that mean the ship is about to founder. You issue memos or whisper words to the captain and he issues the commands you have suggested which save the ship. The others only think they are the key people with their wild rushing and frantic activity. You are the hourly savior of the business; you police trickling little losses that would turn into torrents if you weren't there. As the master scorekeeper and conservator you must be cold, passionless, without emotion. You can't afford to be loved because you might let a little leak turn into a big drain if you were ruled by your emotions.

Yours is a higher responsibility, and your manner and dress should reflect this weighty burden. Your pleasures are simple as with all men whose every decision is a weighty one. *You're rigid if you see business only as figures.*

THE RIGID STAFF TYPE

You don't make anything, or sell it, but you are custodian of something which is vitally necessary to the preservation of the business—it's called a procedure. A procedure implements a sacrosanct guide called a policy, which is never subject to question. Life in the office is to you one of great frustration in which people who don't follow procedures cause you endless work and trouble. You tell them about procedures but they persist in doing things in their own foolish, individual way.

You are pressed by numerous competing forces, the hostility of line people, the demands of top management to which you have no recourse, and the frustration of never really completing a task because people in the line ignore procedures. The solution, you know, will come when you can devise more procedures which will prevent further lapses from policies and procedures not now being followed. *You're rigid if you think a business is no more than a set of procedures.*

CORRECTIVE ACTION

To break people of rigidities is a job of enlarging people. They've got to become generalists instead of specialists.

This provides us with the key to breaking people out of the rigidities which they build into their behavior on certain jobs.

1. Job rotation. One way of breaking a person out of a rigid attitude is to let him or her see the other's viewpoint first-hand by putting him or her into the other's position. The manufacturing expert who goes out and faces adamant customers as a salesman gets a good look at what marketing really means. The controller who spends some time in the plant finds out why certain extraordinary expenses are often required. The staff member who came to the position from a line job is often better than the one who has held nothing but a home-office job. The salesperson who does a tour of duty in manufacturing learns some of the problems of making the orders brought in for rush delivery. The engineer who follows through on designs to manufacture goes back to the drawing board as a better engineer.

2. Coaching and counseling. Because job rotation is sometimes impossible and often too expensive, a more practical method of breaking people out of their mold is to hold regular coaching sessions with them. These are talks on "How'm I doing?" between the boss and subordinates which deal with some of the subordinate's acts and behavior which indicate rigidity and lack of appreciation for other departments' problems.

Such coaching can be on a planned and formal basis, and is best supplemented by frequent, informal chats on a day-to-day basis. If the boss is a people-centered generalist, his warmth and humanity may shine through and be imitated.

3. Civic and community activities. Sending executives out to work on community activities is an excellent way of giving them some broadening, and seeing that the formula for success they have adopted on the job isn't the only way things get done in the world. The manufacturing chief who heads up a volunteer campaign for funds shortly discovers that persuasion and diplomacy are arts which have their place, too, and will come back a bigger and better person for it. Letting executives serve on boards of community associations is a good way to accomplish the same goal.

4. Management courses and seminars. Sending people away to general management courses and seminars is a widely-tried and proven way of helping a rigid manager see him- or herself in his or her true light. Placed in a strange situation where everybody is a big wheel, he or she may discover that the tried and true attitudes are not necessarily the only ones or even the best ones. Where such courses entail free-wheeling discussion, this manager may discover that he or she has to examine the personal attitudes and methods of handling problems if he or she is to convince others. This is good for creating flexibility.

5. Psychological counseling. Occasionally a top performer just doesn't respond to any of these treatments and may be rigid because of some deep-seated attitudes dating back to childhood.

It's wisest, at this point, to try to get professional assistance. If the company has a staff psychologist, the problem might be explained, and a series of meetings for counseling arranged.

The principal purpose here is to have the psychologist help the executive see several basic facts:

- Certain attitudes affecting job performance are damaging the person's future and are affecting company operations.
- That only he or she can make the necessary changes in attitude which will result in more human behavior.

The psychologist often is able to give the person greater insight into his or her own behavior, and help program a change in work behavior.

6. Surround them. Some companies and certain executives won't stand still for psychological counseling for a variety of reasons.

Under these circumstances, many companies organize around the problem person so that special skills and abilities can be used effectively, while disruptive habits are ameliorated by people who act as assistants or colleagues.

In one large company, for example, a noted scientist in top management was constantly disrupting the operations of the lab through his arrogance and inflexibility.

Top management assigned an administrative assistant to handle his housekeeping chores and to deal with customers, accountants, manufacturing people, and others. Not only did the assistant learn a lot, but the scientist himself was relieved of less important tasks to perform his specialty.

The top manufacturing executive who is inflexible may require bolstering with clerks, administrative assistants or understudies who protect the organization from the disruptions growing out of this executive's inflexibility.

In an age when the specialist is more often in demand, we find more and more companies taking conscious steps to offset some of the bad effects of specialist behavior that becomes overspecialized. The need isn't to eliminate specialization, but to get the specialists who have become rigid to bend to the needs of the whole enterprise.

GOALS CAN UNFREEZE BEHAVIOR

Often the rigid person is caught in an activity trap. That's the sad situation which exists in many large organizations when people become so enmeshed in activity that they lose sight of the reason for it. Thus, the activity has become an end in itself. People started out for what were once clear objectives, then got too busy. What was first a momentary lapse becomes a habit, the habit becomes a procedure, and then the procedure becomes a profession.

The antidote?

A countervailing system, something like management by objectives, averts some of the bad effects of the activity trap. At the beginning of each year, all managers and subordinates regularly sit down together and discuss the objectives of the subordinate's job, and continue talking until an agreement is arrived at. These objectives have the following characteristics:

1. They are specific and most likely, measurable.
2. They are stated in terms of outputs rather than activities.
3. They are a mutual commitment of both boss and subordinate; the subordinate is committed and accountable for results, while the boss agrees that meeting those commitments will comprise successful job performance.
4. The agreements are confirmed in writing, with copies for each party.
5. During the ensuing year, the boss is there to help, to provide resources and training, and to measure results.
6. The subordinate understands the constraints in the job and the freedom allowed to engage in activity which is necessary to produce the desired goals.

Implemented on an organization-wide basis, such a system can go far in alleviating the rigid behavior of people, and help both organization and employee to grow and prosper.

9

USING BEHAVIOR MODIFICATION TO CHANGE POOR WORK HABITS TO GOOD ONES

"Those who think must govern those who toil."

OLIVER GOLDSMITH

No single tool or technique of scientific management gives a company more competitive advantage than a staff of people whose work habits are good.

Where do employees get their work habits, and how can they be improved?

A work habit is built up from four basic sources:

1. Genetic factors and early training, including schools and family.

2. Experience in the company, especially the earliest experience. Many work habits are set the first day on the job, and unless corrected, they never substantially change.

3. The group with which the employee is located. If we're with a hard-working bunch we'll put out more to keep up with them; if we're with a more casual team, we'll match our pace to theirs.

4. The boss. Responsibility for work habits over time can be laid almost fully here. Since he or she is in a position to make amends for the other three causes through constructive action, management can change habits.

Basically, there are eight principal ways in which the boss can change the work habits of an employee. Sometimes a single one will do the trick. In more persistent cases, it will take a combination of all eight. The formula must be tailored to individual circumstances. While psychologists can explain many intricate motivation and aptitude factors, it's more practical for the working manager to approach the subject from the viewpoint of work habits than to plunge too deeply into the employee's total personality. It is primarily job performance that interests the manager. If the employee lapses into lazy habits outside the job, that shouldn't be of too much concern.

Admittedly, this is a rule-of-thumb method, but it gets at the main point and is relatively uncomplicated. The eight ways in which work habits can be improved include:

- Watch the work pattern of employees.
- Replace the bad habit with a good one.
- Start the new employee right.
- Show the employee a reason for changing.
- Try the job yourself.
- Set a good example.
- Work through the informal organization.
- Get participation.

Let's see how each of these steps works in practice:

WATCH THE WORK PATTERN

Both simple and complicated jobs will settle into repetitive patterns of work activity. This pattern may be of the employee's own devising, or it may be taught. Once acquired, it will be adhered to. This pattern is characteristic of complex jobs as well as simple, routine ones, except that the pattern may be more extended in scope and is often called a procedure.

These work patterns are not rationally evaluated. In the day-to-day routine of the job, a person will follow the repetitive cycle in a more or less unthinking manner. This isn't necessarily undesirable. Without such patterns, our lives would consist of a series of deliberations and decisions about such things as walking, chewing, writing, and other routine things. The rub comes when we build into our routines a lot of time-consuming activities that mean we don't get the things done we would like to. We build in trips to the watercooler or to the stock room, or social chats with fellow workers simply because we haven't formed the habit of bearing down on the top priority jobs ahead.

The person with poor work habits spends as much energy as the hard worker, but fritters away time and putters around with trivia. Observing the pattern in order to improve work habits means watching for this shuffling and duplication.

REPLACE A BAD HABIT WITH A GOOD ONE

The primary tool in improving work habits is substitution. After getting some idea of the major patterns and finding where the time-robbing portions lie, replace them with something productive. This means breaking the cycle that adds up to undesirable parts. In some cases, this can be done by a physical rearrangement of the workplace at the time the change is introduced. Habits tend to be associated with physical activity. It's also an axiom that the worker will more readily accept the new method if allowed to participate in the change which affects him or her.

In one instance, a manager was able to combine a frank chat, with her employee who had the worst work habits, with a change in desk location. By breaking the routine of work-a-little followed by head-for-the-water-cooler and other similar dilatory tactics, she was able to show the man that the major block to his effectiveness and personal advancement was that he was in a rut. The change of scene, coupled with some candid talk, did the trick.

In another case, replacing a bad habit with a good one took the form of pitching a subordinate with some sloppy work habits a tough chore first thing in the morning. Where the employee previously had started off the day with fumbling, foot-shuffling and floundering that sometimes lasted all day, he now found that he was required to pull together some important information from overnight quickly and accurately, and have it on the boss's desk within twenty minutes of starting time. This momentum began to carry on into the rest of the day.

START THE NEW EMPLOYEE RIGHT

Many a work habit of a decade's standing began with the first morning on the job. A new employee will be most eager to succeed, and will accept the work cycle presented by the first instructor or coach encountered. This means that, before the cycle becomes habitual, it should be studied for idle and observation time and the blanks filled up. With good training, proper method and procedures will be taught the first time the employee encounters the job. The induction step can't be entrusted to people whose work habits are poor.

More than one manager has been heard to say that "I can't waste time doing a full-scale training job for the new employee." Pressed for details, it often turns out that the reason he hasn't time for training new employees is because he's patching up the faulty training of old ones, who, like the present recruits, couldn't be adequately inducted because of the pressures of time.

SHOW A REASON FOR BETTER HABITS

Changing work habits with any degree of permanence requires some motivation. In some instances profit-sharing, incentive or bonus plans already exist and are a ready-made reason for the employee to work more effectively. If it can be demonstrated that the new work pattern will benefit the employee, he or she will tend to hang onto it.

Where no monetary incentive exists, if often helps to show that the new method is really less fatiguing, less dangerous or eliminates some difficulty. In some cases, opportunity to advance is good motivation. Where these elements are lacking, it may be necessary to stress benefits to the company.

In these instances it can be pointed out that working more effectively actually increases security and opportunity in the job, since it improves the company's competitive position.

In a few instances of a youngster without prior work experience or an employee who has been spoiled by poor supervision, more strict action is demanded. After all explanation and selling is complete, it becomes necessary to inform the employee that he or she must change, or disciplinary action will follow. It's often advisable, in such cases, to make the disciplinary procedure a three-step one, letting the employee know each step from the beginning.

1. Inform the employee that his or her work habits are not up to company standards; show the evidence and suggest some specific steps to improve them.

2. If the employee ignores or refuses to follow the suggested steps, he or she should then be disciplined. It's better to be specific than to generalize.

3. Continued lapses from better habits should result in temporary layoff, or possibly discharge. In any event, don't use transfers to another department within the company without some evidence of physical or mental inability to do the job the way you want it done. Transfers have no magic power of improving work habits, and are only justified when they bring about a better fit between the employee and the job.

TRY THE JOB YOURSELF

In some cases, it's a sound idea to take a stab at doing the job yourself, to find out if the employee actually has good work habits but is performing at what seems to be low output because of things in the job which aren't apparent to the naked eye. Many an experienced employee is working at peak performance but makes it look simple to outsiders. He or she may have vastly greater efficiency than you imagined. This is often true of the best employees. Before criticizing the person who seems to be relaxed and comfortable on the job, you'd better quietly take his or her place for a little while. It's not always easy to judge how hard a task is from observation.

SET A GOOD EXAMPLE

Not long ago I walked through a medical supply plant with a company executive. Several yards away, he spotted a small piece of debris on the floor. Breaking off our conversation he walked over and picked up the scrap and put it in his pocket.

"I wouldn't think of letting that piece lie there," he said, "not after all the pressure I put on people to maintain cleanliness and good housekeeping in the plant."

This manager knew that, unless he demonstrated habits of good housekeeping, he probably couldn't expect others to have them either, no matter how loudly he ordered them.

The work habits of the boss have a way of transmitting themselves to the entire organization by example.

Tie this together with a genuine interest in how well people are performing on their jobs, and with periodic talks to let them know how they can improve; you are then on the way to better work habits in the organization.

USE TEAM BUILDING

One of the most influential factors in shaping work habits is the work group to which a worker is assigned. All workers join informal groups, based upon occupational groupings or any one of a dozen or more sentimental or emotional ties, such as sex, age, school attended, occupational groups, physical surroundings of work, and so forth.

The important thing for the manager is knowledge that these cliques control the output of their members, and exercise controls though exclusion and ostracism of people who don't stay in line. A good worker may be soldiering because he or she doesn't want to be on the outs with fellow workers. The key to working through informal groups in the work force is the first-line supervisor, who is in a position to belong to both management and the clique, using modern team-building methods.

With such leadership in first-line positions, the work habits of individuals will be policed by the group. Without group support of company standards of performance, there is little hope of forcing individuals to swim upstream against their fellow workers.

GET PARTICIPATION

One of the surest ways of getting better work habits and making them stick is to get the wholehearted co-operation of the worker through asking help and support in improving skills and habits. As the expert on the job, the employee can offer more concrete suggestions than anybody.

Once involved in changing the pattern, the employee stands a better chance of staying changed for good than if a hundred experts studied and dictated what should be done.

Since changed attitudes are vital in altering work habits, participation is another way of saying we get the worker involved in seeing the importance of doing a better job.

In one eastern plant where hand operation on an assembly line was the limitation of output, management let the operators set the speed of the conveyor which carried their work to them. They not only exceeded records previously set, but also produced so much that they caused a problem in the packing station which came after them. Asking people to set their own pace doesn't mean they will set it too low. Convinced that management is genuinely interested in them and their views, they will set it higher than might have been anticipated.

Work habits can only be changed by leadership. Experience shows that today toughness alone won't do it.

BEHAVIOR MODIFICATION IS THE KEY

These eight steps, together or singly, comprise an approach to behavior modification. The gist of behavior modification requires that the boss keep in mind these rules of management.

1. Have in mind the desired behavior and compare it with the present behavior. The objective is to produce the desired behavior.
2. Break the total change into small, successive steps.
3. When movement is exhibited toward the right behavior, *reinforce it* with *favorable consequences* to the learner. (Payment, rewards, verbal praise, thanks, and recognition).

4. Withhold favorable consequences when progress stops or if the wrong behavior comes forth. People change habits (behavior) when the balance of consequence is favorable for doing the right things and not favorable for doing the wrong things.

10

GETTING AND USING THE IDEAS OF OTHERS

> "The trend in America generally, in our schools, in our homes, and in our communities, is toward giving the individual greater freedom and initiative. There are fewer direct, unexplained orders in schools and homes, and youngsters are participating increasingly in decisions which affect them. These fundamental changes in American society create expectations among employees as to how they should be treated."
>
> RENSIS LIKERT

Henry Ford was asked one time what he expected of his workers. "We expect that our workers will do the work that is set before them," Mr. Ford was reported to have replied. While this was a perfectly typical method of getting results through others in the early days of the assembly line and scientific management, it's no longer true of today's business. It has changed in that management expects more of its workers than doing simply what is put before them. It has also changed in that the workers expect that more can be had from them than simply working according to the directions of the boss. The worker expects to be asked how he feels about his job, and what his ideas are on how the work can be done more easily, better, and faster. A number of reasons account for this change in emphasis.

1. The definition of "worker" has changed. Today there are more professional, technical and white collar people employed than there are factory workers. The number of unskilled workers has declined steadily. During the depression, it fell by some 7 percent. During the decades that followed the depression decade of the thirties, it fell by some 30 to 40 percent. Such changes in the composition of the work force toward professional and white collar work means that the emphasis is upon ideas and creativity from each individual, rather than the specific performance of engineered tasks.

2. The values of our society have changed. The child, the citizen and the employee have been conditioned to receive explanations of the purpose of their work. They have also become accustomed to the environment in which their own ideas and suggestions may be incorporated into the actions they are required to take. This transformation in the overall society has had its impact on the workplace. Each person wants to feel that his opinions about the job are of concern to those who direct the organization.

3. Business has discovered that there are tangible business values in soliciting and using the ideas of people at all levels in the organization. The improvement of the value of the people in an organization becomes a strategy for business growth and profit, as well as being a socially desirable goal.

The implication in these changed conditions is that there is no corner on brains in an organization. The concept of the single thinker at the top, surrounded by peons who execute the work, no longer has any merit; in fact, it tends to arouse hostility and resistance where such a condition is implied by the policies or supervisory practices of management.

Competition between organizations is most often a competition in the realm of ideas, far more often, for example, than competition between accumulations of money or patent rights.

This competition is obvious to the salespeople for the various firms who call on the same purchasing agent. They see the competition, and know directly the effects of better products and more adroit choices of marketing methods. While less obvious, the competition is, nevertheless, just as vigorous between all other people in the organizations that make and sell in the same markets as well. The foreman of Company A is in competition with the foreman of Company B, as are the secretaries, clerks and engineers. The fact that they don't *see* their competitors doesn't lessen its effects in the slightest. It's a competition of ideas, excellence of performance, and ability to keep costs within limits.

Such emphasis upon ideas and their nourishment will not be abated in the least by the trend to automation and such new management tools as data processing and electronic systems for handling information.

> Paradoxically, the trend toward the disappearance of direct human contribution to product creation will be accompanied by an increased need for the recognition of workers as people and more tolerance for the constructive nonconformist.

HOW PARTICIPATIVE MANAGEMENT WORKS

Tailoring this general philosophy of willingness to let employees participate in the decisions that affect them is easily misunderstood. Often it's construed as a form of "softness" and sentimental democracy in which the boss asks workers' permissions before making decisions. Such a system obviously has extremely limited uses, if any, in a business organization.

Yet we know that this "soft" and permissive approach is exactly what is required to make anything happen in voluntary associations where people work of their own free will, and sometimes for whimsical motives. The social club, the service club, the church organization, and the professional organization, run by volunteers, are led by people whose leadership rests wholly upon the willingness of the governed to assign leadership powers to their leaders.

In a business organization, the work contract implies the power of management to hire, fire and otherwise direct the operation of the resources of the company. The principal difference then becomes that, in voluntary associations, one *can't* act in a certain arbitrary way against the collective will of everyone who must do the work. It's suggested here that in business where you *can,* it's often wise not to do so. The reasons have little to do with the moral or social propriety or lack of it in such autocratic behavior, but rather with its soundness as a business strategy.

Participative management, even in such circumstances, still doesn't indicate that management becomes so passive that it abdicates its principal requirement—to lead. The role of leader in the group is a real and necessary one which is recognized by the group. It does mean, however, that certain actions, which give workers participation in the decisions and plans of the organization, will make that organization more profitable, efficient and stable. More importantly, it can help the organization to prosper and grow.

These techniques can be identified in one of several categories.

1. Good participative management is tied to incentives. It makes it amply clear to people that their ideas are wanted, and the more tangibly that is made known, the more clearly this management interest in new ideas is accepted and believed by people. Suggestion plans which give cash awards for productive ideas are but one of the several variations of this principle.

2. Good participative management gives people personal satisfaction. In addition to the tangible rewards for ideas, workers find great satisfaction in identifying themselves with improvements in their own working conditions. As one factory worker told me:

> I suggested a new layout of the time card and time clock system to prevent the big lines and delays in getting in and out. It was adopted, and I still get a little kick out of seeing people pass in and out without delay or tie-up because they adopted my idea.

3. People are better team players when they are made to feel that they are important parts of the organization. Good participative management reduces the helplessness and latent hostility which people feel toward an organization in which they are considered "lost" or simply a number. Even large organizations can permit people to feel that their individuality and special qualities are important if they are consulted and asked about what should be done. In a large meat packing company, one driver of a company fleet vehicle told me:

> This company makes its drivers feel like important guys. They ask us about our routings on over-the-road trips. They let us tell them how long it will take for long trips. They explain about the importance and value of

the stuff in the load, and why deliveries are important. I pull out of the garage with thousands of dollars worth of stuff on the trailer and I can feel the weight of my responsibility setting in. I want to deliver the goods without mishap.

4. People should grow in knowledge and responsibility. Good participative management should be an educational experience for the people making the suggestions. Even a suggestion that can't be used gives them some insights into the overall company problems. An engineer in a pharmaceutical plant suggested that a new evaporator be purchased. It was turned down with a complete explanation, and the engineer didn't seem put out. He explained it thus:

> I learned that the average life of a product in this industry was only 1.3 years, and that the product I wanted to improve the process on was already on its way out in favor of a new one which was being tested in the development lab. They taught me something about this business I didn't know because I put in that suggestion. If I'd been in their shoes, I'd have turned my idea down too.

5. Participative management should be a means of identifying people of above-average abilities. In a climate where new ideas and comments about the job are welcomed, the opportunity for evaluating people's potential becomes easier. If participative management works well, it may go a long way toward screening out the exceptionally talented people. Good ideas, not only about the overall performance of the organization, may uncover individuals who think bigger than one might suppose from simply judging their day to day performance. It can be a tip-off on people with inventiveness, imagination and exceptional ability to manipulate ideas and facts to come up with new combinations.

6. Participative management should let off pressures. People who have some gripes or major grievances against the way things are run, will ordinarily not let such things convert into long-standing and pathological hostility, if they have an opportunity to get it off their chests, and see it corrected early. Suppressed dissatisfaction among the worker group can lead to big blow-offs and mischief later. Good participative management taps it often and early.

> In a large eastern city, a laborer from a factory was arrested for slugging his plant manager with a pipe outside the plant while under the influence of liquor. Asked why he did it, the worker at first pleaded intoxication, but later confessed that he had harbored a grudge for many years against the manager because he "walked through the plant and never talked to anybody."

Obviously, such cases aren't typical in their drastic consequences. It's typical, however, in that aloofness and unwillingness, especially the unwillingness to listen, to exchange amenities with people, breeds great resentment.

LEARN TO LISTEN

Getting and using the ideas of others obviously means that there is communication with employees. It also means that effective listening takes place, a skill which is not as common as we might be led to suppose.

> "Most of us have a filter which we keep constantly in place when we are listening," says management consultant Harold Schmidhauser. "That filter is a trap for ideas that might have gotten through to us if we'd let the filter down. In most people, that filter is simply *attitude.*"

Take the case of the engineers who were laying out a tank house for a chemical plant. The house was to be twelve feet square, of brick construction, and was to house a tank seven feet in diameter. The liquid in the tank would be piped to several adjoining buildings by a pump. One of the laborers in the yard happened by and looked over the shoulder of the engineer, at the drawing he held spread out before him.

"Better make the door a little wider," he suggested. The engineer looked at him as if he were some form of interloper and shrugged his shoulders.

The laborer shrugged his shoulders too, because he'd noticed that the door on the plan was only four feet wide and the tank to be installed was seven feet in diameter. Sure enough, when the building was completed, they had to rip out half a wall to install the tank.

In another instance, a truck driver for an over-the-road trucker was given a route by his dispatcher.

"Now follow this route!" he was directed.

"But..." he began.

"No buts. We'll decide the best route from now on," the dispatcher stated emphatically. The driver shrugged and took off down the road. He knew that he would shortly come to a low overpass which his trailer couldn't get under. After waiting a couple hours in a nearby coffee house, he called the dispatcher and explained the reason for his delay. Naturally, the dispatcher felt cheated that he hadn't been told the thing he wasn't prepared to listen to.

Bad listening falls into several types.

1. We're naturally bad listeners because we're preoccupied with ourselves and our own ideas, and this filters out a clear reception of other people's ideas.

2. Because most people speak slower than the ear can handle what it hears, as much as 50 percent of our listening time is unused. This gives us time to let our minds wander, and often it never gets back to what is being said. Most people can hear and understand 400-600 words per minute. The average speaker ordinarily talks at a rate of 200-300 words per minute. This differential causes a tendency to let our minds drift away. This is especially true when we think we know what the person is going to say after we've heard a few words.

3. One of the causes of bad listening is that we tend to generalize the person's ideas to something about the person himself. If he uses poor English or has an annoying appearance or mannerisms, we are apt to disregard what he says. Good listening starts out with the assumption that there's a nugget of a good idea in every suggestion.

4. We listen passively. Good listening requires sharp attention and active interest. This means that we not only hear with our auditory sense, but watch for facial expression and evidences of attitude. Often the person speaking is saying one thing and implying something else which is far more important. Here's how one labor relations manager put it:

> Most of the grievances that we get at step one aren't actual statements of the real gripe at all. The foreman

acts high-hat with everyone and the boys in the shop are unhappy about that. They can't file a grievance over that, so they scratch around and find something else, something that violates the contract, and they grieve about it. When they get to my office, I listen carefully and probe a little, and more often than not, I can get to the real root of the problem.

5. The best listening is for *ideas,* not facts. A study by Dr. Ralph Nichols at the University of Minnesota showed that the student who listens for facts generally makes poorer grades than one who listens for ideas. This becomes even more important when getting ideas is the first purpose of listening.

6. Listening means *relating.* Good listening means that as ideas and facts come in through the auditory sense, they are classified and compared against what's already there. They are then compared and weighed for accuracy, usefulness and pertinence. Often they can be handled critically and completely. Where the facts or ideas are sketchy, a pointed question will bring out the answer to the inconsistency.

SOME DEVICES FOR SPRINGING OTHERS' IDEAS INTO ACTION

Research at Cornell University has shown that managers and supervisors spend between 1200 and 1500 hours a year meeting and talking with people—including listening to them. Making the most of this time in getting the benefits of good listening and obtaining employees' ideas takes some definite steps. Professor Earl Brooks of Cornell lists ten steps which will make such contacts pay off:

1. Listen with interest, sincerity and friendliness.
2. Make the employee the central figure.
3. Recognize your own prejudices.
4. Be careful in giving advice.
5. Recognize that people hear what they want to hear.
6. Listen to understand, and make that your only purpose.
7. Be sensitive to feelings, attitudes and motives.
8. Respond in a neutral manner.

Getting and Using the Ideas of Others 133

    9. Repeat or rephrase something that has been said by the other person.
    10. Use questions carefully.

These methods go a long way toward proving to the worker that you are genuinely interested in his ideas. Gordon R. Taylor, the sociologist, once said that people by and large have a desire to cooperate with management in accomplishing its goals, if they are convinced that their purpose is a good one and that the leaders deserve to be leaders. Such devices and habits can help achieve that feeling, but there is more.

How, for example, can we be assured that workers and employees at any level will be capable of generating good ideas for innovation and improvement?

Many firms including Texas Instruments, provide for this through a continuous series of training sessions in work simplification, which are designed to tap the pool of ideas latent in every employee. Managers, engineers, staff men, and machine operators have all been through this course. Basically, the program teaches a five-step plan that any operator can apply to his own job or any other, and come up with ideas that cut costs, eliminate waste and make the job easier, safer and more productive. This plan is:

Step 1. Pick a job to improve. Start with your own job or any job that is costing too much or is inefficient.

Step 2. Study the job in detail. Put all the facts down on paper. Make simple flow charts or diagrams. Show distances traveled, weights lifted, etc.

Step 3. Question all the details. Ask the five questions: *Why* is it necessary? *When* should it be done? *Who* should do it? *Where* should it be done? And finally, *How* should it be done? The ultimate question to ask is: Is there a better way to do it?

Step 4. Develop a better way. If the person doesn't find a sound answer to any of the questions about the details of the job, he or she is to figure out a way of doing it better, faster, cheaper, or easier.

Step 5. Install the new method. Once the new method is mapped out, try it for practicality. Sell it to others, the boss and the industrial engineers, then start using it.

Many millions of dollars in savings have been gained through the polled ideas of ordinary employees. Every person becomes an idea person, and innovation in methods and products isn't limited to the "idea departments" of industrial engineering or research.

"Brainstorming" is a technique often used in connection with idea-getting which has produced some amazing results. The term and its application grew out of advertising man Alex Osborn's attempts to improve the creativity of copywriters, and has been adopted wholesale by industry. Many firms report amazing success in the use of this stimulating technique, which uses the group approach to idea-getting.

The procedure is to gather together people with varied experience in a conference room and throw out a problem to them. The major rules are that no negative reactions are allowed. Every idea, no matter how wild, that might solve the problem is sought. Since one idea suggests another, this association of minds often pulls out unique ideas that might have been discarded before evaluation under ordinary circumstances.

With all of the ideas out and listed, a smaller group then takes the record of the brainstorming and evaluates each fully for any possible applications. This freeing of the imagination has the effect of eliminating the barriers to ideas which stem from supervisors' resentment of subordinates' ideas, of the fellow who says "we tried that before," or of the person who suggests that "our business is different." Moreover, people report it to be stimulating, and it often results in an attitude change in the hardshelled individuals toward the reception of new ideas once presented.

Ultimately, however, such ideas must be evaluated from the viewpoint of their value and practicality. This ordinarily falls to a few people who have the broad picture of the needs and procedures of the firm, and can fit new ideas into operations.

> Continental Can Company found some profitable savings through brainstorming the question of how to use the angle irons which came to guard corners of tin plate from the mill. Previously these had been scrapped, and sold for a fraction of their value. Over 50 usable ideas for commercially producible items or money-saving uses came out of the scrap-iron piece.

The use of any ideas from employees, however, will only occur when the relationship between the manager and his subordinates is one that is satisfactory to both. If the worker feels that his or her opinions are wanted or even sought after, they'll be forthcoming. This implies a condition that has been described as democratic leadership.

HOW DEMOCRATIC LEADERSHIP WORKS

Using such a term as democratic leadership can bring about some confusion in the minds of people who have associated the terms with political democracy, the mechanics of party politics and elections. As it's used in industry, however, the mechanics are different. The real justification for the term democratic means the underlying philosophy of political and industrial government, rather than the mechanics by which each is applied. Obviously these procedures are different ones for the two different circumstances.

Perhaps a more accurate way of describing democratic leadership in management is to apply the term *responsiveness*. Where the manager is not at all responsive, and simply makes decisions and announces them for others to execute, there is certainly no democratic leadership. The degrees of responsiveness to the wishes, needs, desires, and aspirations of his or her followers is the true measure of how democratic leadership really is.

Friendliness toward employees may have little or nothing to do with responsiveness to their needs. Employees may hold the most friendly feelings toward an autocrat who has provided them with security. Even a dictator is aware of the need for avoiding hostility in the ranks of those ruled, and simply meeting this standard implies no great virtue as a democratic leader to the manager who accomplishes this. Since every leader must achieve at least this much to survive, there's little merit in claiming such an accomplishment.

Responsiveness implies a mutual regard, and becomes important to the manager who wants to make things happen in the modern company because it will thus make available to the organization the pooled talents of the subordinates. This pooled talent can be voted positively or negatively as the group decides and, when thrown into the struggle, favorably provides a distinct advantage to the leader who elicits it.

The minimum requirement of responsiveness is a willingness to change a decision if we detect that the prevailing opinion is such that it is not acceptable to the majority of people, unless the overpowering considerations of urgency require that it be done. Perhaps the dividing line between democratic management and other kinds is where the supervisor presents problems rather than solutions.

> There's a law of administration which I'd suggest holds true in almost every situation. That is, if the boss presents his solution first and asks for opinions about it, a vote of approval will follow almost every time.

Responsiveness and democratic management means that the boss asks for others' solutions to a problem which affects the people whose opinions are solicited, and listens to their suggestions before announcing the decision. The ideas of subordinates widen the flow information upon which we can make the decision.

> One large company holds pre-bargaining sessions with their supervisors before going into contract negotiations with their union. Each is asked to comment upon possible union demands, and to comment upon the present union contract as to workability. These comments are taken into consideration when bargaining gets under way.

Still even more responsive, and perhaps an untypical example for that reason, is the form of leadership which permits the group to make its own decisions. Employee recreation committees often function within the framework of a budget allocated by management. The only provision is that the committee must fairly represent the employees' interests in recreation and spend no more than the money allocated or chargeable for specific events. Quality circles, joint employee committees on safety, housekeeping, and the administration of certain employee-oriented functions such as the credit union, the welfare fund and other functions, come close to this form of management.

Less frequently applied, but stoutly defended by its advocates, are those forms which let employees set their own work standards. Professor Bavelas of MIT conducted numerous research projects on the use of employee participation in decision-making, and almost unanimously, the results have been favorable from a management viewpoint.

The important variable in such management methods isn't in its techniques, however, but in the philosophy which underlies it. The presumption that employees are responsible and mature, and will arrive at responsible decisions if entrusted with the power to do so, isn't one of gadgets and methods. It's a function of the basic attitude of people.

Two pressing reasons indicate that newer techniques are needed which press further in the direction of more democracy in management.

1. Our nation is democratic, and the needs for extending this democracy into the places where people work are quite pertinent. Many serious people of conservative bent are asking if we can keep alive the democratic instincts and abilities of citizens to make free and intelligent choices if they lack opportunity in the place they spend most of their waking, creative hours—their jobs.

2. There is a preponderance of evidence showing that responsiveness to the needs of people and democratic management are the only feasible ways to obtain the benefit of pooled employee brainpower in a firm seeking innovation. The value of the worker's asset is immense, and tapping this is worth the efforts of the best management knowledge we can muster.

11

USING COMPETITION TO SPUR THE ORGANIZATION

"Winning isn't everything—it's the only thing!"

VINCE LOMBARDI

When Europeans come here on junkets to study the American character, then return to their native lands after three weeks armed with complete data for analysis, they universally report one facet of our character. We work hard and play hard. After a stiff day in the office or factory, we often return home to work equally hard at "do-it-yourself" projects in our cellar or expansion attic. Over the weekend or on vacations, we drive three hundred miles to ski, or water ski in season. We play 27 holes of golf on Saturday, climb mountains on our vacations, or crank the mimeograph machine all evening for the PTA.

"I wish to preach not the doctrine of ignoble ease," said President Teddy Roosevelt, "but the doctrine of the strenuous life." His words would fall on ears as receptive today as they were around the turn of the century.

This passion for activity—sometimes just to be doing things—results in a general climate of competitiveness, in business and in the community generally, which is important in understanding and motivating people at work.

A. C. Spectorsky has described graphically the vigorous manner in which we approach leisure. The rule seems to be that off the job and around the house the pace must be maintained, and the people across the street in the imitation Cape Cod mustn't be allowed to get ahead of us.

This *new competition,* as we see it through the eyes of the manager, is somewhat different from the old style competition taught us in freshman economics in college. The old style classical economics has a lot of different assumptions which, as we now know through the studies of social scientists, are neither correct nor appropriate as a guide to management decision-making and policy. Take, for example, the basis of the old style economic competition: John Stuart Mill once wrote that,

> In the case of most men the only inducement which has been found sufficiently constant and unflagging to overcome the ever present influence of indolence and love of ease, and induce men to apply themselves unrelaxingly to work for the most part in itself dull and unexciting, is the prospect of bettering their own economic condition and that of their family.

Whether or not this was true in the nineteenth century when Mill was alive isn't pertinent. It's more important to note that we've discovered some additional insights into human motivation since then, and the smart manager uses these new insights to get action from an organization.

It's equally pertinent to note that the competition that made up the engine of classical economics—being a kind of invisible hand which kept people efficient—doesn't work exactly the way Adam Smith and David Ricardo pictured it in the nineteenth century. Modern competition isn't ordinarily price competition, and the workings of supply and demand in the classical sense is more of an academic exercise than a description of the way competition works in reality. Nonetheless, competition as a moving force in business is just as vital—if in a different way—as the economists of the last century pictured it. Competition in modern business does the following things:

- It brings about a demand for innovation
- It spurs research and development

- It is the core of modern advertising and merchandising
- It is more often rooted in quality than price
- It is based upon service rather than cost to consumer
- It forces people to work more closely in teams
- It sharpens individual rivalry between teams
- It demands that individuals stretch themselves to hold their positions on the team on which they serve
- It brings about the downfall of inept team leaders
- It emphasizes cooperation between rivals for position
- It's conducted without hostility being openly expressed
- It places great demands upon individual performance of team members to produce for the team
- It demands special skills of conformity to the team's goals.

THE BASIS OF HEALTHY COMPETITION

Because it has this different complexion, it offers some fruitful opportunities for the manager who wants to make things happen. If he or she clearly understands the way competition works and the good results which come from skillful fostering of competition, his or her results can be phenomenal.

1. Technology and engineering. If a single thing has confounded early predictions made in 1800 that population would outstrip food supply in the world, it is the fruit of modern scientific research and engineering. Creative chemistry has made the American farmer more productive than any other in the world. Breakthroughs in electronics at IBM, Bell Labs and other major electronics firms have produced a new world of computers, communications and information.

2. Product development. A major form of competition has been the creation of new products. This is the conversion of scientific and technical principles into new and useful products for application in every aspect of human existence. This includes traditional areas of comfort and leisure, but even more importantly, areas of transportation, health improvement, nutrition, safety, communication, and human services.

3. Human resource development. One of the major areas of competition between firms is in nurturing the talents of the people they hire and employ. In the late seventies, General Motors was reported to have spent $1 billion on training and development with other similar amounts being spent by the Bell Telephone Company, IBM, Xerox, Ford, and other major corporations. This investment in human capital, said Nobel Laureate Theodore Schultz "may be the most distinctive feature of western economies." Reaching minorities, women and previously left-behind segments of the people, such human development itself comprised a social movement as well as a competitive strategy.

4. Development of strategic management. Combining all of the resources of the firm, strategy itself became a basis for competition. New and sophisticated techniques of planning appeared using systems management, backed up by computers which became more sophisticated, smaller in size, and sold at a fraction of their original cost as intensive competition between computer manufacturers intensified. The strategies, however, were human systems of logic, which sought to find more relevant goals, live within social and governmental constraints, and use resources more effectively.

Competition at this macro (overall) level is matched by making the competition in the giant organizations more personalized between the individuals in their jobs. Overall, competition is aimed toward creating excellent performance at every level of work. When competition produces individual efforts, which tap the full human potential of every person from janitor to executive, it has a humanistic element. People grow from pursuing disputed and opposed ideas.

To a large degree, this results because the manager has created the aura of importance which surrounds such work for the people involved in doing it. He makes each person's effort seem important by showing how it relates to the necessity of meeting the competitors efforts. He isolates the employees from any questions or doubts which might be aroused in their minds about the worldshaking significance of their product.

Most workers will respond more quickly to the challenge that "if we don't do it better, those other people will beat us out" than to any ideological arguments about vital importance of better cakes—

or jet engines—to the world. Workers in defense plants during World War II were more often pushed to herculean levels of production by the possibilities of breaking records, or of beating out Lockheed or North American—or the crew on the next line—than they were about saving the world for democracy. Men in infantry platoons were normally more oriented to what the men in their platoon thought of their conduct in battle than they were about the ideology for which they had been drafted to defend.

> The results of healthy competition, then, will be achieved more often through relating people to those in their immediate group than to some global and theoretical goal.

This isn't to say that the larger goal won't have an effect. People who have a larger goal that they can identify with, as well as a keen sense of personalized competition, will probably perform at closer to their maximum capacity than those who don't have such long-range objectives. Yet, for the manager who wants to move his people into action most effectively, the basic problem over which he has control is this internal competition. Healthy internal competition *within the small group or between small groups* has these effects:

- It moves the members to put forth their best efforts
- It taps the latent abilities of the group
- It brings out the full energies of people
- It gives vent to their natural desire to be active and vigorous in their activities
- It springs creativity and productivity into full use.

WHY PEOPLE COMPETE

People compete in business, and accordingly exert themselves far more than they might without this drive which energizes them, because it meets many of their needs. Here are some of the human needs which are met in business by competition:

It's interesting. The sad fact is that many jobs in industry are either dull, monotonous, repetitive, or trivial. People need to have their interests piqued by what they are doing in order to throw themselves fully into it. Ego involvement can come from doing important work. Yet, with the great rationalization of work into specialized tasks, it's nothing more than fact to say that most industrial jobs, including staff positions, are fraught with the possibility of colossal boredom. A manager can attempt to add interest to a job through several means. He or she can assure people that their work is important; and, tell them how they are a cog which can stop the whole machine. These have limited appeal. More importantly, he or she can build interest into any job through getting the ego of the worker attached to the results achieved. This almost always requires some element of success or failure being attached to the job. Competition is perhaps the most effective way of arousing this interest, since it has to do with the work itself.

The hope of winning. In the large business organization, where the demands of simple management mean that people must be treated in a standardized fashion, competition gains some special advantages. Where the worker becomes part of a competitive group, he or she gains the opportunity to win special attention which seems to accrue to winners anywhere. The combative instinct, while not a dominant one, is strong in our culture. It's ingrained in workers from childhood, and the prospect of winning makes the ardors of competition seem worthwhile.

The fear of failure. The other side of competition is that in pitting one's efforts or abilities against others in the group, or in joining a group which is in competition with another group, there is a negative spur which prods the players on. The prospect of appearing less adequate than one's competitors, or of being laughed at, or perhaps even of missing out on an award, can be a motivator that causes the worker to rise to new heights of excellence and endeavor.

USING RECOGNITION AS AN ACTION-GETTER

Keeping a competitive spirit alive in a group is best done through the adroit use of recognition as a motivator. What kind of recognition is best?

A study by the Survey Research Center of the University of Michigan shows that both supervisors and employees agree that *pay* is the best form of recognition. The second most important form, employees declared, is training for a better job. Some of the commonly-held views that praise, a pat on the back, or being called to the attention of supervisors are highly desired forms of recognition, proved to be not nearly as important as supposed by bosses.

The United States Steel Company's "Creed of Human Relations" marked "recognition" as its first specific principle.

Five major reasons why recognition is an important tool for the supervisor or manager are:

1. It gives people a sense of belonging.
2. It prevents the same mistakes from happening again and again. (This implies a recognition of bad work as well as good work.)
3. People work harder and longer when they get credit for doing so.
4. People grow through recognition—stagnate without it.
5. It requires that the supervisor know the business.

Competition of a productive kind grows out of the best uses of recognition. There are a number of ways in which a manager can use recognition to spur people into action:

- Give them a raise or a bonus
- Tell them when they exceed the standards
- Enter exceptional performance records in their personal file
- Make public announcements of good performance
- Train people for better positions
- Tell superiors about the employee's achievement
- Promote the best people
- Give more responsible work

AVOIDING UNHEALTHY COMPETITION

Despite the virtues which are implicit in competition to spur people to greater effort and higher quality work, there are methods of achieving competitiveness and types of competition which have a bad effect.

Some of the poisons of unhealthy competition would include the following:

1. Competition which aims at destroying the other person rather than getting to the goals faster and better inevitably becomes senseless and counterproductive.

2. Poisonous competition occurs when people divert their energy more toward winning a small battle rather than on forwarding the overall purposes of the organization. When one department tries to beat another by sabotaging its work or withholding information which would have helped the whole company succeed, it's poisonous.

3. Poisonous competition feeds on itself. When one group has been dealt with unfairly or unethically by another, it naturally tends to seek revenge. This, in turn, produces a stronger counter-response in even more damaging form. The revenge ethic ultimately destroys both aggressor and victim. When they work for the same firm, it destroys the firm; when it becomes widespread in a specific industry such as printing or paper, it weakens the entire industry.

4. Poisonous competition emerges when too much power and clout centers in a single competitor. Power corrupts, as Lord Acton put it, and absolute power corrupts absolutely.

5. Poisonous competition is not developmental of people, but causes them to diminish. Such motivators as envy, greed and hatred are inevitably destructive of the person feeling them. When competition requires that we exhibit such behavior, it ruins us in time.

In each of these cases, competition deteriorated from a healthy rivalry into cut-throat competition. The healthy instinct which causes people to pull together aborted into a desire to get ahead by making the others look bad. There are several danger spots where sound competition can become unhealthy competition. Here's when a manager should keep an eye focused to watch for such deleterious effects—and remedies for improving the situation.

Between partners at work. Where two equals are paired in a common task, it's possible that they will focus their attention on beating one another, not in using the other's example as a stimulus to improving their own performance. The smart boss watches for signs of this inward turning between competitors, and squelches it promptly. Some of the first signs of it are when one begins to report the other's mistakes to the boss, or fails to cover for the other and permits him or her to fail in the job. *The remedy?* Telling the two in no uncertain terms that this lack of unity between them is viewed as more serious than any failure of either to perform.

Between cliques. When informal groups having like interests band together to bring about the downfall of another group, the ill effects of competition can be painful to the company and the boss. Breaking them up doesn't always provide the answer. *The remedy?* Don't rush in too fast. Study each clique, its members and the way in which they operate. What are the goals of the clique? Are there any common members between the two? If so, appeal to the common members of both groups to bring about reconciliation. Failing this, take a firm stand on any evidence of discord and indicate that you expect them to pull together in harmony. Perhaps the most useful method is to effect interchanges between groups. Getting them to *know* the other group and what it wants will often temper the hostility which is the immediate cause of the problem.

Between the line and staff. Staff people may take a strong position and attempt to usurp the functions of line management. Line people may ignore or even attack staff groups because they seem to threaten their position or function. *The remedy?* The first step is a clear definition of what line authority consists of and what the staff's responsibility is. If the staff has advisory power only, this should be spelled out with some clear examples of how this advisory power is to operate. If they have functional authority to move in and make decisions (as in quality control in a pharmaceutical plant), this should be made clear as to both limits and scope. The line manager should be taught how to use the staff departments. Any evidence of conflict and competition should be explored by getting all the facts and explaining jointly to the people involved what the rules of the road are.

INSTILLING THE DESIRE TO WIN

Competition isn't the only influence that moves people to excellence. It's a strong one, but it's only effective when it's combined with a desire to cooperate: with the other members of a team, with the company as a whole or with an individual. There are some tested methods used in instilling a desire to excel and to win:

1. Let people know they're competing. There's something stimulating and challenging in saying, "I'll race you to that corner," that adds zest to the trip. In all too many cases, management doesn't let people know they are in competition or in a race, with the result that they don't extend themselves to win.

2. Give an incentive to win. The game must be worth the candle if people are to extend themselves. Often this may be merely a symbol. In one factory, for example, the foreman would buy coffee for the crew that came out best each day. The monetary amount was trivial, but it provided a symbolic yet tangible means of rewarding the people who had extended themselves. Coffee or other small prizes won't work with many groups, however, and a more substantial incentive must be applied. Perhaps the best form of reward and incentive is money, in the form of bonuses, merit raises, or opportunities to advance with greater pay.

3. Let people experience the benefits of winning. With such incentives for excelling, it's only half the battle to quietly call the person aside and pass out the bonus or reward. Give public recognition to the winner by presenting the reward in a conspicuous fashion. This doesn't mean that the Michigan Marching Band must be brought to the plant every time a bonus is handed out. Sometimes simply listing these on a bulletin board, or mentioning them publicly where they would reach the ears of less successful competitors, can have the desired effect. The more intense the competition, the greater the need for letting the victor bask in his or her glory.

4. Ask for that little extra effort. The benefits of competition and the desire to win come through the little extra output that resulted in one person being on top. Nobody gets a prize for simply entering the race, although this has benefits too. The prize goes for moving faster or being smarter than the others who entered and who also ran. It's this little extra effort that gets the reward and moves others to put forth that extra effort next time. Making it clear through rewards that the sole reason for awarding first prize is that the person not only competed, but competed better than the others, is the core of using competition to get the extra results which are inherent in competition.

12

COACHING A WINNING MANAGEMENT TEAM

"I'd define coaching as the job of getting men to play up to the best of their natural endowments."

FRITZ CRISLER

Any youngster who's ever followed the circus knows that one of the miracles of the business is the setting up and taking down of the show. The job most commonly seen by the public is that of driving tent stakes, in which three muscular men armed with sledges all drive the same stake into the ground with blows struck in quick succession. For the roustabout who let his hammer strike atop another, or permits his own to be so slow in pulling away that it is struck by the next, would be laughed out of the gang. In stringing the lines, raising the canvas, breaking up the side show, or linking the caravan into a mobile unit, the roustabouts show teamwork which is a circus tradition. However this system of teamwork was originated—some say by P. T. Barnum—the effect of early coaching has been felt on circuses ever since. The ultimate effect of good coaching is one of effective teamwork in business as well.

Assuming a managerial position in an industrial organization where such coordination and teamwork doesn't exist presents one of the great challenges of the management job. The major reason for this is that the fruits of good coaching are apt to last longer than any single change a manager can bring about in an organization.

BE SYSTEMATIC IN COACHING TEAMS

Coaching is far more than simply preaching to people or making locker room speeches. It starts with a clear fix on the behavioral objectives the coach has in mind. You want people to perform up to the maximum of their potential. You want all members of the group to work in close collaboration with others. You want people to do their regular work, to see and solve problems, and to innovate. Four keys to systematic coaching will be of some help here.

Step 1. Make sure the physical environment is right for the right behavior to take place. In one college, a talented faculty member was seen by his colleagues as being a "loner" who didn't show collegiality—a campus word for collaborative effort. A visiting industrial executive noticed that the loner's office was located in an isolated area away from his departmental colleagues. "Move him up on the main floor next door to two or three of the most cooperative people on your staff" was the executive's advice. This was done, and within a month, everyone had discovered a new high level of cooperation, interaction and "collegiality."

Step 2. Organize work around teams. Arrange the physical format of work so that people must share some common space and funnel their work through others. Let the success of individuals be dependent upon the assistance and collaboration of others, and teamwork will emerge.

Step 3. Reward teamwork when it appears. Issuing favorable consequences to teams when they achieve things jointly will produce more teamwork.

Step 4. Deal with people one-on-one after the first three steps have been taken. Usually, issuing reprimands to an entire group is less desirable than identifying individual problems and handling such nonperformance privately.

Teach Basics First

In assigning the worker to the job or sharpening individual skill, slowly and patiently go through all of the *basic* requirements of the job, one step at a time, until you are sure he or she has them. This stress on fundamentals continues with every employee, until each person's confidence and adeptness are solidly built into performance. This is more than selection for general abilities. It consists of matching the worker to the individual job, and to the team with which he or she will have to work.

Condition the Group

The supervisor conditions the group to accept the new member. If it's an already existing group, the supervisor spends some time getting to know each member of the group and smoothing out frictions and confusion between the individual members. Ways are pointed out in which helping one another makes things easier for all. Approval is shown for team play, and disappointment at selfishness and obstreperousness.

Show Interest

The coach who sits in the stands and reads the newspaper or listens to another game isn't going to generate much support from the team. If it's a productive, competent team, the players want the coach observing, saying a good word, giving them tips on new jobs coming up, and asking them how things are going.

Make Changes Carefully

A smoothly functioning work team is often governed best by the rule of "hands off." Changes of a minor nature for specific individuals involve some individual coaching and instruction. These are generally quite acceptable. Drastic changes in the entire format—presumably the same team will exist and must execute them—are best approached cautiously, with the acceptance of the group achieved through discussion and participation.

PICKING AND TRAINING GOOD PLAYERS

For the action-getting manager, his coaching plan begins with a hard look at each person on the team. Does he or she have the capacity to do the job? Is there a better way of assigning work? Is the worker learning and growing?

> A staff department of a large corporation had a vacancy for a top-flight engineer who had lots of operating experience. After some careful screening—or so they thought—a twenty year man from a plant manager's position in the field was transferred into the staff department. Within a short time, it became apparent that he wasn't going to work out at all. For one thing, he could not write a decent letter or memo. His plant job had not required it, so he had never developed the skill. More than that, his relations with others were awkward because of his rough language. With young secretaries and clerical people who saw themselves as more genteel than his former associates in the mill, his habit of addressing equals with clubbiness and profanity isolated him from the group. Eventually he had to be reassigned to the plant—a much happier man.

Good assignment and selection doesn't always mean that every member of the team must be a paragon. In one metal working plant, it was customary to take the most troublesome employees, the roughnecks, the mavericks, the rebels, and assign them to the foundry. The foreman of the foundry had capitalized on this fact—without necessarily letting management know what he was doing—and greeted every newcomer with:

"What did you do wrong to get assigned here? Every one of us down here in the gang has been kicked out of the civilized society upstairs. I want you to know that we can show those guys how to put out ... you've got to be rough to live down here. If that doesn't suit your taste, then get the hell upstairs now."

This reverse motivation worked beautifully. The work output and tolerance for the noise, heat and back-breaking labor was fantastic. The language was rough, the work brutal, but morale and output were unmatched anywhere in the shop. To have picked an overly sensitive or "promising" person would have ruined both the worker and the team.

Occasionally, the very hardships and special difficulties of working conditions can become a rallying point for a team. Certainly the most effective teams ever built were those of the infantry or Marines.

Training people to function effectively with the group begins with simple job instruction. This will always follow sound instruction in the basics of their individual job. The Job Instruction Training programs of World War II proved wonderfully effective for quickly training persons without experience in factory operations to assume defense jobs in vital industry and arrive at peak effectiveness within the shortest possible time. This formula went as follows:

1. Prepare the learner (make him or her want to learn, etc.)
2. Present the operation (patiently show and tell one step at a time, until you're sure he or she knows)
3. Have the learner try the job, and correct any errors
4. Put the learner on his or her own, then follow up to see how he or she is doing.

Before beginning a training session with a worker, the instructor prepared to instruct through studying the job fully, and making a job breakdown sheet. On this sheet was listed the key points ("anything which will make or break the job is a key point") and all materials and the place of instruction were readied before training began. These basic steps in training are still sound.

Once the worker is on his or her own, it should be crystal clear what is expected in the way of output, quality, housekeeping, safety regulations, maintenance of equipment, and all other details of the job. It's not enough to be able to say, "I told her all those things." One of the basic precepts of job instruction is that "if the learner hasn't learned, then the instructor hasn't taught."

Until the new worker has been properly trained and followed up on to insure complete familiarity and acceptance of the basic skills of the job, the extra coaching for the fine points of advanced teamwork should be played down. Constant attention to basics will pay great dividends in the coach's scheme of things.

Occasionally, a group session with a demonstration that reviews basics in single areas such as safe working habits, quality control, machine maintenance, or others is required.

In one personnel department, it was a regularly scheduled event to hold brief meetings with all clerks, typists and file clerks on the need for confidential handling of personnel records. As a result of this regular check-up instruction, the personnel office never became the source of rumors and scuttlebutt involving people's pay, their personal records and other information, which would have been harmful to the individual and the company if allowed free dissemination.

In another company, the firm hired a famous designer to redo all of their packaging designs. As a result, the cartons and shippers in which the product was shipped and displayed were highly attractive to potential customers, and caught on for the "impulse buyer" in the store. Yet, too many cartons arrived at the store in dishevelled condition. Sealing tapes were either crooked or loose, and there were coffee rings, rips, dents, and dirt on the outside. The plant manager, upon hearing of it, called small group meetings of all the employees, explained how the company had made the choice of the new design, and solicited their cooperation in making the packages as attractive as possible when they left the shipping dock of the plant. This coaching of the group, followed up by reminders from the supervisors on the job from time to time, completely licked this troublesome problem.

The point here isn't to suggest how a manager should train machine operators, packers or even clerks. The important point is that sound coaching begins with training people in basics of their job, and advancing from there to the fine points, niceties, and professional ramifications. This latter stage may be done either through individual talks with employees or small groups, or through a combination of both.

TEN RULES FOR GOOD COACHING

Within the pattern of coaching, there are ten basic rules for good management coaching:

1. Know each person. The first rule of good coaching is to know each employee as an individual. The more information you can obtain, both personal and professional about the employee, the better use you'll be able to make of his or her capacity. You'll also be able to do a better job of matching strengths and weaknesses of the respective members of the group to the best advantage of the department.

2. Know what good performance looks like. The coach can't generally do an effective job of improving performance by dealing in generalities with individuals. They want to know specifically what they are doing right or wrong. They want to know what is expected in every detail of their performance, and hope to receive credit for doing it well. This doesn't imply that the coach must be able to do every job better than the person doing it, but he or she must know very well what proper performance is and be able to judge it accurately. The manager as a coach sees this *judging performance* as an important part of the job.

3. Stretch people to capacity. To get high standards of performance, it's necessary to set tough but attainable goals which tax employees and give them something in which they can take pride when successful.

> A young lawyer joined the legal department of a large corporation and worked under the direction of the patent department head. Immediately he was thrown tremendous loads of research, brief writing, investigations, and analysis. He had to learn not only all the law he'd failed to master on patents, but also most of the technical details of the company's products.
> "I thought it was impossible for awhile and hated the old slavedriver I worked for, but I'll have to admit he made a corporate lawyer out of me in a short while."

4. Show confidence. The manager as a coach is probably the most important source of optimism and confidence the work team can have. Groups have a way of swinging up and down in levels of enthusiasm, and require a stabilizer who remains aloof from the swings of emotional fluctuation. Here's what one advertising man told me:

> We introduced a new line with a direct mail campaign, and every day we counted the sales returns from the field. Most of the copywriters, artists and production people in the creative departments were ready to open a vein, things looked so gloomy for awhile. Bill, the promotion manager, never wavered a second, though.

He kept telling us that we'd done a great job, and that things would turn upward any time. Sure enough, they did, and we were all vastly relieved. Bill never changed. "I knew they would come out OK," was all he said. Either he's got nerves of steel, or he's a terrific actor.

Such confidence and steadiness in leadership is a basic requirement for the coach when the team is under pressure. It's the team that doesn't get rattled which wins over one that falls apart under pressure. Under stress, the manager's coaching job may simply be one of setting an example of confidence, and shoring up the more timorous members of the group.

5. Taking the long view. The manager in a coaching role holds the major responsibility for keeping the larger objectives of the organization in sight. Under the stress of daily pressures of getting the goods out the back door or meeting that deadline, there's always the possibility that the long-range plan gets gobbled up in reaching for short-range objectives. The tyranny of the problems of today too often prevents us from doing the long-range planning so essential for our corporate success.

6. Build flexibility into the group. Basic to good management coaching is working constantly for flexibility. This means more than simply teaching people more than one job—even though that's important too. It means that plans for the future must be adapted quickly to unanticipated or adverse changes in the circumstances of the business.

This flexibility in people is especially tough to achieve if most of the jobs are held by specialists. This specialization causes a narrowness of viewpoint and unwillingness to bend in some instances, which must be overcome through coaching.

7. Pull diverse specialists into a single team. The manager as a coach is apart from all of the specialists who make up the working corps of the company. It's his or her job to point out how the behavior of each specialist must be adapted to fit into the overall pattern of the company. Here's how Charles Thornton, chief executive of Litton Industries, puts it:

> We think of ourselves as specialists with different backgrounds who, as a team, are capable of relating our collective effort to the reality of both today and tomorrow.

Such pulling together means that the manager who is coaching to accomplish it, makes certain that each specialist has an opportunity to see the other person's viewpoint, and to know the requirements imposed by the situation of the whole company.

8. Rate employees by performance, not on personal traits. The business firm is not a family. Accordingly, the coach of a business team should have little concern over the personalities of the employees, except as they directly affect their performance. It's actually this *performance* on the job which is the coach's first and most important concern. Using abstract lists of characteristics to rate employee performance is not only beside the point in a business firm, it's also almost impossible to coach an employee in how to change these things. Rating such things as "attitudes" or "loyalty" is fruitless without specific reference to other performance results. For example, it's worthless for the coach to try to rate a subordinate on "ability to hold his temper" as an abstract item. On the other hand, if somebody is slowing things up or failing to get results on the job, because of temper, then this becomes a legitimate item of discussion by the coach. The emphasis is, of course, on the poor performance, and the coaching on how to change (control the temper) grows directly out of a performance failure. It's rooted in objective facts, not in the opinion or prejudice of the coach.

9. Coaching requires rewards and punishments. Building a hard-hitting team comes from the high motivation of the employees on it. The first requirement is that people be told when they are doing a good job and be given some intangible and tangible rewards for exceeding what might be expected in the job. Monetary incentives—especially in business—are important motivators. Although used with more economy, reprimand and discipline are important motivators as well, and must be used without compunction where they are clearly indicated, in order to protect the team from declining in performance. The size of the incentive may have an effect on the improvement which can result. A range of three to five percent has no incentive effect, and a minimum figure of 10 percent may be needed in order to have an appreciable impact.

10. Boss-Subordinate relations are the key. When a manager sets out to do a better job of moving people into effective behavior, the success or failure of this effort will hinge upon the quality of the relationship between superior and subordinate. This isn't always everything it should be. Psychologist Irwin Taylor once surveyed 138 middle managers and found that most respondents received less time and attention from their boss than they felt they needed, that such talks when held weren't too helpful, that instruction rather than praise or criticism was the main reason for such get-togethers, and that few supervisors could actually help their subordinates since they seldom observed them at work. What did supervisors want their bosses to tell them? Most often it was something about the quality of their work and their work methods. Taylor concluded this from his study:

> Before embarking upon a frenzied hunt for a program, companies would be better advised to see to it that their senior executives are provided with time and are trained to use the tools needed to carry out the basic managerial function of developing their successors.

Still another student of the subject of coaching, Mr. D. E. Balch, formerly vice president of personnel for General Mills, put it this way:

> Coaching requires that the person being coached know that the boss holds him or her in high regard, or the coaching won't work.

Here's how one sales manager reported his highly successful coaching program:

> When I took over the Northwest territory, it was a sick region. The previous manager had violated every rule possible, and most of the good men had left. Before swinging the axe, I made up my mind that I would try to make these present people perform better than they thought they could. I started in by getting to know each man personally and intimately. I met their families, studied their records. I sized up their real capacities, and started working on making them better than they thought they were. It was slow work in the beginning. Finally, one month we came through with the highest volume and profit for the country. You never saw such an elated bunch. I worked my tail off coaching, showing, cajoling, eliminating unnecessary steps, increasing the number of calls per day, per man, tying into advertising and merchandising promotions and all the

rest. But the results were worth it in the rejuvenation these guys had when they saw that they weren't really the duds their former boss kept telling them they were.

GETTING SUBORDINATE COACHES TO COACH

For the manager who has gone up through the organization and is in the general management level, coaching presents unique challenges. For one thing, the general manager is coach of a more highly-talented and able group than many who are lower in the hierarchy. Not that the lesser people aren't as smart, but the higher-level people generally have more experience and knowledge of the company and its products. They've also been through some successful experiences and a screening process which brought them up to their present position. Therefore, they rightly feel that they need less coaching than the rookie at the bottom or the supervisor who is only one step above the worker level.

For this reason also, general managers may not have as much inclination to develop the necessary skills of coaching. As one such manager put it:

> I scrambled up through the pack; let the rest of 'em do the same thing. I believe in economic Darwinism, and think that survival of the fittest is the best selection and development device for management.

In the depression days of the thirties, when managers of great capacity were often doing menial jobs, this indicated no need for extensive coaching. Yet the shortage of skilled managers for growth organizations today is an entirely different circumstance. Furthermore, technical changes in processes and products have made many successful managerial skills obsolete, and the demand for coaches in management positions today is more pressing than ever.

> Coaching subordinates isn't an addition to a manager's job; it's an integral part of it.

Getting subordinate managers to become effective coaches of their subordinates in turn takes several distinct actions on the part of the upper-level management.

1. The top person must be a good coach and work at it. If the president takes time to work with his or her subordinates, in coaching them and letting them know that it is expected that they develop suitable replacements, then coaching will take place.

2. Subordinates follow their boss's example. Where the subordinate is coached effectively, he or she will not only emulate the coaching in practice, but will model his or her own processes on those of the boss.

3. In some instances, the recalcitrant may have to be told flatly that they're not doing enough coaching. When a general manager is faced with outright resistance, it may be necessary to talk cold turkey to the subordinate. In an eastern plant, the plant manager was required, in the face of growth plans for the company, to tell his assistant:

> Look Fred, you know the business okay, and you are turning out the goods, but you aren't doing a damn thing to bring along any of the general foremen to take your place. All you ever tell me is how lousy they are. Yet you picked most of them, and you've supervised them for five to ten years. If they're no good, who should I blame? I think what this means for you is that you sit on your chair and map out a good, solid program of development for all of the general foremen, and come back to me when you've got it. I wouldn't wait over a month to do it either....I'm going to be talking performance review and bonus amount in three months, and this is going to be high on the list of things I want done, and you're going to have to get into the ball game.

Obviously, such blunt talk isn't the first approach with most important members of the management team. Yet, when the circumstances demand it, it shouldn't be evaded.

Coaching subordinates is a business strategy and one of the vital ways a manager makes things happen; not just in this accounting period, but over the long haul.

13

HOW TO USE A PERSONAL STAFF

> "The attitude that 'the only way I can get anything done is to do it myself' is a dangerous one if the tasks referred to can and should be accomplished by a subordinate. Being busy is no virtue in itself—not if you're doing other people's work."
>
> *How Are You Fixed For Time?* SPIEGEL, INC.

You may be spending more time than you think in doing trivial chores. Perhaps you spend more time than you should in such things as making appointments, calling meetings or simply talking to people who could be screened by others. For the manager who makes things happen, this choice of how his or her own time is used may be the key to the dramatic results achieved. Yet many managers who find they can't get the things they would like done are surrounded by personal staffs of secretaries and assistants who, on the surface of things, would appear to be more than adequate to relieve themselves all but the most vital of decisions.

In managing this retinue, the manager has several distinct problems which must be coped with to get the important jobs under way and show the overall results the business needs.

Your old time stereotype of the executive who grabs telephones and sends minions scurrying about like chickens before a Greyhound bus, whose principal skill is pushing buttons that summon frightened subordinates onto the mat is extinct in most companies, as Auren Uris of Research Institute of America put it:

> If he did exist, he owned his own business. It's doubtful that such an operator could long remain in the modern business organization where executive behavior is, to a large degree, social behavior.

Not long ago, I talked to ten general managers about the use of their personal staffs. All of them agreed that this skill was essential for the top person in a division or company who was to get anything done at all. As one of them described it:

> It's a darn ticklish thing, running your personal staff. You see, I've got two basic sets of relationships. One set of relationships is with my subordinates, who have great responsibility and authority for running the major segments of this division. These are the sales manager, production manager, personnel manager, engineering manager, comptroller, and traffic manager. They certainly aren't to be treated as if they were extensions of my arms and legs. They're strong and self-sufficient people with decision-making powers of their own. Then there's another group that immediately surrounds me that's far lower in rank and pay, but who are vitally necessary to run my immediate office, and be my hands and feet in just getting all the things done that I can't take time—mechanically—to do myself. This personal staff can make or break me. They include my secretary, a clerk, my personal "assistant to," and a confidential clerk.

What these managers told me can be summarized this way when it comes to running the personal staff.

1. They've got to be hand-picked. One of the general managers had inherited a secretary who didn't like her, and whom she didn't like. Things went from bad to worse and she found herself getting mad over certain behavior. This sometimes carried over into her relations with the major executives in her division.

> Suddenly, it dawned on me that I was a fool to continue what was obviously an unsatisfactory situation from

both our viewpoints. I had that secretary assigned to another executive, and they got along fine. Then I carefully chose another who seemed to suit my temperament better. Things were much easier for me after that.

2. Close personal contact. Although a major executive might well be able to remain aloof from some people, it's almost impossible to function effectively without establishing warm and congenial relations with the personal staff. Taking an interest in them as people, and paying attention to the normal courtesies are imperative with a personal staff. It may be true that "no bosses are heroes to their secretaries," yet it's necessary not to become an iceberg with people with whom you have the most frequent personal contacts in the organization.

3. Keep them informed. One of the major requirements of using a personal staff is to keep them informed. Since they'll inevitably be handling confidential information, it's necessary to emphasize the need for a tight lip. It's quite pointless, however, to expect them to assist in the management of the personal office of the manager without being aware of what they need to know in order to get the job done.

4. Know what they're doing. One of the basic requirements of the manager in using a personal staff is to know just who is doing what. Said one manager:

> I discovered that some decisions were being made by people in my office who shouldn't have been deciding such big issues. It grew out of my lack of familiarity with what general responsibility each one had. I clarified it and made certain that the major policy decisions came to me.

5. Make them adapt to you. The prime requirement of a person serving on a personal staff is that he or she be flexible in adapting his or her work habits to those of the executive. Certainly, it's a major mistake to do the reverse.

> One section head in an advertising department found that he was altering his dictation practices to suit the schedules proposed by his secretary. This was perfectly okay until one day he discovered that he wasn't getting his letters out on time, and wasn't operating at peak effectiveness.

"I'm always open to suggestions," he said, "but we changed back to my pattern instead of hers to get my work done better. I guess she wasn't too happy about it."

6. The boss should "shoot"—the staff sets up targets. On the rifle range, while the expert riflemen are shooting in competition, down behind the target, in a pit, are men pulling targets. This analogy would fit into the use of the executive's personal staff. The boss is responsible for the shooting; but it's the staff's job to set up targets and pull them down. Here are some of the things a personal staff might be doing for the boss:

- Making travel reservations
- Posting regular reports
- Filing
- Placing long-distance phone calls
- Opening and sorting mail
- Setting up conferences with other executives
- Initiating letters which require no policy decisions
- Seeking out information
- Writing speeches
- Maintaining appointment schedules
- Preparing travel agendas
- Obtaining dossiers on people with whom contact is planned
- Maintaining the office
- Screening callers
- Operating tickler files
- Preparing daily schedules for the executive
- Reporting information which is needed
- Initiating thank-you notes and other customary amenities
- Issuing reminders to the boss to follow up.

7. Make decision-areas clear. The boss should make it crystal clear to the staff what sort of decisions he or she will make and which will be made by the staff. Generally, in those things on which there is a policy, the staff may respond by stating the policy. Where there is no policy or its application is unclear, these matters should come to the manager.

> The manager of a large leather plant found that he was achieving a reputation of being inaccessible since he had taken on an assistant. The reason, he discovered, was that the young man holding this position was injecting his personal judgment into problems, rather than carefully applying the boss's judgment as he himself would have decided it. The boss withdrew this right to engage in such contacts until the assistant was better acquainted with the boss's philosophy and policy framework.

The important point here is that the personal staff of a manager isn't designed to be an independent decision-making group. They are expected to show great initiative, but always within the framework of "what would the boss decide if this matter were presented to him or her personally."

The best personal staffs have the capacity of even making their secondary use of the boss's authority bear the stamp of the boss's personality and managerial style. One speech writer said:

> My job of writing a speech is well done when the executive reads it and says that "it sounds like me." In one case, I was required to prepare a speech for a man whose thinking was diametrically opposed to mine. I wrote it in such a way that the executive told me, 'I like this, you think the same way I do.' This was not the case. It did indicate to me, however, that I had captured the man in the speech I'd written for him, and that's my job.

Not everyone can serve as a personal assistant. This willingness to subject our own whims, likes and individuality to that of some master pattern isn't possible for many people. If such is the case, it's better for both the individual and the boss not to have such people on the personal staff. Internal conflict and discord between the manager and assistant will result. One psychologist put it this way:

> In screening a man or woman to be an assistant for a long period of time, I generally try to find someone who has great intelligence and wit, but who hasn't any

stamp of leadership ability in the old-fashioned sense of the individualistic leader. Frankly, being a good executive secretary or personal assistant requires the personality of a chameleon.

YOUR SECRETARY CAN DOUBLE YOUR EFFICIENCY

Most managers have a single secretary as their personal staff. For that reason, it's vital that this important person be carefully selected, trained and utilized. For the manager who knows how to make the most use of his or her secretary, personal effectiveness can be doubled, in the opinion of some experts. This entails some preliminary diagnosis before selecting or retraining your secretary.

The first step is to identify what kind of manager you are yourself. Then you can describe what qualifications your secretary should have, or what work habits he or she should develop to get you further along in personal productivity.

Let's assume that you are, by nature, a detail-lover. You love checking the minutiae of the work of your department. Your secretary should then have the soul of an FBI agent when it comes to patiently seeking out and obtaining information you'll want for your decision-making processes.

On the other hand, you may be a "big picture" type. You like to operate with sweep and a wide scope. Better have a personal assistant who is good on details, and who will pick up all the little loose ends and do them for you without being reminded, or without even caring whether you know she's covering up for your indifference to the fine points.

Or, perhaps you're still another type, or a combination of them. The first step in selecting a secretary is to find one who bolsters you up in the places where you are apt to be weakest in managing your office, and who complements your strengths with similar strengths of his or her own. One manager said this:

> I get my best results by selling people rather than hitting them over the head. I picked as my secretary someone with a warm, friendly manner, both in person and over the telephone. Everybody agrees that my assistant is part of the office scene because of these qualities.

TRAIN YOUR ADMINISTRATIVE ASSISTANT TO YOUR WORK HABITS

Once you've sized up the kind of executive you are, you're in a position to start training your personal staff, and especially your secretary, to adapt their pace and style of working to you. Here's how the vice president and general manager of an agricultural products firm did it:

> I once had a new secretary who'd worked in the pool, and whose work standards—especially on quality—didn't come up to what I wanted to come out of my office. I cogitated on it for awhile, then I began rejecting letters with errors in such a way that they had to be done over. Being a bright person he caught on that haste made slow progress and a startling improvement in quality came about. Now I know this isn't a universal tool of managing, but in this case it worked beautifully.

For the manager who wants to enlarge the responsibilities of his personal assistant, here's what another manager has done:

> I began to turn out a volume of work which kept my assistant at least half a day behind at all times. Then I'd pick a single job which was new and bigger. I'd call her in and teach her the new job—maybe setting up and maintaining some new control log I wanted to establish. She very shortly found that she could do a lot more of the routine stuff faster in order to get at the "project." Most office employees don't get "stretched," and accordingly don't enlarge their skills and capacity. Simply pitching more of the same stuff on top of the pile won't do it. You do this by adding on interesting and challenging jobs that flatter their intelligence. As a result, the volume and quality of routine work gets done better too.

The concept of "job enlargement" or adding to the responsibilities of assistants until they reach their full potential is a definite source of help for a manager. This requires some careful scheduling of these new aspects of the job, and patient training until they are under control by the learner. Such methods add greatly to the satisfaction which the assistant gets from the job, especially as the less skillful demands on time shrink proportionately.

There's one warning in all this, however. When you enlarge the responsibility and function of your secretary or assistant, don't be penurious about pay. If someone is carrying more responsibility and doing more of your personal work, make certain that they're compensated for the added demands and better skills.

One of the obvious ways in which a secretary's time and your own can be conserved is the use of dictating equipment and word processing. I surveyed two groups of executives, at the general manager level in two management development programs not long ago, on how many used dictating equipment instead of calling the secretary in with a pad. Less than 30 percent of the groups used a machine. The advantages in using such equipment in making the most of your secretary are something like this:

- The typist isn't duplicating your talking time—but is working from the machine while you're dictating the next memo.
- A machine can take verbal instructions from you, even when you aren't there.
- The machine can be talked to at odd hours.
- You can give your secretary instructions and correspondence, even when you aren't in the office, by mailing your tapes.
- Even though you waste time in dictating, the typist won't waste that same time, nor will he or she waste time transcribing, since he or she can work at a uniform pace from the machine.
- You can read your correspondence and dictate answers as they are finished, without tying up the stenographer while you read.

Such machines require, however, that you be more articulate and precise in your dictation, since the secretary can't ask the machine for a clarification or what you mean. There are other limitations upon the machine. On the whole, however, it is a source of personal effectiveness which should be capitalized on when using your personal staff.

Your secretary, like your subordinates, should be sent out of the office at least yearly for added training or information. Memberships in professional societies, in the form of dues-payment and expenses for dinners, are a small investment when such activities can—through better secretarial performance—improve the manager's performance. The National Secretaries Association, in collaboration with a number of universities, including Rutgers, Michigan and Hunter offer special seminars and conferences for executive private secretaries. The topics for such meetings include human relations, public relations, grammar and spelling, systems and procedures, and basic management principles. All of these skills can be put to work, making your office run more smoothly and put out a greater volume of work. It's a double advantage that you can improve your own effectiveness without personally attending the training sessions by which this improvement is brought about.

WHAT ASSISTANTS CAN DO (AND CAN'T DO)

There are several practical rules in making the most of the "assistant" to a manager.

1. He or she shouldn't duplicate or assume secretarial duties. The type of assistant who serves merely to pick up the miscellaneous duties which the boss isn't especially fond of, normally ends up as being over-paid and very hazy in usefulness. Such duties should be handled by added secretarial staff if they are absolutely too much for the boss to handle.

2. The assistant is the most logical way of handling new and special projects for which no permanent organizational spot has been decided. For example, when the general manager finds that personal public relations responsibilities are piling up and he or she isn't ready to move into the establishment of a public relations department, he or she may designate an assistant to handle this function. Later, if the function continues to exist, and the rest of the organization agrees that it should fit into some definite niche, it may be transferred to someone else.

In some companies, new technology such as the computer, operations research, organization planning, or profit improvement may be temporarily placed in such a category.

British consultant Lyndall Urwick describes the job of the assistant as being:

> Study, research, analysis, recommendation, and above all, to help the chief get things done by handling the publication of instructions, etc., watching the organization, and foreseeing and forestalling any failure in coordination between the specialists and the line, but no executive duties.

Basically, the assistant should relieve the executive of routine work. He or she should do the dog-work in planning and controlling which the executive initiates, pull together the use of outside advisors, and, in addition to this, be trained for greater responsibility elsewhere in the organization.

Yet this laudable goal isn't accomplished without some limitations on the use of the assistant. Because it is more than a clerical or secretarial job, it may become invested with special power. Ernest Dale has pointed out some of the ways that people without delegated power may obtain it nevertheless. These include:

- Power through superior verbal skills
- Command through technical competence
- Command through status (next to the boss)
- Command through sanctions (won't send your report on in)
- Command by default (the boss lets the assistant make decisions)

None of these require an ounce of authority to command, since they are based upon the willingness of people to act as if the assistants actually possessed such powers, through either misconception or cupidity. The assistant may actually assume authority if asked to take the posture of expert or boss, or simply fill a situational need. Others in the organization, who don't have the verbal skills, technical know-how, access to the boss, or access to the information which clusters about the boss's office, may elevate the job in power.

In the light of this possibility, it becomes important that the manager who wants to make maximum personal impact on the organization in favor of action and growth understand exactly how much influence and imputed command the assistant is wielding. Not to keep in touch with this trend can lead to the decision-making, not necessarily of the boss's making, growing up gradually.

How to Use a Personal Staff

During his terms in office, perhaps one of the most effective users of the staff assistant was President Eisenhower. Staff assistants, numbering as many as half a dozen in his case, screened every message, report and visitor according to the general instructions and implied objectives of the chief. He read in detail things which his staff assistants stated that he should read, and accepted their word on what was contained in other reports. Through this means, he was able to be briefed on wide ranges of topics and had access to the rest through the people who remained briefed for him.

Using the same system, however, President Nixon was enmeshed in trouble and ultimately removed. In one large manufacturing company, it was found that supervisors were spending up to five hours a day handling clerical duties. The obvious effect of this was that employees on the machines weren't seeing their supervisor who was losing touch with the department. A combination relief operator and manufacturing clerk was assigned to each boss who was then freed to inspect, train and observe within the department. The savings were great since it freed the higher-paid supervisors from lower grade work, and allowed them to use their special supervisory skills on improving the operation of the department and improving the performance of all the employees.

Some of the things which assistants can do include:

- Digesting material and reports received
- Keeping situations under surveillance and reporting problems
- Handling lesser visitors
- Detailing in the broad plans laid down by executives
- Establishing procedures for executive time
- Making "trial balloon" statements to test reactions
- Planning meetings and conferences
- Making out schedules and detailed plans
- Analyzing data received and point out important facts
- Answering routine correspondence
- Handling certain public relations functions
- Managing administrative chores on "campaigns"

EFFECTIVE USE OF EXECUTIVE TIME

The chief executive of a multi-national corporation recently told me how he organizes his calendar.

> At the close of each day, five minutes are set aside for review by writing down each major item which has been dealt with during the day. I also list those items on which more than one hour has been spent. In this way, I find that sometimes I have spent considerable time on relatively unimportant items. I then place on the calendar for the coming day three or four principal objectives, and then matters which are of lesser importance.

Time is probably the greatest investment the manager has. Human power and effectiveness grow out of the effective use and treatment of time—especially our own—with respect. If we have a clearly defined purpose, and develop the skill to attain it, we've developed a valuable asset for the company.

Here's a checklist which one executive developed for his personal use in improving his own utilization of time. You might want to try it yourself:

_____ Could any of the things I did today have been done in less time when I do them again? How?
_____ Did I use all the shortcuts available?
_____ Did I take on the tough jobs first?
_____ Did I wait for others to do something I might have done within a few seconds myself?
_____ Did I get wrapped up in something lengthy which I could have asked someone else to do?
_____ Did I fail to make a project clear to someone, thereby making it likely I'll hear a lot more about it later?
_____ Did I leave a lot of projects half-done?
_____ How much time did I lose due to procrastination?
_____ Did I keep my secretary fully programmed when I was away from the office?
_____ Did I tax my staff assistant with big enough jobs?
_____ Did I keep my energy level high by relaxing occasionally?
_____ Was I punctual for all my appointments?
_____ Did I fill in my idle waiting time with useful work?
_____ Did I waste any of my meeting time?
_____ What's the first thing I should do tomorrow?

How to Use a Personal Staff

From such a checklist, it's sometimes easier to identify those things a manager is doing which can be assigned to someone else.

Perhaps the most helpful principle for using a personal staff is the "exception principle." Under this principle, only the big issues are brought to the manager's personal attention, while the routine, respective and pot-boiling activities will be handled without specific managerial direction by the personal staff. In order that no bad effects result, a control system is set up, whereby the unusual or "exceptional" problems and occurrences will come automatically to the attention of the manager.

The development of procedures and systems to effect this feedback is part of the manager's job. In establishing the routines of his or her office, it becomes important for the executive to think "system," in which information that reflects the larger organization will be handled in routine fashion, with only the new, the significant and the important getting personal attention.

This entails two things:

1. The manager must have a team of trained assistants who work closely with him or her to effect the results he or she wants.

2. This team must be governed by some carefully designed and smartly motivated and trained people to execute the plan.

14

MANAGING CLIQUES IN THE ORGANIZATION

> "No more fiendish punishment could be devised, were such a thing physically possible, than that one should be turned loose in a society and remain absolutely unnoticed by all the members thereof."
>
> WILLIAM JAMES

The management of cliques is a rapidly growing field for executive action. The rewards are obvious: more cooperative people, more productive workers, easier installation of improvements by engineers and accountants, less conflict and confusion rising to the top, and greater unity of effort.

The possibility of better management of informal organizations is the next great breakthrough in management theory and practice. Scientists declare that the dual goals of the clique in business—desire for security and for participation in the decisions which affect them—are finding their way into organizational planning in many firms. No mere academic exercise, the management of the clique is for high stakes.

For one thing cost reduction programs have often pointed up the fact that the people at the top of the organization can't seem to stay in touch with the people at the bottom, no matter how loudly they shout or how keenly they listen. Probes to find the reason have indicated that the clique is a block to real communication.

For another thing, information about policies, procedures, rules, and regulations doesn't come out in the form of behavior the boss originally intended. Systems which are completely logical just don't work the way they were designed to work. Industrial engineers seem to find new heights of employee and clique ingenuity in undermining incentives and methods improvement which would change the social systems on the job.

Still another management problem which seems to center around the clique organization is the failure of specialist groups to coordinate, mainly because they become special interest groups which don't communicate. In many engineering and research labs, for example, the multiplication of technical jargon by the cliques has become almost comparable to a tower of Babel.

Multiplied throughout the company, it's more than the electrical engineers not pulling in harness with the mechanicals; it's the accounting clique battling the sales clique, the quality clique scrimmaging the production crowd, the union bunch fighting everybody, the office fighting the shop, the old-timers fighting the young college Turks, and the company losing in every case.

Finally, the cliques are the building blocks of that much criticized figure, the organization person. The clique makes its members into conformists who suppress their individuality in order to retain membership and popularity with the informal group with which they work. To the extent that the clique places no premium upon individual effort or creativity, the skills of imitation and cooperation become paramount.

As the full dimension of the clique's influence becomes more apparent, many of the methods for handling human relations and communications problems become increasingly inadequate, overmatched by the problems they are expected to solve.

In format, the clique appears as a small group; the graduates of a particular school, practitioners of a special occupation or a few people bound together by ties of sentiment, common interests or like social ties.

The clique is a spontaneous, informal, natural cultural formation inside the organization. It controls its members through social pressures and can act either favorably or unfavorably insofar as the company is concerned.

Since management can neither order the clique out of existence nor circumvent it by industrial engineering or directives, the logical course is to prevail upon the group to act in the firm's interest.

A number of steps can lead toward this result. Summarized, these include:

- Recognize that cliques exist
- Train managers in team building
- Catalog the major segments of the clique organization
- Study the operating techniques of cliques
- Work through informal leaders
- Plan facilities so that they will establish social status

RECOGNIZE THAT CLIQUES EXIST

Cliques exist in every human organization including the family, the church, the unions, and the government, as well as in business firms. No master plan or sinister conspiracy is needed to start one—only a few people having common interests, fear of the boss or pride in achievement. Many large and imposing clubs have grown out of a clique founded on the habits, likes, dislikes, sentiments, interests, and endowments of a group of individuals.

Management which, on hearing that cliques exist, reacts with an emotional outburst aimed at wiping them out, or with a denial that they have infiltrated the company, is merely putting obstacles in the way of steps which might lead to a more sophisticated treatment of the subject.

Acceptance of cliques as going concerns, and an effort to understand their nature and scope, will pay dividends in the adoption of policies and practices designed to enlist them into channels of help and increased productivity.

TRAIN MANAGERS IN TEAM BUILDING

One of the basic steps in getting a grasp on the clique situation must include some basic training of management in group relations and the specifics of informal organization. Human relations training in the past has often been oriented toward studies of individual behavior without attention to the group processes.

Although it's obvious that the group consists of individuals, mere understanding of individual motivation, without some practical knowledge of how the clique modifies this behavior, is only half the story.

Mary Jones may want to produce more work in the typing pool; but she has learned that if she is too productive, she won't be invited to the little luncheon and gossip dates which also are important to her. With cliques in mind, we still study the individual; but we pay more attention to how Mary meets her individual needs through group approval.

John Jones, engineer, may be more interested in what the boys down at the engineering society think of him than what his boss thinks, or even what he thinks of himself.

Putting this basic importance of the group across to the supervisor, the manager, the technician, and the staff man is a key step in managing the informal organization.

CATALOG CLIQUE SEGMENTS

With a management and staff aware of the importance and nature of cliques, a company can catalog the major cliques and learn how they react to one another and to the company. This is best done by the people who are actually on the spot as managers, engineers and staff people. The foreman of Department 10, for example, will know the workers as individuals, and can easily plot out the major cliques in the department.

Mechanics are one clique, the old-timers another, the operators of certain sections a third, and so on. How they get along, who is considered highest on the social scale of the shop, who likes whom, all are part of team building.

Top management can usually spot the major clique divisions.

In one chemical company, for example, the major clique consists of graduate chemists who will move up the line in management. Generally, the four major subdivisions of cliques will include:

- Top management—on mahogany row
- Supervisors—the white-collar bosses in the shop
- Technicians—accountants, engineers, and others whose work is primarily concerned with improving other people's effectiveness
- Workers—the clerks, typists, machine operators, laborers, salespeople.

Within each of these major subdivisions are cliques. Even in top brass there will be cliques. The typists in the secretarial pool from a particular school may be a worker clique; the engineers in the sales force or the Harvard Business School grads in executive row may be another.

In looking for cliques, the key seems to be to identify common ties which people might have. These ties can be affection, pride, insecurity, hatred, or simple gregariousness. The resulting cliques will have similar forms. Usually they are about as strong as the emotion which caused the members to drift together into a clique in the first place. Sometimes direct questioning will elicit accurate answers about cliques.

People are especially aware of cliques above them in social status or to which they aspire. They often deny the existence of their own, not because they want to hide its existence, but simply because they don't recognize it as one.

STUDY CLIQUE OPERATING TECHNIQUES

The most important operating technique from a business viewpoint is the clique's ability to control its members' actions, especially their productivity, creativity and cooperativeness. A worker, who does more work than the clique has arbitrarily decided is a safe or decent amount, risks ostracism. This control system can work to restrict output or upset the most soundly-planned incentive system. It can also carry through to fabulous success any management plan which fits in with the special goals the clique has set. It also resists change effectively.

The weapons of control most often used are exclusion from social contact, and failure to be included in luncheon groups, small talk or help on the job.

The clique rations congeniality and warmth, and sometimes extends outside the plant into the community. Unless the offender has some hope of being included in a different and better clique, there is little chance of his swimming upstream against the clique.

The supervisor who can identify the cliques and their control systems can go further and seek out the basis of clique standards of control.

The best leaders get the clique pulling for them. In fact, they become informal leaders of the clique as well as being the formal leaders assigned by management. The most effective and productive teams are cliques that have aligned their own goals with those of the administration.

In such cases, the full power and ability of the group will be brought to bear, and the results will be unsurpassed anywhere.

Assigning good workers to a hostile clique or one with low standards can only result in spoiling the worker. On the other hand, putting a loafer with a hard-working group can often boost his or her performance up to the group standard through clique controls.

One key indicator of group operating methods is a special language. Often this is simply a new use of plain English. In other cases it involves development of special jargon, such as "gandy dancer" on the railroads. These words are often functional words commonly used in the day-to-day, technical aspects of the job. In others, they are simply profane. Occasionally, they are inside jokes, or hints and innuendoes.

The manager who is sensitive and observant will find that these things are open signs which a keen observer can interpret. With such indications of group sentiment, the manager can take steps to avert bad results and encourage favorable ones, if he or she can interpret these signs as evidence of the modus operandi of the clique. In some cases, we may be required to proceed regardless of group sentiment, but with a forewarning of resistance.

In other cases, we can try a different approach, or even defer action with a view to winning clique support to the plan.

WORKING THROUGH INFORMAL LEADERS

Every informal organization has its informal leaders. These leaders are not appointed by management or selected by plebiscite, and have no guaranteed tenure. They are the individuals who seem best to articulate the emotional state of the group, and are most sensitive to its sentiments. Once established, they are entitled to lead the group in particular situations, policing backsliders and setting an example for the rest.

It is here that the greatest opportunity exists for working through the clique. If the assigned leader, office manager or executive can earn the support of the clique and become its leader, he or she has a singular role in the group and serves management as well.

If we speak the language of the clique, we hold a key to moving the group toward standards which are satisfactory to the company and at the same time pleasing to the clique.

By controlling the communication system, we exercise special powers over group behavior. In practice, we can hold onto informal leadership only so long as the group identifies us as being one of them. Once excluded because we have threatened the group's solidarity or made it feel inadequate, we lose this control.

The group operates in such a way that a supervisor may also be accepted by a worker clique, because cliques are loose groupings and a single individual may belong to several of them, even those with opposing interests, without such affiliations seeming inconsistent.

A person who is in good standing in several cliques is in a position to bring about teamwork, cooperation and unity of effort.

The evidence seems to point to the team leader as the best manager for getting the clique to pull toward company goals. The nonconformist who wears a beard and Bermuda shorts to work can be productive only so long as the clique accepts this as normal behavior and him as one of the group. Tossed out of the membership by the clique, the loner is likely to become ineffective because he fell out of step with the group.

Managers normally find that they need the cooperation of three or more cliques in order to function with any success.

They are obliged to get cooperation the informal organization way. Informal leadership, as a method of managing, then becomes a skill in joining several cliques without seeming to be inconsistent to any of them. From inside a leader can sway the group toward the company goals.

PLANNING FACILITIES

The physical facilities of the plant or office are important in managing the clique organization. Every desk, chair, office, telephone, rug, and tool used in the technical performance of work has a veneer of social significance in addition to its functional usage.

These serve to establish the social status of the persons to whom they are assigned, so do inequities in the assignment of office space, in tools and in differences in pay.

Being founded on sentiment, the clique cannot rise above the somewhat petty considerations of small differences in working conditions. It will buzz loudly at changes in desks, work layout, conveniences, and facilities which the social scientists call status symbols. Complaints are not based on actual physical comfort or discomfort, but on the social effects of change on the group.

In one case, a group of draftsmen in a New Jersey company stopped work because new air conditioners were installed in their department. Baffled by this reaction, the chief engineer spent several hours chatting with a delegation, explaining how the pieces were chosen, who selected them, and explaining "why the draftsmen weren't consulted."

Consulting key cliques in the careful, detailed planning of facilities, may be an important consideration in managing the clique. Often it means that key cliques must be involved in this planning; or, at best, the managers of the respective departments must be consulted on the possible ramifications of such change.

15

THE NEW LOOK IN EFFECTIVE COMMITTEES

"A camel is a horse designed by a committee."

ANONYMOUS

For the manager who is action-oriented, the invention of the committee often seems like a device designed to thwart us in getting things done. Not only must we serve on many of them (one survey showed that the average general manager is on nine committees), but frequently we must manage the details of leading several. This is especially true when working for a large organization.

One study by American Management Association showed that of 150 large companies surveyed, 110 reported standing committees as a regular part of their organization, with over 50 percent having management committees which concerned themselves with problems on overall administration of the firm. Others have functional committees which have general surveillance over policy in such areas as research, personnel, purchasing, manufacturing, contributions, public relations, and so on. The management committee may have an addition to its plenary group subcommittees, running to as many as five or six on a permanent or *ad hoc* basis.

When should a manager resort to committees to get things done? Basically there are six legitimate occasions for the appointment of a committee in order to make things happen more effectively than by any other method:

1. To get participation. When there are varied and possibly conflicting interest groups who will be affected by a decision or policies, appointment of a representative from each involved group will provide a forum where dissents and viewpoints may be included in policy *prior* to its being made. The obvious advantage here is that the latent opposition of conflicting groups can be ameliorated, circumvented or eliminated by having representation upon a committee. A positive advantage lies in the ability of the various groups to contribute to the scope of the whole policy through their special knowledge of one facet.

2. To bring about uniformity of direction. It's almost inevitable that humans will differ on objectives and paths for reaching them if left to their own devices. These differences may have some advantages in originality, but they may also result in conflict between goals of the groups, and confusion and lack of unity in the whole organization. Committees serve as control devices for bringing the respective parts of the organism into line with the total objective by accomplishing some uniformity between the respective units represented on it.

3. It trains the members. The narrow specialist or the obstreperous person with selfish attitudes will grow through committee membership. There's an attrition into excessive individuality in an organization through committee membership, and the maverick may continue to be a maverick after long exposure to committee techniques, but will also be aware that others have equally strong views. Occasionally, the strong member will convert all of the others if they are indifferent to the decision being made, and, in such cases, will achieve uniformity of direction by giving in. In any event, the training experience from committee membership is a strong argument for its use. It not only brings knowledge, but also has some effects upon changing attitudes as well.

4. Strategically it packs more weight. There's little doubting the strategic values of committees in complex organizations, in terms of the weight their conclusions carry. The board will be more apt to endorse a management committee action than the decision of an individual. For those down the line, the fact that many people (a committee) have deliberated and decided will make the final policy more palatable than a seemingly arbitrary decision made by an individual.

5. It's an effective morgue for foolish ideas. For the action-oriented manager, there's often an occasion when ill-advised, poorly-timed ideas will need tactful disposal without the outward appearance of flat refusal. Committees, although costly for such purposes, are often a convenient manner of unloading and buffering the idea from seeing the light of day. While this buffer role of committees is more often used for bad purposes (killing good ideas rather than bad ones) it has its place in the scheme of things for the action-getter too, as a means of handling tough interpersonal situations involving aggressive, but wrong, suggestions.

6. It's a good repository for destructive criticism. The manager who makes things happen is more apt to come under fire from his or her associates than the time server who simply keeps things at the status quo. Handling such criticism can be a time-consumer for the action-getter, and a committee can serve as a convenient depository for such criticism.

> For example, one industrial engineering manager was making great strides with a cost reduction program when several managers, made insecure by the program, protested that the program was disruptive to morale. The industrial engineer accepted these protests seriously, and asked several members of the protesting group to serve as a committee to study "in depth" the problem of how these considerations should be handled in installing the new cost reduction program. She promised to open her books to the committee and give it access to her files. The committee entered a lengthy, but enthusiastic, study of the entire program. It came up with some minor suggestions for procedures, which she promptly adopted. Meanwhile, the entire program had been installed and proved extremely effective in cost-cutting.

WHEN INDIVIDUAL ACTION IS BEST

Despite these obvious tactical and managerial advantages in appointing committees, there are limits upon their appointment and usage. There are circumstances under which committees are both time-consuming, inefficient and costly. Each circumstance should be weighed carefully to discover where the preponderance of benefit will lie. Since there will be advantages in both methods (individual and committee) in most circumstances, it may seem that the decision is moot. Yet, there are some guides when individual action is better in terms of getting action, without serious side effects which will undo the action taken over time.

1. Individual action is best for directing action. The organization principle of "one boss" is a sound one which is proven again and again in practice. Having an employee responsible to a committee is a multiple form of the evils of reporting to two bosses. Directions, orders and discipline are best the matter of one leader. Action leadership tasks in the hands of a committee are almost always poorly executed, or executed with timidity, lack of resolution and extreme caution.

2. Innovation is rooted in individuals. Committees and task forces who brainstorm may have certain valuable functions in solving jurisdictional problems, in communicating the information of the members to one another, and in overcoming future obstacles in execution, but the great creative work must be done by an individual. These creative acts occasionally are bettered by buffeting them around in committees, but many creative tasks are solitary. No committee ever wrote a great novel or painted a masterpiece. Yet it was a committee which created the Constitution of the United States. One format which can be used here is a combination thereof:

- The group meets and drops ideas, which the creative person notes and fits into his or her thinking
- The creative person does his or her innovating in private
- Tests of creative innovation upon the group are healthy

3. Where immediate action is demanded. For all of their virtues, the committees do not have great mobility and decisiveness. By their nature, they are deliberative groups. In execution of decision and policy already decided, the individual is superior to the committee. This is especially true when speed of reaction is the essence of the situation. The football huddle, for example, is not a conference but an order-giving situation. The shop supervisor faced with a breakdown and the need for immediate decisions must have the power to direct others to move. The forcing of decisions, down to the lowest possible level, is based upon this principle, and group decision-making under such circumstances can only result in what Admiral Rickover described as "a train on which every passenger has a brake."

WHO SHOULD BE ON A COMMITTEE

When "Engine Charlie" Wilson was made Secretary of Defense, he called a meeting, it is reported, which he estimated should have brought forth six people, or ten at most. Over thirty showed up. Glaring around the room, he snorted:
"What are all these people doing here?
At the next meeting, it's said, less than six showed up.
The point is that committees have a way of attracting people who have a natural proclivity for attending meetings, even when they aren't required.
Since committees and committee meetings aren't always the most productive place for a person to be spending time, control over the number of people who are members, and equally stringent control over those who attend the meetings, should be maintained. Some companies have done these things to control committee size and attendance of members at committee meetings:

- Eliminate from membership people whose contribution or usefulness to the committee is only sporadic. Invite such people to attend those meetings where things that concern them are to be discussed.
- If the work of the committee is complex and might require the work of subcommittees, appoint members of subcommittees who are not members of the committee as a whole. The member of the full committee then reports back on the actions or recommendations of the subgroup without having everyone on hand at the original meeting.
- Use "task forces" of staff people to do the work of committees, with the proviso that they be discharged from the committee upon completion of the required staff work.

Who, then, should be included on a committee?

As a general rule, only those people who will make a contribution to the objective of the committee most of the time. Yet this entails some *caveats* if the effects of the committee action are to avoid disruption and require redoing the work of the committee because it omitted some vital interest group. Here are some guide rules:

1. Policy committees. Membership on committees, which can make or effectively recommend policy, should include the chief manager of every department who must execute the policy. For instance, the salary committee should include the major executives of the divisions and staff departments who must abide by the findings of the committee. The result of not including such people is failure to comply, with the justifiable excuse that they didn't understand, didn't agree or didn't believe that the policy applied to them. Others who might be asked to join or sit in on such meetings are people on "the verge" of top management, who might acquire a feel for such deliberations by taking part in committee activity.

2. Problem solving committees. These are normally ad hoc committees established to do such necessary things as cost reduction, profit improvement or other similar problem areas. Here the committee should represent the various areas of the business which must execute the plans developed, as well as some technical experts from staff departments who can provide expert analysis and advice on specific subjects such as accounting, industrial engineering and so on. Such committees may be designed with steering groups of top employees and temporary members to bring in special reports or perform special functions.

3. Training committees. Certain companies, such as the McCormick Company of Baltimore, have formed "junior boards" that serve to train their members in problems which have significance to the senior boards of the company. Members of such committees have ordinarily been selected for their potential advancement and for their positions as representative of certain functions or departments of the company. They deal with specific issues and make recommendations to the senior boards regarding policies that affect the lower echelons. Membership is rotated to permit as wide a distribution of membership and training opportunities as possible.

One of the great plagues of the committee system is the use of committees as a means of drafting people to do extra work without adding it to their job description. University faculty committees, and occasionally such committees as employee recreation, junior achievement, fund raising, and similar peripheral activities, are managed in this fashion. While they serve the purpose of getting free work, they frequently sap the time and energy of busy people in a way which places some doubt upon their ultimate efficiency. Perhaps a more efficient manner of handling such assignments would be to enlist some full-time people to perform the chores, and rate them on their performance in them. The ultimate cost in terms of hours would be far less. As a cold, hard matter of personal career planning, such committees are to be avoided if such avoidance doesn't put one into direct violation of the stated desires of a superior. The ideal person for such committee work is the least busy, and perhaps the least able, person. He is apt to find such activity pleasant and enjoyable, and a means of garnering honors and responsibilities which he might never otherwise obtain.

KEEPING COMMITTEES UNDER CONTROL

The Standard Oil Company of California and other companies have established systems of annually reviewing committees to keep them from becoming a great jungle that strangles the efficiency of the organization.

The manager who hopes to keep the fat from accumulating in his organization may find that such a procedure is worthwhile in his organization, too. Here are procedures for keeping the spawning of useless committees within reasonable bounds:

Draw up a committee organization chart. The first step in controlling committees is to draw up an organization chart of the *committees* which exist. One effective way of doing this is to start with the top nine or ten men in the company, and ask them to prepare a brief memo stating what committees they belong to, how frequently they meet and how many subcommittees each has. These can then be compiled into a master committee roster, and plotted graphically to show the overlap and duplication existing.

This step in itself will suggest ways in which simplification can be made.

Then test each committee. This can be done by asking of each committee *what* its purpose is; *why* it is necessary; *who* is on it that might be eliminated; *when* it meets; and is this the proper timing (does it meet too often); and, finally, *how* could the work of this committee be eliminated, changed, simplified, or combined with another. Such hard questions asked of each committee yearly will wring out some of the grossest cases of committee-itis in an organization and free executive time for more productive efforts.

FIVE GUIDES TO EFFECTIVE COMMITTEE MANAGEMENT

In studying any single committee, or in studying the whole structure of committees, the manager who hopes to keep the organization vital and trim should look at five factors with regard to each committee:

- Committee economics
- Weighing committee contribution
- Using the principles of group effectiveness
- It should have tight procedures
- It should deal only with "committee" topics

It might be worthwhile to explore each of these a little more in depth.

Committee economics. The costs of committee operation are often hidden, but are extremely high in most companies. A committee should be weighed against the out-of-pocket costs of secretarial help, of the salaries of those attending, and of time and space used. Beyond this, committees cost even more through poor execution of their decisions which might better have been made elsewhere, and the immunity to criticism which improves performance and inhibits sloppy performance. Often, the committee is costly in the internal politics it generates through its activities. In many instances, this is because the "least busy" member of the committee, and perhaps the least-informed member, has the greatest influence because he has time to do the busy-work of the committee. This least-busy member will ordinarily initiate more vetoes and demand more by way of preventive action by managers than any other member. All of these costs should be considered in weighing a committee's effectiveness.

Weighing committee contribution. Placing a strict cost and profit analysis against committee output is probably impossible to do. Yet a general yardstick of profitability should be applied in every case. Does the committee contribute more than its cost in terms of training, problems solved, acceptance gained for ideas and programs, coordination of related functions, and tightness and logic of policy? The committee system can hardly contribute to profit during the coming fiscal period, and it's often pointless to even attempt to evaluate it on this basis. It isn't impossible to ask, however, what the committee has added to the stability and growth potential of the firm through its actions in the current period. There are committees which have added immeasurably to these growth and stability factors in a firm. The facts are that there are good committees and bad ones, and the good ones have contributed to growth and stability of the social organization of the firm. The experienced executive must use his or her intuition and experience to evaluate the contribution. The standard is intangible, but nonetheless real. Like individuals, committees may be subjected to performance appraisal. One useful standard is to ask how the committee performed against its *stated objectives*. Another is to ask for a listing of its contributions and weigh these against possible alternative ways of accomplishing the same goals.

The committee should use the principles of group effectiveness. Being a good committee leader requires experience and skill. It takes an equal amount of skill to be a good *member* of a committee. Courses and programs aimed at sharpening those skills are economically sound where the committee system is well entrenched.

Ernest Dale has spelled out some criteria which guide group effectiveness. They include some of the following:

- The members should have skill in verbal expression.
- Conflicts must be resolved by integration, not by domination on the part of a single member or the leader, not by compromise which leaves both parties sullen about the result.

- Committees should emphasize the concrete and practical, and avoid the blue sky topics, the philosophical or the speculative questions not solidly rooted in fact.
- Productivity in a committee comes through its being given urgent problems, the power to make decisions or recommendations, easy communication between the members, an orderly system of treating problems, and the intelligence and originality of the group.
- Agreement in committees, research shows, comes through strong attraction between the members for one another, through personal friendships in the group, through uniformity of background and interest, and the presence of few dissenters and mavericks. (The latter may not be desirable, since a maverick may often bring in original ideas.)

Committees should have tight procedures. Every committee should have its scope and function defined clearly before it is allowed to function. It should be the proper size. Research at Harvard's Social Relations Department indicates that under five is undesirable and over 15 is unmanageable. Its chairman should be weighty in status and skilled in conference leadership, should not dominate and should not be passive. The secretary should be chosen from among the weightier members, since his or her impact on the results through preparation of minutes is considerable. To get action from committee meetings, the agenda should be circulated in advance, and other information related to the decision should be in the hands of members in sufficient time for them to study the materials.

> "I never can think clearly in some committees," one executive reported, "because they throw things out I haven't had time to digest. They should send them out in advance."

In one company, all committee meetings are scheduled one hour before lunch or before quitting time, in order that the chairman will not let things wander and the groups won't tend to drag things out. It's been found in this company that few meetings run overtime when they're scheduled this way.

Committees should deal only with committee topics. The ideal topic for a committee is jurisdictional disputes. Here the manager can throw the dispute to the people who have been most heavily engaged in such disputes, along with some neutral figures. Under the duress of committee procedures and a firm charge from the person appointing them, solutions are often found by which the members will abide. Still another committee purpose which is beneficial and productive of unity is where people who have little opportunity to see one another in daily work schedules will become better acquainted and both formal and informal communication will be forced into being. This is a valuable function of a committee and in some instances is the major purpose of the committee. Policy-making which entails both of the above problems can legitimately be identified as a good communication area. The topics to be avoided are:

- How to do something
- The administration of an activity
- The execution of a plan

In short, committees can be vehicles for getting things done. They require careful planning and managerial control if they are to become effective tools of the action-oriented manager.

16

HARNESSING AGGRESSIVENESS IN MANAGEMENT

> *"The rung of a ladder was never meant to rest upon, but only to hold a man's foot long enough to enable him to put the other somewhat higher."*
>
> THOMAS HUXLEY

Aggressiveness ranks high among the qualities sought in managers. Every company is looking for self-starting young people who can show initiative and follow-through.

But the overly-aggressive person arouses resistance. Others will go out of their way to block his or her progress.

For this reason, top executives declare, they spend much of their time doing two things:

1. Trying to stimulate subordinates who don't show enough aggressiveness.

2. Trying to straighten out those who let aggressiveness get the best of them.

Methods of attaining the first objective—salary increases, fringe benefits, status symbols—are generally understood and applied. But how to put brakes on aggressiveness, once it gets out of hand, is more complex and harder to manage.

It is not impossible, however, once we recognize the motives that lead to aggressiveness and the personality changes that show it is becoming a handicap.

A number of studies show that, although other motives may exist, those that drive a person to accomplishments are primarily three:

- A desire for power
- A desire for a good reputation
- A desire for wealth

Let's look at these motives and at the danger points in each. In every case we will find a stage where caution is indicated. If this stage is recognized, the still effects of having too much of a good thing can be prevented.

THE DESIRE FOR MASTERY

Deep inside nearly every successful one of us is an intense desire to be best. We might want to be number one in the organization. Every action is calculated to carry us toward that goal. Naturally, this requires that we acquire some skills in outwitting our competitors or, more often, outworking them. There are six stages of this desire to be top dog.

The first stage is the highly sought-after desire to excel in a chosen field. A sense of craftsmanship and pride in our work that we simply won't turn out an inferior job or be bested in quantity dominates. This is the basic building block by which most managers and employees achieve mastery of their field. One of the great problems of modern management is to develop more tools and skills for instilling this desire in more people.

Usually this desire to excel propels a person quickly into the next stage. Here we become the joy of the boss, because we demonstrate a self-development habit that leads us to acquire new skills as well as to do effectively the things we already know. We study our own past efforts, correct our mistakes, and learn how to repeat our successes in new situations.

In the third stage, we raise our eyes to see how the other person is doing. Rather than working to meet some personal standard, we tend to increase our efforts and performance to exceed the best efforts of our best competitors. We get real enjoyment out of rivalry with other good people. We especially enjoy winning against tough opposition.

The next stage involves emotions and ego in our work to a degree which wasn't previously apparent. When we face a tough competitive situation, we learn to stretch ourselves to win, and develop the capacity of working at paces that we didn't know we could maintain.

In these first four stages, we see an ideal manager for a modern company.

The danger point comes in the fifth and sixth stages, where we begin to blow our top when frustrated in our drive for mastery.

In these last two stages, basically sound drives have turned into belligerence and hostility. In its mildest form, this crops up as maliciousness and nagging. At worst, it appears as temper tantrums.

A hothead can add a touch of drive and energy to the management team, but sometimes at a cost the company can't afford. A midwestern banker learned this. He hired an aggressive man to head his new-business development. Blessed with a keen sense of competition, he shortly began to go after, and get, the taken-for-granted customers of other banks. His attitude was one of open competition for customers. For a while, his own bank president was delighted. Then one day a customer decided to withdraw his account. The new man made a hard sales pitch. The customer, also hotheaded, gave him some sales resistance. Soon they were out in the parking lot behind the bank swinging at each other. Police intervened before damage was done to anything except the bank's prestige.

This is an extreme case, but uncontrolled temper can constitute a problem for the manager who tries to build a hard-hitting team of aggressive people.

The too-aggressive person often develops a general attitude that other people are inferior. This puts a limit on where he or she can be assigned, because subordinates and associates quickly sense such an attitude.

Such a person will be surrounded soon with compliant people, since only passive personalities can stand being around him or her long. Such reactions to opposition are usually painful, not only to the objects of wrath, but also to those who deserve it. Such bosses are quick to fire people: a loyal subordinate who thinks independently or an advertising agency that doesn't agree with their whims are both dispensed with.

THREE CURES OF EXCESSIVE DESIRE FOR MASTERY

How do you help an angry person control his or her wrath and channel it into useful lines?

1. Most people learn it by feeling the hard knocks others give them when they behave that way. Letting them get the cold shoulder from colleagues, or being left out of the social niceties of the work group, is one way. Anger as a system of obtaining mastery is a self-feeding device. If it works once, it will be tried again. If it produces only hard knocks or slapped wrists, it will be used with more reluctance.

2. A knuckle-rapping by the boss can be equally effective if done early.

3. For the person who has an advanced case which is causing over-all output and quality to suffer, there's no cure unless the person recognizes the condition and tries to control it. Normally a superior can point out that work and personal progress are being adversely affected by tantrums, and can seek agreement that the ondition exists and needs improvement. This is often slow work and occasional lapses are to be expected, coupled with some guilt afterwards. Failing this, the superior might seek professional advice to an advantage.

In one case, a competent young sales manager for a large company was suffering from a bad case of egotism. His records in selling were excellent. Not stopping there, this aggressive fellow undertook to tell manufacturing, engineering and just about everyone else about their shortcomings.

Not wanting to lose his excellent abilities, but pressed for action by his subordinates, the general manager rotated him into a position as plant manager. After two months of trying to apply some of his methods there, he asked to be sent back to sales, a chastened and wiser man.

The factory wasn't hurt too badly because the professionals at the next lower level had kept things going in spite of him. They had also contributed greatly to his growing-up processes by pointing out the effects of his impulsive and ill-formed decisions. Not everyone can have such valuable and quick training, but the principle is sound. An unjustified feeling of mastery can be brought into line by putting the man in a spot where he can taste failure.

DESIRE FOR A GOOD REPUTATION

Every person on the rise learns quickly the value of a good reputation, and quietly works to establish one, since it's obviously one way of getting where he or she wants to go.

The realization that reputation is valuable comes when a person is noticed and possibly praised for doing good work. More important than the praise, however, to the aggressive person, is the fact that now he or she becomes a candidate for jobs further up the ladder.

"The first time I really began to feel that I might make the grade in this company was when I heard that two managers were squabbling over who was going to get me for a vacancy in his division."

That's a statement by a company president looking back upon her career. The realization that a reputation is an extension of the good work you've done is a key phase in reputation-building. Soon the aggressive and competent performer finds that he or she is in a position to select the spot to move to.

As one general manager put it:

"At one time, after five years out of college, four different executives asked that I be assigned to their departments. I sized up the situation and applied for the job with a small division which was growing fast and needed somebody who could do a job. It was the smartest thing I ever did. I rode with that division until I was the only logical candidate to be general manager."

Having arrived in a position where he or she is now proven, the manager develops and creates reputation-building opportunities. Here's how one such manager did it:

"When I first took over the X division I sized things up carefully, and asked myself, 'What the tallest weed that I can chop down here?' The answer was in manufacturing costs, and this was where my experience lay. I mapped out a cost reduction program that trimmed away the fat left and right. Naturally, the profit of the division improved considerably, and I was tabbed as a profit-maker. This paved the way for assignment to the Y division, the biggest one in the company."

All this is desirable and should be cultivated in a manager. It is when we get to the next stage that the first symptoms of danger begin to appear. At this stage, the person has built up supreme confidence in his or her ability to lick most any problem. The confidence sometimes extends to other things about which we have little real competence, but which we assume are just as easy to solve.

In extreme form, this desire for reputation turns into a feeling of infallibility. Confronted with contrary views of opposition from subordinates, however sound the reasons, produces rage. In this advanced and harmful stage, the desire for reputation has turned into an unfortunate set of behaviors. Adrenalin flows, blood pressure rises, rationality and civility disappear, and all of the powers of the person are reduced to that of the aroused beast latent in humans. Rage, when used as a system of leadership, produces bad decisions and compliant and passive subordinates.

It's when we go beyond this into the sixth stage that we are likely to have trouble—along with the company. At this stage, we're out of touch with reality, and only hear the things that agree with our preconceptions. We lose our skill in listening to others, especially those below us in rank, assuming that we needn't hear the whole story to see the truth. We become immune to criticism and irritable when we hear it.

As this attitude hardens, we become less tolerant of opposition, considering it impudent. Here's how one such executive's subordinate described her boss.

"Nobody dares to tell her the truth if it's against her opinion, and everybody tries to guess what she wants to hear before opening their mouths. She can destroy months of work with a single snort."

When such a person takes a fall, as they almost always do, they'll resort to tricks to feed their egos. We deceive ourselves first, become more skilled in alibis, and avoid hard tests of our skills in order to avoid further failures, however small. If facts get in the way, we'll duck them. If our predictions fall short of reality, we'll question reality rather than our own judgment.

WHAT TO DO WHEN DESIRE FOR REPUTATION LEADS TO EXCESS VANITY

Once a manager has gone beyond the danger point in building a reputation, there's still some hope. The guide for solving the vanity problem (which is what passing the danger point creates) lies in prevention, rather than cure.

Here are some steps in prevention and cure:

1. Every young person on the rise should be coached in the techniques of reputation building by a boss who still holds his or her future in hand. This may be done by the manager, or by a management development counselor, if necessary.

"One method I've used to show young people on the way up how to avoid getting a swelled head is to point to some examples that are commonly known in the company or outside," one counselor states.

2. Several training courses for managers are therapy-centered and attempt to hold up a mirror for such people to see themselves. Commonly known as "sensitivity training," these courses have done wonders in helping people see themselves, when competently led.

3. Occasionally a survey of employee opinion will reflect images of top management. Such results seldom cut through the hard shell of a tough case, but in some instances, they startle the executive who has recently fallen into this pattern.

In one company, a general survey of management practices included the question, "How do you see your boss?" and gave the subordinates an opportunity to check one of several frank answers. The result was that the boss did a sharp reversal on her practice of not listening, squelching ideas and treating subordinates like dolts.

4. The company's management-appraisal system permits the subordinate and the boss to sit down together and talk frankly about such problems as this. The limitation here lies in the incapability of the average line manager when it comes to dealing with complex personality counseling.

One large food company's appraisal procedure provides that the content of such talks be limited purely to the subordinate's performance. If performance is bad, then the reasons become legitimate items for frank discussion. If the reasons lie in the vanity and unwillingness of the person to listen, then this is discussed as a part of the performance. The theory is that, unless a habit or trait has affected performance, it's none of the company's business.

5. Our peers are the best people to tell us our problem in instances where we are too high up the ladder to be treated by normal methods.

The executive vice president of one company was suffering from a severe case of inflated ego. One of his subordinates convinced him that he should attend a management course.

After trying some of his tactics on his classmates there, all of whom were just as important in their companies as he was in his own, he caught on to the idea. On the last day of the course, he asked permission to address the class.

"I'd like to apologize," he said, "for being the insufferable fathead that you saw when I came here. I'd like also to thank you for the kindly fashion in which you took me down a peg or two. I think this has been the most valuable experience in my business career."

Another executive was asked to serve as chairman of a volunteer community chest drive in her city. Her insufferable vanity shortly got her into trouble. Finally, several executives who were also working on the drive cornered her. She saw the whole drive threatened with collapse unless she tempered her ego, and began to listen to others. The experience had substantial carryover on her behavior in the company.

THE DESIRE FOR WEALTH

The next stage comes when an executive gets many of the things that he or she associates with a better standard of living but discovers that he or she can probably do even better.

"When I was foreman in the plant, I decided that we would some day live in one of the nice old houses on Main Street," one executive said. "When I became assistant manager, we made it. After we'd lived there a while, we began to eye one of the bigger houses up on the hill. That was a big turning point in my career. I began to figure out a five-year plan for moving into the plant manager's job, and I made that, too."

The next stage comes when he or she has achieved most of the outward symbols of success and can afford most of the dreams he or she had as a youth. At this point he or she either levels off or sets his or her sights on gaining the big successes. The new goal may become an estate and financial independence, or he or she may begin to eye the cruisers at the boat show with a new interest, or maintain two houses, one at the lake and one in town. He or she may start talking to architects about that dream house in the fashionable part of an exclusive suburb. He or she finds that managing his or her personal affairs is a fair-sized business problem in itself. Here's how one executive put it:

"I found that owning a house in a community with the inherited-money types was heady stuff. I got an old farm, modernized it, bought six Aberdeen Angus steers, and joined a country club."

This step occasionally leads ambitious managers into the dangerous fourth stage. This is where they begin to discount against the income they expect from the next promotion. They stretch their standard of living too far, neglect their estate-planning, and let spending exceed income. Often they find that the expense account is keeping them going, and they treat it with a liberality which is just short of outrageous.

The family budget is a thing of the past. The tension and strain of maintaining living standards which are beyond their incomes result in some tension in the job which may have the beneficial effect of driving them to terrific levels of output. The truth is that most people who get into this position carry it off. An unhappy few stumble and fall. It takes strong nerves.

One executive search consultant reports:

"I always consider it in my favor if the people we are trying to hire away from their present company are living beyond their income. This means they'll likely listen to our offer if it means a boost of that eight to ten thousand dollars which they think will solve their problems. Usually the money won't help."

The final stage comes when their financial woes catch up with them. One sales executive was taken off a traveling job when his expense account became too big; he was put in an office job. This caught him in a financial bind and he wound up in a trap he couldn't handle. The company spent huge sums bailing him out, and he finally quit. Financial problems growing out of overextension are frequent. When they occur, they create company problems.

THE CURE FOR TOO MUCH DESIRE FOR WORLDLY SUCCESS

As with many serious ailments, an ounce of prevention is worth a pound of therapy. One executive describes her method like this:

"Whenever I can, I talk to the younger people about their personal estate-building program, and try to get them on a long-range plan that includes savings, insurance, a retirement plan, annuities, and a sound real-estate plan."

Many companies offer special programs which advise their younger executives on estate-building, and make counselors available at no cost.

Other companies try to prepare their people through adroit planning of the compensation and benefits they provide executives. This is coupled with a management newsletter that includes some professional and down-to-earth advice on personal planning for executives.

One insurance company requires executives to file annual statements of their financial condition. Those in hot water—or on the verge of it—are told bluntly to get things in line.

In a large midwestern bank, the senior vice presidents are held responsible for the private financial affairs of the younger subordinates reporting to them. If one begins to live beyond what seems to be normal means for his or her income, he or she is invited to explain.

Drastic as these steps seem for most companies, there is still room for informal chats on performance which slide smoothly into more personal aspects of finance and personal estate-planning.

Under such a plan, the executive can appraise how eager the subordinate has become for worldly goods, and, from his or her own experience, drop broad hints about curbing what appears to be undue emphasis on outward evidences of success. The latter would appear to be most workable for the average company.

Part III

PERSONAL TECHNIQUES FOR ACTION-GETTING MANAGEMENT

> "This body of ours is something like an electric battery in which a mysterious power latently lies. When this power is not properly brought into operation it either grows mouldy and withers away or is warped and expresses itself abnormally."
>
> D. T. SUZUKI

17

HOW TO BE A LUCKY EXECUTIVE

> *"Fortune is the ruler of half of our actions, but she allows the other half or thereabouts to be ruled by us."*
>
> NICCOLO MACHIAVELLI

Survey the average corporate employee and you'll learn that the reason you're not further along, or the top manager got ahead, is because the successful were smiled upon by Lady Luck. The concept of luck is a vast face-saving device for many of us, for it prevents us from having to confront our own personal shortcomings and inadequacies. The best part of this entire system of reasoning is that there is an element of truth which can be demonstrated regularly. Pure chance and blind luck exist and affect the course of companies and the careers of people. They also provide a wonderful excuse for failure, a rationale for not working hard and an alibi for poor performance.

While it's probably impossible for an executive to eliminate luck, there are ways in which we can put it to use in our competitive plans, and can become a "lucky" executive and make our company one of the "lucky" few which succeed and grow. There's no disagreeing that luck is a factor in success and company growth. Even the august Stanford Research Institute lists *luck* as one of the factors which has characterized growth companies along with identification and orientation to growth fields, willingness to drop dying lines, courageous and energetic management, and so on.

One of the persuasive arguments for *luck* as a factor in management success is the lack of uniformity in management practices which brought success to one organization and disaster to another. One firm follows all the textbook rules of management in such things as organizing, planning, controlling, motivating, and developing people. It would be a joy to the case writer from the university school of business administration. Yet it staggers along with mediocre growth and profit, while another, without a bit of attention to these things, coins vast profits and grows at an exponential rate. In another instance, one company follows certain practices and loses money, where its competitor follows the same rules and makes great sums. In still a third instance, two firms follow entirely different approaches to management practice and end up equally profitable and successful. These three instances would make a good case for the presence of luck and its significance as a cause of failure or success of a business and its management. Yet, to impute the differences to luck alone would be to oversimplify. What are some rules which can put luck on the side of an executive and prevent its going against him? The basic rule is a simple one:

> Luck shows its power in business where there has been no provision to resist that power as it appears.

Applying this rule consistently, and through large and small decisions, can improve the odds of the phenomenon of luck, and increases the chances of its being "good" instead of "bad" luck. Let's take an example:

> One large medical products firm, in its controller's department, has a group known as the "profits committee." In the early part of each year, the profits committee meets with the management committee to review forecasted operations. Throughout the year it periodically reviews performance against forecast. These provide the basis for switching efforts and resources if one area falls down and overall profits are threatened by "bad luck" in one product or market line, and capitalizing on "good luck" in another.

Our point here isn't one of financial management, but the control of fortunes and changes in luck as they appear, through making provision for bad effects before they actually occur. We must provide for safeguards against the ruin which can come through changes in circumstances beyond our control. Blind trust in luck can bring about ruin if the manager counts on luck alone to provide all of the favorable advantages. Control of luck means setting up barriers to contain the flood of bad luck when it runs high, and these defenses must be constructed during the periods when things are running smoothly.

This change in outside conditions which affect the business accounts for the differences in results which can come from diverse management methods. It likewise accounts for the success of one person and the failure of another, where both use the same approach.

The lucky manager adopts every strategy to gain a superior position that can be protected against loss in the future. This superior position is comprised of many different features, and being lucky means knowing what these components of a superior position are and when each should be used.

> One concern stresses its reliability of service, another its low prices, this one its wide selection, that one its exclusiveness, and still another the style of its products. One newspaper will become distinguished for its wide coverage of news, another for its special features.

Such choice among alternative courses of policies demands a wide knowledge of trends.

KEEPING ABREAST OF LATEST TRENDS

The control of luck, and of being prepared for competition, means that the executive identifies the trends and conditions which must be controlled to prevent great losses resulting from reversal in fortune. What are some of these areas in which we must keep our flanks covered to offset the possibility of "bad luck" overtaking us?

1. Know-how. Through research and development, and through training, we must keep the firm ahead of the competitor—

domestic or foreign—who can smash into the market armed with new know-how and put us at a disadvantage.

2. Changes in taste. Consumer tastes are fickle, and you may find the firm which is too greatly wedded to one style or model left in the lurch. Annual model changes in automobiles demand that careful attention be paid to predicting styling changes several years in advance, for example.

3. Trends in location. Not only do markets change—from the city to suburbia, for example—but the availability of low cost labor and the proximity to raw materials may be important. Some companies take advantage of low labor costs and favorable governmental assistance to meet competition from European and Asian countries, thus forestalling competition from abroad.

4. Competitive products. Established products may find themselves hard-pressed by new products which compete for the same markets without being identical in kind; glass jars competing with tin cans, for instance. Offsetting the possible ill effects of such changes can be made through buttressing the product with services, quick delivery, easy replacement and parts, or other distribution and service advantages the new product can't hope to provide.

5. Trade connections. The connection with a good supplier or distributor can help offset catastrophic effects of new products or new processes entering the market where they must compete against such connections. Yet, trade connections wear out, and changes in distribution systems, consolidations of suppliers and similar modifications of trade connections must be watched and allowed for constantly.

Other trends which may be equally important and have a direct bearing upon management luck and the supports which must be built to protect against "bad luck" include such things as:

- Reputation of the firm for quality
- Labor supply
- Changes in labor leadership
- Political climate
- Changes in tariffs

- Technological changes
- Supply of raw materials
- Change in wages and salaries
- Particular manpower shortages (engineers, etc.)
- Retirement or death of key executives
- Price inflation
- Price collapses
- Price cutting by competitors
- New merchandising methods
- Changes in government regulations

Let's look at some examples of how managers have faced up to bad luck that confronted them, and came through without damage where others failed.

> Dayton's department store in Minneapolis was faced with a possible decline of business in their downtown store because of the construction of shopping centers in the outlying sections of the city. Rather than simply renting space in such a center, it constructed one of the largest and most unusual shopping centers in the country in its Southdale center. Thus it not only met the competition of such centers, but actually assumed leadership through outdoing all other centers, drawing shoppers from all other shopping areas, not only to its own store, but also to the other stores in the center.

Such provision for harmful changes can extend to the personal career planning of the manager as well. In one large utility, the middle level of accounting supervisors was confronted with the problem of data processing equipment being installed and making many of their skills obsolete. One group in such a company requested the management to organize a study group to instruct them in electronics and computer languages to put them abreast of these newest developments. Management eagerly complied, and not only trained them in programming and the grammar of machine language, but also probed into possible future changes through courses in operations research and managerial economics which refurbished the skills of the staff attending.

PREDICTING THE HOT ITEM OF THE FUTURE

Hard luck often takes a heavy toll in people who have continued doing things the same old way, busily occupied with their daily tasks, oblivious to the new things which are already on the horizon. Fortunately for most alert managers, such new innovations are a long time in coming, and offer the vigilant a chance to foresee what will be ahead and to prepare for it. Generally there are four major ways in which a manager can keep abreast of what the important agenda items will be in the future.

Keep abreast of the current literature. Most management magazines today are keenly alert to anything new. The pressures of editorial deadlines, and the demand of the readers for current and new information requires that its writers and editors be more than simple reporters of the existing methods. The great pressure in the giant publishing houses is for new and novel things. Often these are researched and scouted out with great resourcefulness, and presented with clarity for the management reader. The amount of information about new and promising methods, techniques and trends contained in these publications is a vital factor as management peeks into the future. As W. J. Arnold put it:

> We're more interested in what's going to be common practice five years from now than we are in what is going on today—although we like to watch what the leaders and successful firms are doing right now, too.

Still another source of information on the important topic of the future is the **management** or **trade association meeting.** Speakers here are selected for their experience in novel and pioneering practices. The American Management Association, for example, prefers the company which adds something new and interesting to the same old stories of ordinary practice.

Watch the leading companies. This is a likely source of ideas for the future. Every new idea finds its roots quickly in some large and already successful company. Such pace-setters as IBM, GE, K-Mart and the Bell System often innovate in management methods and provide a useful guide to what the thinking manager should be watching with interest.

University business schools. These schools and social science departments are often the focal point for new ideas.

Colleges of industrial engineering often generate new ideas that find their way into industrial practice. Seminars by such universities can provide the executive with some guides as to the trends he should watch.

In all four ways, there is the assumption that the manager who would avoid bad luck occasionally gets out of the office and his or her own company and talks with other managers. From them he or she gets the feel of new items and how important they are apt to become. This can be extended to stating that he or she often gets out of his or her own town or region, and attends national meetings where executives from all parts of the country are in attendance, in order to avoid provincialism and inbreeding of ideas.

PLANNING FOR THE UNEXPECTED

Luck seems to fall hardest on firms when their executives were unprepared for a change.

> One large newspaper chain has a plan for dealing with shortages of newsprint, through an arrangement with an alternate supplier, and a mutual agreement for exchange of resources for limited periods during emergencies.

This preparation for emergencies or unexpected catastrophes is never easy to lend a sense of urgency to (until the firm has been through one sad experience), but it's a basic to averting the effects of hard luck. The key ingredient is a long-range frame of mind for all managers. This frame of mind is based on:

- **Application:** Planning is work.
- **Study:** All angles must be taken into consideration.
- **Brainpower:** The qualitative aspects of planning should form a backstop for the quantitative to avoid misdirection of effort.
- **The will to plan:** If planning is a chore, the results will reflect the planner's poor attitude.
- **Communication:** Everyone in the organization must understand plans in order to cooperate in carrying them out.

The underlying philosophy here isn't one of being defensive against the ravages of change and bad luck. It's more likely that it will bring bad luck to competitors who aren't as vigilant in planning the future and making provisions for changes. Company weakness, internal or in relation to competitive position, may be spotted and exposed for correction. The capabilities of key personnel are highlighted, the necessity for providing sufficient depth of personnel and the uncovering of latent talent is brought out.

If there's a place where this logical process can break down, it's in the area of assumptions which must be made about the future. Every manager must have some clear ideas of where the over-all economic trends are headed, and know why he or she feels that way. Some of the areas where a manager must make such assumptions include:

- Whether high government expenditure will continue
- Changes in composition of spending (from aircraft to missiles, etc.)
- Rate of population growth
- Growth patterns in basic industry (housing, autos, etc.)
- Direction and rate of consumer buying power
- How effective research and development will be

Human Resource Planning has an especially important role to play in preparing for the unexpected. A force of managers and professionals who are competent in dealing with change is perhaps just as important in preparing for the unforeseen as any forward-looking projection could possibly be. As one manager put it:

> If I can build a strong flexible corps of managers at every level, I won't worry about changes and unexpected occurrences because they'll be equipped to handle them. If I don't have such people on my staff I'm licked, even if I have done the best planning in the world.

Such planning includes the more rapid development of managers than would take place through such methods as trial and error and the passage of time. This can include periodic appraisals and incentives of management manpower, early identification of successors to management position, a program for introducing outsiders where they are needed, and the fitting of manpower development needs with overall corporate growth plans.

> Long range planning is a necessity if one's competitive position is to be maintained and improved; and it may prove to be a life-saver if economic conditions—overall or within an industry—should take a turn for the worse.

While this logic is unassailable, it's also important to note that long-range planning doesn't mean that the company is thereby fitted for a strait jacket. Flexibility and agility are two essential ingredients in providing against the ill winds of chance.

HELPING YOUR WINDFALL

It's perfectly true that basing your future on luck alone may be costly if luck runs against you, but this doesn't preclude running with your luck when it makes its shining appearance. Having the wit and agility to move quickly and adapt methods to circumstances is a vital part of helping your windfall and capitalizing on "breaks."

> A small floor tiling company struggled along through the war years into the middle forties with barely enough business to keep its head above water. Shortly after the war the housing boom got under way, and the demand for floor tile rose sharply. Keeping its eye on the rising housing curve, the management went in debt up to its ears to build new plant, hire new help and modernize. Its most optimistic hopes were exceeded, and within five years it was operating at a level far exceeding the growth rate of many of its slower competitors.

Of course, the exact opposite can happen as well. One of the classic stories is that told of Montgomery Ward under the management of Sewell Avery. While Sears was building after the war at a phenomenal rate, the redoubtable Mr. Avery was reported to be lecturing his officers and directors on the necessity for maintaining a high liquid position in preparation for the forthcoming depression. When a store burned down, it was not replaced. No new locations were researched and none opened. As a result, it continually lost market position until after Mr. Avery's retirement and a new management who saw the growth pattern of the economy more lucidly took over.

The real trick is to adapt the manner in which management functions to the circumstances. This is as true in large companies as in small firms, and in individual departments as well as whole corporations.

> Cost reduction seemed to be the major problem in one small company. A consultant studied the situation and discovered that the supervision in the plant was wishy-washy about demanding a fair day's work from the workers. Investigation proved that, in the past, there had been extensive labor trouble, and the supervisory group had been trained and instructed in a particularly soft approach to human relations, which came out looking like pussy-footing. Presented with these facts, the management instituted a program of improving discipline and rigor. Without returning to the old days which had caused the labor trouble, they began to insist that employees produce according to standards, and that wasteful practices be eliminated. The results were immediate and startling. Among those most pleased were the old-time employees who had been dismayed at the new laxity which had followed the human relations binge.

The current debate which rages in management over best methods of supervision, "the hard versus the soft line" in management, seems to be moving in the direction of firmness and discipline. This, in all truth, is probably more a product of the times and necessity than of any newly discovered principle of management. In management practice, there is a time for diplomacy, for cunning, for sincerity, for immediate obedience, and for participation. None are universal tools, for all of them must be available to exploit the competitive demands of the circumstance.

> Take the example of the man who entered the construction business through a franchise to sell metal buildings. Seeing further opportunities for profit in laying concrete floors for such buildings, he added a floor division. His customers proved interested in other types of buildings as well as the type he sold, so he rushed into the construction business of all types of buildings. All of these things happened to fall into a rising market for contractor work and he was phenomenally successful. Since he had done no investigation into the overall possibilities (he hadn't time), he

took a chance of great failure. Yet it paid off handsomely, simply because he was impetuous. If he had been prudent, he might still have been a dealer in buildings instead of being a large contractor with substantial assets.

MORAL COURAGE AND LUCKINESS IN LEADERSHIP

Such instances are often the typical example which is cited to show that a person was lucky in management. Yet, the example of the contractor isn't without a valid principle. It's the axiom that *planning may prevent the ravages of ill luck, but boldness, audacity, energy, and a certain amount of fierce drive are needed to exploit good luck.*

Once all the odds have been weighed, the economic and social trends assessed, and the possibilities of gain and loss assessed, *boldness is better than caution.*

P. J. Lovewell, one-time director of economic research at Stanford Research Institute, had this to say about management leadership and courage:

> Occasionally we see a company with all of these visible success characteristics—but it still isn't going anywhere. Plans are carefully prepared by a competent staff; product possibilities of real potential are staked out; the company's record of service is outstanding; and yet progress is disappointing. When this occurs, the usual missing ingredients are management leadership and moral courage. In the final analysis, planning cannot be meaningful without management foresight, management support, management decision, and management follow-through.

This drive and willingness to assume risks—uninsurable risks—are the basic elements in the management job. Despite the rationalization of management, the division of the management job into logical portions, with staff and line experts in charge of each, there is no escaping the uninsurable risks of being an *entrepreneur.*

Because large corporations are collective in their efforts, they are prone to the conservative's viewpoint. Cooperation between many people to make the organization operate at all makes the center of power and decision more difficult to identify. Many of the risks they take are less serious in the overall life of the organization, since they have resources to ensure its success through simple ponderousness and persistence in overcoming obstacles. The ever-pressing need, in such an organization, is a corps of people scattered throughout its ranks who are impelled by the instincts of the business entrepreneur. These are the traders, the risk-takers, the profit seekers who will exercise their talents as employed managers with the same zeal and boldness which they would exercise if the gains were to be their own.

The quality which seems to be most associated with the lucky executive is not one of forbearance and restraint. Rather, it is performance and action.

18

HOW TO KEEP AND USE A SECRET

"Trust not him with your secrets, who when left alone in your room turns over your private papers."

JOHN LAVATER

One of the troublesome problems for the executive in the modern corporate business system is handling information with discretion and judging what should or should not be considered secret. This is no simple dilemma, for the modern executive who wants to rise through the great organization, and at the same time hopes to make a personal imprint upon it, is faced with a paradox with regard to *information*. On one hand, the organization runs on participation and committees to a large degree. On the other, if we tell everything we know, we limit our progress to that which any good conformist can make if tuned to the proper signals from the mass of people in management.

The hard fact is that conspicuous and personal leadership that makes things happen through organization requires that the person who would develop skill at rising and achieving must not only confide, but also must "communicate." From another viewpoint, for the executive to build and extend his or her orbit of control, he or she must, at times, withhold information and facts which might transfer control to the group. This control to a committee or a team all too often has the effect of deadening the impact of leadership and vitality in the firm, substituting in its place a sort of administrative nudist camp where such old fashioned virtues as privacy, secrecy and circumspection may be considered as evidence of maverick behavior, and a violation of many companies' concept of the accepted pattern of leadership.

Consider the plight, for example, of the person who would make things happen who must function in a firm where, as one president put it:

"Our company is managed by communication. We do not have leaders over people, but working with them." Naturally, the manager who would make things happen must pay some token obeisance to such statements. At the same time, he or she must not take it too seriously to the point where he or she allows the norms of the organization to be his or her own, or he or she will discover that he or she does indeed, merely work with people rather than move them. The climate, of course, must be one of candor and thoughtful answers to questions which the employee requires in order to perform. Yet, the leader must ever retain the seventh veil, beyond which he or she withdraws occasionally to formulate goals toward which he or she will persuade, direct, order, cajole, or manipulate people. This places him or her under some tension in deciding which matters are secret and which are not.

HANDLING THE ENJOINED SECRET

Perhaps the first level of problems in managing secrets is the matter of the enjoined secret, in which the manager is privy to information with the direct understanding that it will not be divulged. A new product has been developed in research and will be marketed in six months. We are invited to a briefing session—sworn to secrecy—and allowed into the temple. Obviously this is one we may use only through taking preparatory steps for the forthcoming changes which will result from the new product without telling anyone below the reasons for the steps. Perhaps we cut back on improvement project budgets for existing products which will soon become obsolete. Despite the puzzlement of engineers, who would prefer to continue their project to completion, we must cover reasoning with an appearance of confusion, incompetence, or outright lies.

Perhaps one ancillary rule here is that there are certain kinds of information which a manager should be cautious about in being sworn to secrecy. Matters such as confronted one bank personnel officer might illustrate this.

> Mr. Jones, personnel manager in a large firm, was asked for an appointment by the lady who was president of the employee credit union. Upon entering his office, she said:
> "I've got to ask that you promise not to repeat what I'm going to say to you."
> Foolishly the personnel man promised, perhaps thrilled by the confidence being placed in him by this old and loyal employee.
> "I've been stealing from the credit union's accounts," she stated, "and am $450 out of pocket. I'm so glad that *you* know it, too."

Respecting confidences is a virtue under some circumstances, but it requires that the manager have in mind the possibilities for the future if he or she accepts or seeks out secret information accompanied by any such promise of secrecy extracted in advance. Matters which make us an accomplice, whether to a crime or simply to something inimical to the company or himself, are to be avoided like the plague, and once received should not be accepted quietly and tucked away in the inner compartment of the mind without further action.

Loyalty to persons is an admirable trait. Yet this same loyalty extended to "the organization" often results in immense stress upon the manager. This is more than simply refraining from shipment of defective products to customers, which most companies do not desire to do. Nor does it merely limit itself to avoidance of unethical practice or sharpness in commerce which the typical corporation today does not approve. It does extend to having a sense of responsibility to the individual dignity of people which occasionally runs into conflict with the organization.

> Take the instance of old Gary X. who was performing poorly, and was being considered for separation. It was decided by the personnel committee that he would be asked to leave after six more months when a suitable replacement would be ready. All members of the

committee were sworn to secrecy. Shortly after this his manager, a member of the committee, overheard that Gary had been offered a safe and better paying position with another firm where he might finish his career with dignity. A quick survey of the committee found them adamant against taking any action which might expedite Gary's expulsion in order that he might capitalize upon the offered position. His manager weighed his regard for the man against the integrity of the committee and let Gary pass up the offer.

Others would have handled it exactly the opposite by violating the committee rule and tipping off old Gary.

BEING JUDICIOUS WITH INFORMATION

Practically everyone expresses admiration for the stuff called "communication." This isn't idle talk, for it's part of a larger plan by which most modern corporations run, that the leader gets results through raising the dignity of the individual, giving information and participation in the affairs which affect employees.

Yet the judicious handling of even routine and factual information about the job isn't without its limitations.

Take the case of the electronics company where the product was a stabilizing device for aircraft used by the navy. The workers on the assembly of this equipment were prone to talk incessantly on the job. This worried the management no little bit, since a failure of the equipment might cause a plane to go down and even result in a flyer's death.

Determined to communicate the importance of quality, they called a meeting and had a navy officer tell them that if they "didn't stop their talking on the job, they might make a mistake which would cause a naval officer to be killed."

This had the desired effect of stopping the talking, but it was also noted that many quit their jobs within the next week or two. Upon exit interviews, they stated:

"For the money I'm getting I don't want to do work that can kill a sailor if you just turn your head for a minute."

Management threw up its hands. It laid low on communicating stories about drowned sailors, and set up a tight quality control system to catch any defects which might result from talking on the job.

The point is that simply telling people your reasons or letting them in on your secrets doesn't necessarily mean that they will respond by seeing things the same way management does.

Telling people certain types of things can have no effects but harmful ones, and may include such matters as these:

1. Tentative plans which may never be carried out.
2. Information which would help one person against another without benefiting the company.
3. Matters of personal information about employees which come into the hands of management in the course of routine personnel administration.
4. Rumors.
5. Gossip.
6. "Hard facts about the business" which aren't commonly known and which might serve as useful strategic information in the hands of a competitor (technical information, cost data, etc.).
7. Allegations about people or groups which have no solid basis in fact, or remain unproven.

Another pertinent kind of secret for the manager which we might find is wise to be judicious with, is personal information and opinions which, if divulged, would constitute an invasion of privacy. In the large corporation today, there is an almost insatiable desire on the part of many, especially personnel people and psychologists, to probe deeply into the attitudes, motivations, personality traits, and feelings of employees, especially at the managerial level.

Ostensibly, this probing is for purposes of predicting success. The pattern goes something like this. The psychologist, trained or otherwise, assumes that certain personality traits will lead to success and others will bring about failure. (In some instances this is right, in others there is no empirical evidence to support this thesis.) Probes are then made into the personalities of people in the organization, in order to inventory these attitudes and traits. With this inventory, the analyst recommends promotion, job assignment or the withholding of such benefits. Privacy becomes nearly impossible for an individual under such circumstances, and constitutes a problem of maintaining secrecy for the individual being put under the microscope.

William H. Whyte once published an article in *Fortune* on "How to Cheat on Personality Tests." It was exactly this protection of personal privacy, call it secrecy if you will, which he pointed up.

> "The important thing to recognize," Whyte points out, "is that you don't win a good score, you avoid a bad one."

Recognizing that the probers are being impertinent in asking you to incriminate yourself and your career chances in the first place, it shouldn't be at all a matter of conscience to judiciously withhold information which will prevent you from getting the job you might like *as long as you are confident that you can handle bigger responsibility.* Here is the real test of how completely you let yourself be exposed by the manipulative devices of the company.

> The manager who can make things happen and do a job for the company has a responsibility to be discreet about divulging information about these feelings and habits that might bar him or her from getting such a position.

Whyte lists six statements which might, if kept firmly in mind, get you through the majority of such tests and interviews.

1. I loved my father and mother but my father a little more.
2. I like things pretty well the way they are.
3. I never worry much about anything.
4. I don't care for books or music much.
5. I love my wife and children.
6. I don't let them get in the way of company work.

Most psychologists, in selecting people for organizational jobs, won't understand in the slightest the leader who has unique personal confidence to make things happen despite the strictures of conformity and committee forms of management. Therefore, it's pointless to play into the hands of outsiders.

Perhaps the kind of secret which is most vital to keep in personal advancement strategy is the kind that responds to such questions as "What are your major weaknesses?" Don't, for heaven's sake, give any real ones, such as the fact that you are afraid of the dark. It's far safer to invent a few which seem to be assets to the investigator, but which you list as liabilities. "Sometimes I am too energetic in getting my work done." Don't overdo this to the extent that you let slip your opinion, "When I get in charge here I'll knock a few heads together and clean out the gold bricks." This is entirely too much dominance, and will indicate to the interviewer an unhealthy desire for control.

WHEN TO GIVE IN ORDER TO GET

Being in the mainstream of useful information in an organization means you are able to tap and use the information flowing along the grapevine. This means two things.

1. You must know where the grapevine is and how it operates.

2. You must not appear to be an originator, or even a vital link in the process. Yet you must be able to offer a morsel occasionally, in order to get some in return.

The problem here lies in the possibility that you may inadvertently find that you are really letting slip more than you are getting, thereby becoming a generator of major importance. Usually there are two or three places you can tap to get most of the useful information on what's going on, that will give you some tactical advantage. Such crude tactics as picking over wastebaskets and thumbing through papers on another's desk are gauche, and will inevitably result in a closing of the channels. An occasional crisis may arise where the ability to read material upside down is of some value, but even these are to be considered as unlikely sources of important information.

Probably the best source of information is the horse's mouth itself. Most executives and staff people have trouble guarding their remarks to the degree that they can't be patched into a consistent story that's useful to know. Naturally, this requires some extensive personal contact, and the luncheon table and golf course are places where you will be tapped without your knowing it; in return, you can construct a picture from the parts. Coffee breaks are often occasions for the rumor mill to grind. Under such circumstances, it's wise to be able to give something in order to get more.

From our knowledge of how the grapevine works, it functions through "clusters" of people, reports Dr. Keith Davis. One person tells three or four others. Only one of the cluster will repeat the rumor and pass it along; the remaining members will keep it to themselves. Such carriers of rumor and secrets operate through the firm so that the grapevine is probably only made up of one-fourth or so of the employees. Yet it carries the tales it bears to the entire group through the cluster phenomena.

This particular individual in the cluster, sometimes identified by the social scientists as the "liaison individual" is more apt to dispense gossip, rumor and secret information than others. Other people in the work group seem to have a lot of influence over the opinion of others beyond this, and are resource persons when it comes to interpretation and conjectural materials on what's apt to happen around the office.

This leads to a principle in getting and using secret information:

> If you are going to be ahead of the crowd in getting inside information, you must be a liaison person with the grapevine.

Now this may provide you with inside information and afford you the opportunity to get something through giving something else by way of information. It also is a distressing fact that such people who function as transmitters through their cluster can't remain anonymous to others for long. You become known as a "link," and accordingly over time, this means you will be labelled as a person from whom the really vital information is withheld.

In short, in order to get and use secrets, you will need to become a rather specialized form of information carrier. This means that you'll want to be known only to a select few and with them only for useful stuff. The important thing to remember here is that you shouldn't use the grapevine as an ordinary person might—to fill a psychological need for knowing the gossip or relieving some emotional strain within you. For the manager who sees the secret and the inside information as a tool of action and control, it's a form of intelligence activity which he manages quietly but in an orderly fashion.

How to Keep and Use a Secret   231

    Since the rumor mills are ordinarily quite thorough, even for the receiving members of the cluster, there's no necessity for joining the carrier chain in order to be kept abreast of what the grapevine is saying. The only requirement is that you belong to a cluster which is serviced by an efficient carrier. In this capacity, you can get all of the important material without giving anything in return. You won't get it first (that requires that you be a carrier) but you'll get it quite soon. Only the "loner" who has no cluster never hears what's running along the informal channels and through the rumor mill.

THE HARDEST SECRET TO KEEP

    The rumor which comes to a manager can often be handled without comment or simply by saying, "Hm, isn't that interesting?" It's not as easy to keep a particular kind of secret in which everyone knows that you have information or could make a decision which must ultimately be announced, but for purposes of timing mustn't tell just now.
    Surprisingly the hardest secret to keep isn't the one which is not even known to exist, but the secret everyone suspects exists and upon which they feel enough confidence to make a direct question asking for facts. The reverse of this is true also:

> The best way of finding out a secret is to ask the person who knows one.

    Turning down information is a tough job for anyone. Unless especially reinforced in determination to keep the matter absolutely silent, we are very apt to tell it to a person who asks point blank for the facts. Occasionally we may add lamely, "Now this isn't known yet, and I must ask you to keep it quiet, but..." At this point the secret probably isn't a secret anymore, but you've cracked the silence barrier and can put the information received into use in your personal planning. It's a hard-shelled or especially enjoined person indeed, who can resist communicating what he or she knows in today's company. Certainly it's more honest, clean cut and simpler if you want to know a secret to go right to the person who knows and ask them. Surprisingly often, things that are presumed secret will prove to be somewhat less restricted then you supposed.

The other side of this coin is that others will have discovered this fact if they've thought about it at all. In this case, keeping a secret may require that you plan in advance how to resist such raids on your storehouse of secret information. In some instances, you're just as apt as the next fellow to let slip information with the provision that the hearer not repeat it. It's a wise idea to have your response planned. Simply saying, "I can't say," or some similar response will do if you are armed for inquiries and are determined not to lie or divulge your information.

There are several categories of what might be termed hard-to-keep secrets.

1. The I-told-you-so type. A manager of marketing argues against a certain line of promotion and predicts that it will rebound to the company's disadvantage if tried. Sure enough it fails, and the bad results are barely in before he or she tells people I-told-you-so. Along with this crowing, they also let slip some other information about sales, profits or other techniques, that should be kept quiet.

2. The hurray-for-me type. This secret is hard to keep because telling it provides a boost to the ego of the teller. He or she scores a victory or a coup over opponents and wants to let others know about it. Perhaps its a promotion that's all fixed but hasn't been announced yet. This is often prefaced by, "It hasn't been officially announced yet but..."

3. The bad-news-for-you type. In one eastern plant, the executive committee decided to let a vice president go. Since he was out of town, it was decided that it should be kept secret until he was told. When the president finally called him into his office and informed him the next morning, the ex-V. P. reported sourly, "Yeah, I heard it from the elevator man on my way in this morning."

SMALL TALK

Perhaps the most fertile source of rumors and information which ought to be kept secret is the small talk which comprises the lubricant for human relations on the job. Small talk which turns to the company often finds itself turning to matters of speculation and personalities. Often, the small talk circuit and pattern can develop independently of any information or factual support. Let's take the case of the large chemical company where three executives were competing for the general manager's position. During the six weeks ahead of the final decision for this position, one of the three carried off an especially clever coup over several competitors. He not only stole several valuable customers thereby, but he pulled the organization along with him to make the new deliveries on time. As a result, everyone speculated that he was now the number one competitor for the promotion.

When, in fact, he received the promotion, which had been a carefully guarded secret insofar as the top management was concerned, it came as a surprise to no one. Here was a case where everyone was able to anticipate what the answer would be as accurately as the top group, and any attempt to keep it a secret would have been foolish. Stock splits when a stock runs over 100, are often predictable from experience of past actions of the same kind, and are difficult to keep under cover simply because small talk both inside and outside the company concludes—independently—that it will happen.

Social scientists have often been amazed at the accuracy of conclusions reached by the small talk circuit, which exists so independently of the grapevine that it needs no feeders, clusters or transmitters to have everyone arrive at the same independent result. A fight between executives, even when conducted in secrecy, is often the topic of small talk and independent observations that sense the state of affairs, without any outside feeder adding to the input of facts.

> If the secret is one that is being commonly chatted about in small talk through independent speculation, it's not really a secret and should be verified or denied wherever possible.

This is most often true of "talk" involving the reputation of key people in the organization regarding their personal lives. Take the case of the executive who was reputed by the small talk circuit to be an alcoholic. No single "bit" of information toured the grapevine to verify this opinion. He was seen once by the secretaries reeling into a restaurant where they had gone for dinner. Several people had run into him in the men's lounge drinking Alka-Seltzer early in the morning. Some visitors noticed liquor on his breath another morning shortly after starting time. Without any organized story running in the grapevine, the accumulated small talk concluded that he had a serious drinking problem.

Small talk has the characteristic of being different from the grapevine in that it wells up independently in numerous places at once, without any single bit of information being transferred from ear to ear by a hidden communication chain. It reflects the sense of the group that something is so, and often the best guarded secret, well preserved from any leak to the grapevine, may be commonly known through this welling up in the small talk which goes on constantly in the organization. Keeping the obvious, and sometimes the subtle, from getting through the grapevine still may not quiet its being known and accepted throughout the ranks, if small evidences of the truth are available to casual, but sensitive, observers.

SECRETS VERSUS GOOD COMMUNICATION

In the light of these complex methods by which information is transmitted, despite the best efforts of a few individuals to keep it from being known, the question then arises as to the balance which must be maintained for effective operations. Secret information which is impossible to maintain as confidential requires useless, pointless energy and effort on the part of many people. Where information is apt to be leaked or presumed true with some accuracy, it's often the best plan to deal with it frontally and let everyone in on the facts. Take the case of communicating with management people during labor negotiations. Closed meetings are held, offers made and counter-proposals given in return. Some companies now make it a point to issue bulletins and statements to foremen during the progress of negotiations. As a director of industrial relations for one firm puts it:

> They'll find out anyway from the workers, who learn it from the union. We might as well tell them the straight facts rather than keep them in suspense and let them feel that they are less informed than employees on the bench.

News of impending changes have greater impact to the employees if they get the facts immediately after the decision is made from the company, rather than indirectly from another worker.

Despite the necessity of maintaining silence on certain kinds of information, the situation in most firms is that more information should be transmitted openly and quickly.

INTEGRITY AND SECRECY IN LEADERSHIP

The guides to the maintenance of secrecy in leadership bring us into confrontation with the issue of integrity and what constitutes intellectual and personal morality in such matters on the part of the leader who makes things happen. Henry Taylor, the English statesman, suggests that there are two classifications of conscience; a strong conscience and a tender conscience. The overly tender conscience may be illustrated by the manager who pays too much attention to the small responsibilities at the expense of his larger responsibilities.

> Take, for example, the person whose conscience winces at asking people what he or she would detest doing personally, such as dealing with unpleasant customers, discharging old time employees or closing a plant which is the major source of employment in a small town.

Because a manager winces at this, he or she usurps most of the dirty jobs, or even fails to step up to the larger responsibility of preserving the health and vitality of the firm in the competitive market. This manager lacks the capacity to be cruel in order to be kind, and in this ends up being ultimately the cruelest of all leaders.

Often this conscience, which is all tenderness and has no strength, will breed in its holder a great tendency toward inaction and become a "quagmire in which the faculty of action shall stick fast at every step."

Secrecy often becomes a guide for inaction, and the person who wouldn't hurt a fly, will hurt the whole company and the economy. Because of anticipating the response of people so accurately, the manager flinches from saying what needs saying, and spreads a tender cloak of anonymity over what should be said forthrightly. Secrets which protect others too much, or create a false sense of security among those concerned, are a negative result that comes from an overly tender conscience.

Here, too, lies many of the areas of misunderstanding between the social scientist and the business leader. Social scientists have, by and large, a tender conscience. The business leader who makes things happen must have a strong conscience. The blows and cuts which are suffered by individuals in the modern company, in terms of its ego and social needs, are often the only concern of the social scientists who enter the business firm to study what goes on there. They are almost wholly in sensitive (especially when there to inculcate managers in sensitivity) to the rationale and virtues of the strong conscience. This leads to different perception about the extent to which managers must communicate, both in urging too much and in urging too little, as the conscience of the observer permits.

The action-oriented manager deals with the problems of secrecy, in short, through developing a sense of integrity which is controlled by a strong conscience rather than a tender one.

19

HOW TO PICK A FIGHT AND WIN IN BUSINESS

"With the jaw of an ass have I slain a thousand men."

JUDGES XV:16

Practically nobody talks about the subject of fighting in business. It's normally considered crude, and furthermore, it is implied, it shouldn't be done at all. This folklore, that fighting leads to career oblivion, is in diametric opposition to the basic fact of business in a free society. Competition is, in fact, nothing more than defeating another person through economic superiority, greater agility, being quicker witted, having a sharper tongue, or having more resources than the other. Conflict of wills is—however much we may disguise it—a basic act of business management, with the minor exceptions of certain complete monopolies. It's also a product of the immense upward striving of many people for the lucrative and high status positions in the hierarchies of business. The prizes for top leadership positions are great. It's not surprising then, that competition and rivalry for them should be quite fierce.

Despite the underlying facts about fighting—call it by any name—there are certain rules of the game which the others in the forest expect will be followed. Since they have the capacity to throw their weight in favor of one protagonist or another, and all the scrapping is done in close quarters where others can alter the outcome, it's part of the strategy of competition not to violate the rules of the fray. Learning such rules early is part of the personal development of the manager who would make things happen. Let's look at a few of the unwritten rules which govern economic warfare for managers.

Rule 1. Always express abhorrence of fighting. Perhaps the cardinal guide to successful combat in business is the avoidance of any outward appearance of relishing combat. It's more a matter of outward mien than inward emotion; in fact, it is a unique combination of pugnacity and driving ferociousness, masked by an outward cloak of complete affability and congeniality. The more completely this split in inward attitude and outward manner can be managed, the more acceptable it will be to those who surround you.

Rule 2. Avoiding petulance and impatience. In entering the frantic world of business competition, it's wise to take special pains to master one's emotions in order that no glimmer of petulance, impatience or sullenness appear, no matter how severe the blow received. For a manager to sulk over getting beat out of a promotion, losing an account or being transferred to the Unimak, Alaska sales office, will immediately arouse murmurs of clucking regret from his peers. "Maturity" in business competition means a self control over disappointment or chagrin, which goes far beyond the phlegmatic and stolid control of the German saber duelist when he receives a fierce hack from his opponent. In business, one must not shout out in dismay and anger, but must behave just as if the outcome were a source of the greatest possible delight. A smile and hearty handclasp, with eye contact, are part of the ritual. Later, over a couple of cocktails, we may express our true sentiments, but with everyone from around the shop it's *de rigueur* to accept such blows with aplomb.

Rule 3. Never lose your temper. Fighting in business is disguised in affability, and losing one's temper is prohibited. This means more than simply refraining from saying nasty things. Anger is easily detected, since it entails a whole sequence of physiological changes in the person. The mechanism of the sympathetic nervous system causes chemical and electrical changes in the body when one gets angry. Adrenalin is shot into the blood stream, the liver injects fuel into the system, breathing increases, blood circulation rises, discoloration of the face and enlargement of the veins take place, and the salivary and digestive juices flow haltingly. All of these make changes in the person which can be seen, indicating that he or she really can't control him- or herself. In even the most composed person, anger may raise signals such as a reddening of the ears or a hearty belch for the ulcerous, which are signals to the cool observer that one's hackles have risen under competition. Thus the other person is armed to deal more rationally and compete even better by appealing to those acts which bring on anger. The truly composed and sophisticated fighter in business never lets the message get into his or her sympathetic nervous system. He or she remains rational, calm and affable.

Rule 4. Winning is what counts in the long run. In the small group of people who know the rules, winning may be interpreted to cover a lot of actions, only a few of which have to do with genuine regard for others. Over the long haul, it's winning which seems to be the most acceptable, and doing so with composure. The kinds of infighting and hanky-panky which schoolboy ethics or ordinary love of one's fellow man dictate, can be reconstructed later through good behavior, once one is securely on top. There are some rules for *winning* in business too:

A. **Keep your value systems in line.** However much lip service you may pay to serving others, the successful fighter for status and position must remember the priority system which ranks:
   the self first
   the company next
   any other casual human who happens to be present, third

B. **Hard work is a great competitive weapon.** In winning promotions and rank, a secret weapon of being a veritable beaver sometimes is down-graded by cynics, but is of highest importance. The briefcase carried home and the work done by the light of the midnight oil arms its bearer with facts, insights and know-how, which comprises an armor that will stand you in good stead in the fray of competition.

C. **Keep your eye on the main chance.** The executive who would rise must always keep an eye squarely on the road ahead and seek out opportunities for scoring hits. The "main chance" seeker is a person who wants to become rich or important, who is willing to make money for the company as a means of getting his own reward. (The social scientists call this "reconciling the goals of the individual with that of the organization.")

D. **Build strong alliances.** Despite the competition between executives, there are certain kinds of alliances on non-competitive matters which must be made and maintained. Exchanging information on management methods improves oneself at the same time it improves others. These alliances are vital in building a reputation among others, since they provide a forum for proving one's mastery of business methods.

E. **Look good in performance—not only on appearances.** There are many who contend that it's fatal to look *too good,* be too well dressed, be too handsome or be too glib in speeches. The "model manager" on the way up attracts the javelins of the lesser lights—many of whom will never make it. Nevertheless, they constitute, like a stream filled with flesh-eating piranhas, a total influence which should never be aroused by attracting too much attention from making big splashes. In one firm, one such superior-looking man constantly attracted attention of the type that caused people to ask, "How can anybody be that good? Let's look for some flaws in his facade." Naturally they found some, and he was routed into a safe niche where he worked for his competitors who hadn't made the mistake of looking too much like perfection.

F. **Look conformist—think maverick.** Attracting attention through odd appearance, non-conformist behavior and erratic actions invites being slapped down. At the same time, in order to win, the up and coming executive must constantly generate new and successful ideas, which means that group thinking doesn't dominate his or her own instincts.

G. **Don't relax when winning.** Once your strategy has begun to pay off and you are gaining the recognition and prizes, don't sit back and enjoy them. Pour your new resources into making further advances, building up a team to run with you, and making breakthroughs into new territory.

Rule 5. Fight to win, not to kill. The rule of affability can be extended to include behavior toward the loser as well as the victor. Reactions always occur when the winner wastes effort and energy in getting revenge upon those who competed hard but lost. The trick after victory is to convince the losers that they lost to a better person, and win them over as allies. This becomes apparent as the winner notes the value system outlined above. The first priority is getting on top oneself, and the second is to advance the interests of the firm. Destroying capable people, simply because they fought and lost, can result in many good people being thrown out and into the hands of a competing company. To execute such a policy over time would only serve to weaken the company and ultimately react to the disadvantage of the executive. Since we must get results through others' efforts, we must be careful not to destroy everyone we pass by in our rise to the top, lest we weaken the organization.

Rule 6. Gather allies by perpetuating the rules for competition. The rules of competition and fighting in business are, of course, designed to assist the superior competitor in rising, and to maintain his or her status in the organization. It's therefore distinctly to our advantage to support vigorously the unwritten code of fighting. In doing so, we insure that we will rule over a stable and successful organization, in which able people will rise, and the less able will level off according to their abilities.

Rule 7. Always consolidate your captured ground. The fight to move in the organization is almost always disruptive, and may result in uneasiness and grumpiness among those not chosen. It's imperative, then, that the top person immediately upon assuming that post, sort out such problems and solve them.

> Take the case of the vice president who was selected president of a small company after a period of several months of doubt as to which of several vice presidents would be chosen. Even before the retirement of the outgoing president, the president-elect began a cam-

paign of punishing the failing candidates. As a result, two of them quit and many other people in the organization stated that they had a great feeling of insecurity about the future.

Consolidating captured ground in business competition between individuals, unlike that between companies, may require that changes be introduced cautiously.

Conflicts of wills, conflicts of interests and personalities are normal conditions of the world of business. Learning the art and the skill of successfully meeting such situations, and teaching them to the up and coming, is part of the way in which a successful executive makes thing happen in business.

Part IV

CHECK AND CORRECT AS YOU ACT—THE IMPORTANCE OF REVIEW

> "... All Men make mistakes, But a good man yields when he knows his course is wrong and repairs the evil. The only crime is pride."
>
> SOPHOCLES

20

HOW TO CONDUCT A PERSONAL INSPECTION

"In life—as in bridge—one peek is worth two finesses."

ANONYMOUS

One of the neglected arts of management is that of *looking* at the situation. Very few courses at Harvard, Northwestern, Michigan, or California have anything to offer in regard to this vital skill of the manager. Yet there's nothing that creates more social distance between a manager and a worker than too much desk leadership at the expense of personal visitations and inspections.

The reasons for the chair-bound manager sticking too closely to a chair are very persuasive. For one thing, the in basket seems to burgeon every time he or she gets away from the office. For another, there always seems to be a stack of phone messages waiting when he or she returns. Even more persuasive is the fact that if he or she doesn't go to people, they seem to find their way to them, giving the feeling of not keeping fully abreast of what is going on in the shop or field without making such visits. This is, of course, a false and misleading illusion, and one which can be extremely costly if continued over a period of time.

Getting out for a look at the actual scene of operations can sharpen the quality of decisions made in the office. It provides a feel for local conditions. More importantly, it adds to management decisions a generally higher quality in the mind of the person affected, because they have the touch and aura of reality which chair-bound decisions seem to lack. There are, furthermore, some things which can only be judged from personal inspections. Housekeeping is but one of these. Let's look at the housekeeping example. Here's what one president says about conducting plant tours:

> I know darn well they clean up special when I'm coming, but this doesn't dismay me. I know from inspecting the place whether or not the manager of the plant has sufficient control over operations to be able to enforce a special program, on demand, if he is able to pull a good clean-up program on short notice.

Here's what a vice president of data processing says about inspections:

> I always attach a lot of importance to my trips, even though the only real thing that is evident is housekeeping. If I go into an installation where everything is neat and orderly, I have an impression that the place is under control. It may be possible that a data processing shop looks like a pig-pen and actually runs like a clock, but my experience is just the opposite. If the manager can't control the things I can see with my eye on a brief visit, he probably has a lot of other things that are more basic that he's let slip too.

As with housekeeping, there are many things which can be awry that will never be reported. No plant manager ever walks into the boss's office and reports, "Our plant looks terrible." It takes an inspection by the boss to find out just how poor things are. Some other areas of the business which can best be observed from close-up inspection include maintenance of the plant and equipment, the general tenor of work and pace of the work force, evidences of unsafe practices, the care of materials, and the general attitudes of people at work.

In addition to seeing what is going on, the manager *is seen* on inspection trips, and this is an important facet of management and morale. The concept of the absentee boss is one which has great capacity to rile workers and managers alike.

How to Conduct a Personal Inspection

One successful chief executive insists that his executives spend much of their time out of the office visiting plants and sales districts. Beyond this, he spends much of his own executive time out in the field as well. In addition, the board of directors changes the location of their board meetings from place to place, to be able to include plant tours in various locations as part of their agenda. Going even further, the company also holds unique "regional stockholder's meetings" in various parts of the country where the company operates, in order that the owners may see the properties they hold on paper.

Yet, a visit in itself can be either good or bad. There are some methods of making such visits most effective that have worked well for managers, and some things to avoid as well.

WATCHING FOR THE IMPORTANT THINGS ON A VISIT

The experienced executive learns what to look for on a visit. Since the chief is probably going to be there only a few days or hours, he or she can't hope to learn everything and see everything that could be seen. This requires that the boss develop a sharp sense of rooting out the vital things to look for, using them as indicators of the things unseen.

Plant and operating people have a vast facility for picking up which items the top person is going to inspect, making certain that they will be correct before his or her arrival. Yet, where this surface polish is all that has been applied, the smart inspector will pry into the basic operations very quickly to find the things swept under the rug. Four general areas seem to be productive in sorting out the important facts from the trivial in a plant or office.

1. Do the people who are supposed to know have the answers? Usually the plant or branch office tour is accompanied by the manager in charge of the operation. The visitation can also be the occasion for a quiet but systematic quiz of the local boss, using items and events as they occur to provoke answers.

"How much scrap do we get from these machines?" or, "What's the grievance rate been in the foundry?" might be asked as these facilities are being inspected or viewed on the visit. The fact that the local manager doesn't know may not be damaging, but it's worth further investigation when someone is ignorant of some local situation in too many instances. You might even do as Eugene MacNeice of Johnson and Johnson did, as a method of conducting such quizzes. MacNeice set up a point scoring system. It went something like this:

> 4—If the subordinate had the answer immediately and it was correct.
>
> 3—If he or she said, "I don't know, but I will find out," then reported back with the correct answer shortly.
>
> 2—If the person was very slow in reporting back with the facts (for example, more than two or three days).
>
> 1—If the person had to be reminded to get the facts and report.
>
> 0—If he or she failed to report even after reminder, or reported incorrect facts.

This rating system wasn't perfect, but it became a guide as to who was on top of the job and who wasn't when a long series of such scores were accumulated. MacNeice found that his best people consistently scored threes and fours, and his problem managers racked up zeroes or ones.

2. Are the easily controllable things under control. In every operation, there are certain parts of the job which are easily controlled by the manager who is abreast of things. In some plants this is housekeeping, and sloppiness is evidence of a lack of discipline and control over the actions of employees. The only alternative here is the assumption that the manager likes to have the place unkempt. One manager puts it this way:

> It might be that a plant with unpainted machines, and disorder and confusion in stock, machine parts and workplaces is, underneath it, a smoothly functioning machine, but most jalopies look like it, and most Cadillacs not only outrun the rattletrap, but they *look* as if they could.

This isn't to say that a foundry should look like a surgical manufacturer, but there are orderly foundries and sloppy ones. Nor are special periods of rush orders and extraordinary crises apt to find the place as neat as when a clean-up has just taken place. Putting these exceptional circumstances aside, however, housekeeping is one evidence of a lack of control. Great stacks of rework product, a high accident frequency and severity rate, workers walking about in obvious violation of known safety rules, and gross evidence (or less obvious evidence) of carelessness and inattention can be danger signs that some of the controllable things aren't under firm control. At this point, the inspector can begin to turn attention to the management of the place.

3. Is the surface representative of what lies beneath? Inspections can be a terrific waste of time, and moreover can be deceptive in some cases. Where an inspection seems to indicate that all is in order, but the quick view isn't representative of what's actually occurring, a false optimism and dangerous sense of security can come about. Probing beneath the surface, in one or two instances, can sometimes unearth any evidence of "glossing over" of poor conditions. Here's how one general manager does it:

> I use a system of one-two inspections as I make my tour. I may pull a sample of something here and there: a product off the line, or have a chat with a worker. If everything seems to be OK on the basis of the first check, I go along and look at the next thing. If I discover something wrong, however, I stop and take a second look, and then maybe a third. Finally, I'll probe just as deep as I need to, to find out how bad things are. It's that first sample that triggers a deeper look, however. It works surprisingly well.

4. Does the inspection check out with other facts? Before going on a plant-or-local office tour, it's a wise plan to get some basic facts about the place before leaving. Some of the figures might include labor relations, morale, cost accounting, spoilage, and so on. If something is showing up very good or very bad in these figures, this is a hint as to where to look. High direct labor cost ought to be borne out with inspection evidence that lines are shut down or delayed. When you have a report that morale is great in the plant, but every employee you talk to seems disgruntled, it might be worth further investigation. The figures should merely be a guide to suggest places to visit and inspect personally. If the figures and the local inspection don't tally, this discrepancy should be followed up and clarified.

SHOWMANSHIP IN PERSONAL VISITS

One of the values of inspection is the opportunity it provides people working in the outside location to see the boss. This is important to them since it gives them a chance to personally size up the caliber of top management in their company. It would be a drastic mistake to assume that, because they aren't all staring directly at the visitor during the visit, they aren't seeing everything that goes on. This means that the boss as well as the people and the plant are on display, and should be governed accordingly.

The first and most obvious requirement is that dignity, friendliness and cordiality be the rule of the day. This doesn't mean one must be a hand-shaker or a back-slapper, but does mean that reactions are positive when you see things you like. If things seem to be okay and management is satisfied with what it finds on such visits, it's sound strategy to express this satisfaction to the employees or in their hearing. It also means a willingness to try to remember faces and names between visits, and to recall past associations, even temporary ones. Here's how failure to do so can affect relationships adversely:

> "I've met our vice president five times now," a mechanic reported in a metal factory, "and each time I had to be introduced again, and I'm sure he didn't know who I was any of the last four times. You'd think he wouldn't be so dumb as to forget."

Admittedly, this vice president met many hundreds of people each year, and could possibly forget. It actually proved to be a habit of the vice president's that he never tried to remember anybody's name, even those whom he saw daily. This coldness toward interpersonal contacts reflects itself quickly in employee attitudes. It's possible that such people might do better to avoid visits entirely, since they do more harm than good.

How much time should an executive spend with an individual employee? One consultant, who analyzed many such visits, reports that the average successful chat with an employee can run around ninety seconds, and during that time the benefits of personal contact and showmanship can be achieved. A simple question oriented toward the employee, not critical in tone or intent, rewarded with an evidence of interest and sincere thanks for the information, is sound visitation and inspection strategy.

How to Conduct a Personal Inspection 251

Personal attire is part of the showmanship of an inspection where the objective is as much to be seen as to see the plant. When the executive is visiting the plant and is on display, he or she should look like an executive. Neat and quietly expensive clothes are probably the safest as a rule. Hand painted neckties, stylish dress fashions and the like have been found to bring out the derision latent in employee views of managers from afar. A visiting executive should, of course, always follow the rules of the shop in regard to hard hats, safety glasses, coveralls, and the like if they are part of the pattern in the shop. Most safety rules are considered by employees as originating in the president's office if not higher, and for an executive to violate them leaves a bad taste in their mouths; it also undermines the local manager's safety efforts.

A sound briefing on the big problems facing the people in the local office or plant is sound strategy. This provides the visiting inspector a chance to ask some intelligent questions, which indicate that at least enough interest in their affairs to inquire and be informed about the plant. Probably the use of this information can be limited to stopping by the machine of the employee working on an important job and saying:

"Hello Harriet, I thought I'd drop around and see how you're making out on this job. As you know, we consider it one of the hottest in the company, and I thought I'd see how it was going."

THE ETHICS OF MAKING INSPECTIONS

One of the reasons that many managers refuse to make inspections is the resistance they occasionally get from lower level management over their too frequent inspections. There's some sound reasoning behind this resistance. Most of it grows out of the fact that, all too often, top management people don't observe the unwritten rules of the game in inspections and visitations. These rules go as follows:

1. Don't undercut the management on the spot. It's a cheap appeal for popularity in the eyes of first line management for the executive to visit the plant and water down the first line supervisors' authority by dealing directly with employees. The employee who has nerve and brass may use contacts with the top person to work for points, and settle an argument with the foreman by going over his or her head. If this is done with the tacit consent—or even the invitation—of the top person, the worker has "used" the top person by whipsawing against an immediate boss.

2. Always build the status of local management. Unless things are so horribly fouled up that the local manager is about to be relieved on the spot—even then it should be done privately—visitations and inspections should be used to enhance local management's importance in the eyes of the employees. State how much confidence you have in the local management, and imply that they have the close contact, communication and confidence of the top.

3. Find fault privately. If things which aren't up to snuff are discovered, it's perfectly acceptable to ask questions, but the hostile, directive or interrogatory question, that puts the local manager on the spot before subordinates, should be reserved for later. If several layers of supervision are between the visiting foreman and the local manager, they should be on hand and all criticism should be routed through them.

4. Don't generalize on too scanty evidence. Take the case of the president who visited a plant and found a man reading a racing form in the maintenance office. He immediately walked up to the man and ordered him to put the "damned paper in the wastebasket and get to work." Imagine his chagrin when the man coolly informed him that he was an outside telephone repairman who was waiting for his partner to come back with some parts from the truck, and furthermore, since he didn't work for that company but the phone company, the executive could go off into a corner and soak his head. Naturally, this story spread like wildfire around the plant and the whole company. The man might better have identified his target before letting loose with his heaviest guns.

While this instance was merely one of foolishness on the part of the executive, more damaging circumstances are those where a visiting inspector generalizes on half the facts about his own people.

> Take the case of the visiting auditor who was touring a regional warehouse for an auto supply firm. As he was walking through the yard, he saw a workman burning trash and noticed that several tires were among the items being destroyed. In his report back at the office,

he reported that the warehouse manager was burning tires—no explanation, just that they were burning tires. Naturally, an explanation was asked for by letter. The local manager was furious at the implication that he would destroy good tires, or even recappable ones. The tires, he explained in a hot return letter, were completely unrepairable, had been taken in trade-in and his procedures followed company policy exactly. He further went on to complain bitterly about "spies and snoopers" who would see such things and not report them to him before going back to company headquarters to write snide letters.

This leads us to the next rule of ethics for inspection tours.

5. Let the local people explain their side. When the inspecting executive sees things which might be wrong, the first step is to ask the local manager in charge to explain why a certain thing is being done. "I don't understand why you are doing this..." is a good preface to bringing up such situations. The act of putting people on the defensive in the face of what seems to be damning evidence, in itself causes all inspections to be viewed with a jaundiced eye. Even when they have a chance to explain, when it is done under the circumstances of being in the trial court, it has numerous bad effects. When accosted by such things as, "I notice that you are doing such and such a thing, and it would seem to me that you are making a mistake," it makes any explanation which follows an alibi rather than a reason, and the fact of being placed in such a position by the inspecting executive is the basis for resentment. In most cases, local conditions have created reasons why procedures have been developed. Asking for these facts and feelings first may make the whole thing seem plausible. If it does not, the executive should then move firmly into explaining the reasons why it must be changed.

HOW TO DETECT COVER-UPS DURING INSPECTIONS

The inspection process itself can have the harmful effect of giving the inspector a false sense of well-being and security where he or she glosses over the underlying facts. This is especially true in such matters as morale and the general attitudes of employees.

> In one steel company, the president toured a mill and, among other things, inquired of the superintendents how they would evaluate the morale in the plant. Either because they didn't really know or because they wanted to present a favorable front, they all reported that things were normal. Later that day, the evening shift pulled a wildcat walkout, which was followed by the other shifts following suit.

How can visiting executives determine whether or not things are not what they seem to be, and when they are getting accurate information? This becomes especially difficult when they must skirt around assigned officials to get this information. Here are some guides to getting at these things:

1. Talk to people. An integral part of many visits should be informal chats with people at all levels. In addition to making small talk and complimenting outstanding people (suggestion award winners, for example) ask such questions as these:

> What is you job here? How long have you worked here?
> How do you like your job? Why?
> What don't you like? Why?
> What could we do to make your job easier, safer, better?

Asked in casual but direct fashion, these questions can produce factual information, indicating feelings and opinions of people, from which generalizations about morale and loyalty to the organization can become the basis of appraising the conditions there.

2. Comparisons with other locations. Standards of performance for the organization can be carried from one plant to another by the inspector who has seen many such plants in operation. If the housekeeping in one plant is better than in another, or if one plant has more people on certain jobs than another, these are evidences that should lead to follow-up and closer examination.

> The manufacturing manager for a can plant with national distribution has a habit of reading production figures from feeder counters at the end of the line as he tours the plants, especially on key lines. Although he probably has a general acquaintance with differences in output, the fact that he sees a figure which seems

low to him can open the door for such questions as:
"I notice you've only made ten thousand containers on this line today, and if my memory is correct, we should be getting fifteen for this line at this time. What seems to be the problem here?"

He reports that this often opens the door to general discussions on what's wrong with maintenance in the plant, the training of operators, relations with the sales department, or the effectiveness of production scheduling against the machines.

The purpose in probing into such specific things isn't to investigate the single instance of low production, but rather to open the door to more generalized discussions of plant operations with the management. In one plant, he found that the fault was his own, for he had vetoed a mechanical overhaul program several months before, and it was having serious effects on direct labor costs in that plant. Getting effective use out of such comparisons can only be done by the person who has knowledge of many plants and the ability to accurately recall the standards and actual performance from plant to plant.

In one large drug firm, where the manufacturing head sees that one plant is way ahead of another in housekeeping, morale or maintenance of equipment, he suggests that the manager of the less effective plant visit one of the better-managed ones and "pick up a few ideas." This ordinarily has a sound effect of stimulating the lesser plant manager, at the same time as improving on the ability to change things through exposure to sounder practices that have worked.

3. Have some information in advance. One of the ways in which inspections can be probing in nature is to go armed with facts and figures which need some investigation. If, for example, a morale or opinion survey has been taken recently, these results can be the basis for focusing attention on visible causes of difficulty during the inspection. In more cases than one might suspect, the tangible effects of bad conditions can be visibly seen and checked by inspection, and with the local flavor in hand, some genuine asistance and counsel for improvement can be made. Working from the accounting report, the morale audit, or the down-time report can be ephemeral and theoretical. The principal use of such information comes in actually using it to effect improvements. This ordinarily requires some personal looks at the scene, as well as generalization and solutions based upon pure logic developed in a corporate headquarters.

THE CASE FOR THE LEADER BEING SEEN

There are few instances in management where the personal qualities of the leader have greater impact upon the organization than during a personal visit. Throughout history, the leader of great movements, the general, the statesman, the monarch, or the president who was able to lead the great organization to excel was the one who had the capacity for being seen favorably by large numbers of followers.

Modern psychology has largely ignored this factor in leadership, despite the formidable array of evidence of its importance. The leader who appears often before the employees can transmit enthusiasm, sincerity and zeal to these people. It is one of the most obvious places where the physical bearing and manner of the leader has significance. Personality traits become crystallized and summed up in the leader's manner during the ninety-second exposure.

Nobody has extensively studied the importance of appearance in a leader, yet in the personal leadership of large groups of people, close attention to this facet of managerial ability is a key that unlocks many doors, and offsets the inability to deliver speeches that bristle with intellect.

In all of our attention to the qualities of management and the skills of the manager in organizing, planning, controlling, and using deskmanship, we have often overlooked the necessity of personal appearances, before large groups of subordinates, as a vital factor. Obviously, dynamic or showy qualities in visits can't offset sloppy staff work, or make up for a chaotic organization plan. Yet it can unite the people behind their top leaders as few other procedures can do.

Many techniques of the modern management of people are designed to allay the evils which come from failure to inspect and visit the scene where the goods are sold or made. Appraisal systems, budgetary controls and similar logical procedures all too

How to Conduct a Personal Inspection

often owe their existence to a desire on the part of top executives to remain apart from their subordinates. Inspection and personal leadership are due for a revival.

What are the occasions when inspections and visits should take place? One of the most obvious is at events where people are gathered for some honor-giving occasion. The safety award dinner, the annual supervisory or sales banquet, the suggestion award, the sales training meeting, or the management development session are all good excuses which should not be missed. They afford a means of making a personal impact by the top person who has arrived, because of the very leadership qualities that would make such inspections and visits to the field or plant bring the greatest return in action and results from the organization.

21

SEE IT BIG—KEEP IT SIMPLE

"The first principle of composition, therefore, is to foresee or determine the shape of what is to come and pursue that shape."

WILLIAM STRUNK, JR.

Being a person of action is more than a matter of temperament, however important that may be. Many persons of impetuous manner have the qualities that make things happen, and frequently their suggestions are proposed with a view to seeing more happen than presently is being done. Yet this carping at inactivity, and railing at inaction and stagnation isn't enough by itself.

Perhaps more importantly, the person who would make things happen must have the skills of generalizing from the information at hand, and encompassing within the scope of thought more than most people can do under the same circumstances. This frame of mind is one of being able to accurately simplify the general conditions which exist in a social situation, and identify what is important and what is trivial.

The principal block to this seems to be the vast amount of information which daily assails anyone in the management position. Not only have the skills and tools of the administrator proliferated, but the outside influences which impinge upon the managerial decision increase daily. Among the former are the many new tools and techniques which are being developed, and which have been used successfully in many companies. The use of cost accounting, electronic data processing, computers, operations research, systems and procedures, wage and salary administration, motivation research, statistical quality control, organization planning methods, strategic planning, and a myriad of similar complex methods, are examples of a small portion of this new technology of management and administration. While they add rationality and system to a world that needs managing, they also bring up the distinct possibility that diversion and side excursion from the principal goal of business may entrap the manager.

In the instance of those outside influences upon businesses and managerial decision-making, the delights of dallying with momentous but peripheral affairs matter from the viewpoint of the firm. Inattention to these outside influences may be fatal, it's true, but for the executive whose primary function is to run a business, they must almost always be viewed first with a view toward long run growth and survival of the firm. This isn't as narrow as it might seem upon first glance, for such considerations always include those actions on the part of the first, which are necessary to the preservation and improvement of the system under which the firm operates.

As a trustee of the firm, the executive manages it for others, including stockholders, employees, customers, and the public. This balance between competing demands isn't one of simply balancing them like the famous billiard balls of Alfred Marshall. It means that we must first see the requirements which are made by the aggregate, and the need for making things happen through the efforts of the leader of the firm. Without seeing this basic objective, we may become so engrossed or hard-pressed in satisfying others, that we ultimately dissatisfy all.

> The shape of what must be for the executive, is simply that the firm must work, must survive and grow toward some goal.

Unlike the economic models which classical and theoretical economists would suggest, the firm works, grows and survives because people make it happen. They make it happen because they have a clear image—clearer than all others—of what can be expected of it, and have a plan for making it occur. This *fixity on ends* is the only possible rule for remaining free from entanglements in the many details of doing business, making and selling products, dealing with unions and customers, and handling the intricacies of finance. It is furthermore the ultimate test of success or failure of the executive. If we run a profitable firm, sell good products at a fair price and pay good wages along with the amenities of decent working conditions, we have succeeded. If we don't do all of these things we will fail, no matter which of the other requirements upon us we perform superbly well. Delighted stockholders, employees with high morale, satisfied customers, and a community that is pleased with its corporate citizens are not, by themselves, indicators of managerial success. Keeping this larger objective in mind, and knowing how to make it happen is what makes the good executive.

HOW TO SIFT AND SCREEN INFORMATION AND OPINION

Sub-optimal standards of business performance are being proposed daily for the modern corporation. The firm should take part in civic affairs, it should support colleges and universities, it should employ handicapped and minority groups, it should cut costs and fight inflation, and it should give its employees a chance to participate in the decisions which affect them. No one would dispute the soundness of any of these recommendations under some circumstances.

Nonetheless, it's the manager's role to remain detached from all of them, and assess each against the general standard by which he or she must be judged. There can be no community donations or support of colleges, unless the firm is profitable. Participation of employees in the decisions which affect them is excellent to the extent that it doesn't hamper unduly the ability of the firm to produce, work and do business.

The art of screening the many facts, opinions and demands upon business must, then, always be against this general standard for executive results.

WHEN OVER-SIMPLIFICATION BECOMES FALSEHOOD

The temptations to look for single causes in management are many. Many definitions of management have this defect.

"Management means getting results through people," goes one such homily. This reduces the manager, as David Moore puts it, to a sort of Tom Sawyer who gets the other kids to paint the fence while he watches. Yet, getting others to work is fruitless, unless their efforts are productive and profitable, and meet the tests of the entire firm's objectives. The implication here is that the manager's only skill is that of delegation. It leaves unanswered the problem of what the manager does after passing out the lesser jobs to others.

"Management means communication," declares another school of thought. While it's perfectly true that managers must have great ability to develop communication channels and methods, this is no test of the success of an executive, since it doesn't exclude the circumstance under which we communicate well, but the company fails. Certainly the executive is more than a walking switchboard or a live servo-mechanism that turns power off and on. We may actually do this, but our skill at this is not the ultimate test of the right to hold the executive position.

Wrong simplifications on management are over-simplifications, which are a form of deception. Even the title of this book, suggesting that managers make things happen, could be construed wrongly if it assumed that in simply making things happen—anything at all—the manager was successfully discharging all that might be demanded. The real test comes in assessing whether or not the things which we made happen were the right things, and consistent with the goals of the firm.

ASSESSING DETAIL AGAINST THE OVERVIEW

In action, this checking of details, suggestions and proposals, the manager may spend much time weighing one countervailing demand against another. The sales department wants lower prices and more liberal credit. This must be weighed against the cost figures and manufacturing demands for higher standardization and control, and the need for more profits. The demands for more dividends from stockholders must be weighed against the long run demands for plowed-back earnings into research and commercial development. This arbitrator of competing demands in executive rank has more than a position of simple mediator between competing demands. We must weight all demands against the total demand of the firm for producing goods at a profit, providing jobs and paying dividends.

In the purest sense, the executive is the paid entrepreneur who allocates scarce resources among many competing demands, and assumes the risk of alternative courses of action. Steps to make things happen are inevitably best when they spur on one part of the organization to bring about a state of balance between them that adds up to more ultimate efficiency for all of them, taken as an integrated unit.

ON THE IMPORTANCE OF BREADTH OF VIEWPOINT

Here lies the key to the so-called executive shortage. Certainly there is no lack of candidates for top management positions. Yet, many aspirants see themselves as generalists when their principal approach is through giving wider scope and enlarging the efficiency of one particular activity of the business. The sales manager who becomes general manager must go through several stages of growth to become successful as the general manager, including an enlargement of perspective which will enable him or her to trim the sales department's proposals with equal zeal as he or she would with any other department inconsistent with over-all organization goals.

The early identification of people who have the potential for generalizing about the functions of the business, and who see the corporate body as something with a life distinct from its parts, that is inextricably linked to them, is at the heart of the executive shortage. This is the lowest hurdle the successful general manager must overcome. Beyond this comes the even more sophisticated art of seeing these competing demands and making things happen in the organization, despite and because of these special claims upon the executive. Basically, these skills of generalization and breadth of viewpoint have six characteristics:

- **They are goal-setting skills.** The executive is able to see the corporate entity and all its parts, and sets goals for the total organization that are attainable.
- **They are organization skills.** Seeing the complex structure in its entirety, the successful executive is able to integrate

the parts into a shape which is envisioned as being the most effective one, filling the slots in the whole organization with able people who can perform their function well.
- **They are standard-makers.** With his organizational shape fixed, made and staffed with able people, the executive is able to set and transmit standards of performance for the people in the organization, and set goals which require their best abilities to complete.
- **They know how to measure.** In the face of this complex structure and the many different people manning it, the manager is able to inform the organization of how well it is performing. Controls and measuring methods that indicate when the organization is performing up to standards and when it is falling short of the organization goals are vital.
- **They are improvers.** The broad-gauged manager is an improver of what exists. Where we set standards, we seek to bring people up to their maximum capacity in order that they meet these standards and develop their personal abilities in order that they will achieve what they set out to do.

RELATING THE ORGANIZATION TO SOCIETY

Perhaps one of the most difficult generalizing skills of the manager is to know the organization intimately and relate its efforts and goals to the over-all goals of the society in which it functions. Industry does not create wealth. God creates wealth, and industry converts in into useful objects through establishing and managing for the benefit of the society in which it functions. Just as society draws on industry for its standard of living, so does the corporation draw on the society for accumulated capital, stable money and banking systems, an educated and intelligent work force, law and order, sound legal systems, and property rights to acquire and dispose of its assets as it sees fit.

This larger responsibility becomes almost impossible for any single unit of the firm to accomplish, without the stated policies of enlightened and action-oriented management to make it happen.

22

THE GENTLE ART OF CHEWING OUT A SUBORDINATE

> " 'Once the compass points north and we know where we're going we stay on the beam. I ain't interested in ideas that are off the beam, and I ain't interested in people that are off the beam. Check!' 'Check,' went around the board table like a whipcrack."
>
> FREDERICK WAKEMAN, *The Hucksters*

There's a necessity for order in an organization if it is to survive, and there's perhaps even more demand for such order if it's to grow. This corporate discipline which brings about unity isn't a natural condition of human groups, and it grows out of the behavior of its leaders. What leaders do to accomplish this unity, without running into counter-facts and ultimate disunity because of *wrong methods* of establishing and maintaining order, is vital.

As Dr. Dallas Jones has pointed out, the new discipline in industry is substantially different from the type which prevailed when the manager acted as the overseeing agent of the owner. Under such circumstances, the employment contract, which every person entered into when he or she went to work, implied that the boss was entitled to be autocratic in directing people who entered the premises. This tacit agreement was part of the entire package, and was a condition of employment.

Two conditions have brought about a major change of the disciplinary concept. The first has been *psychological-social,* and presumes that it isn't always wise to exercise one's property rights in dictatorial fashion. The second is a new, *legalistic* concept of discipline, which requires administrative remedies (union contracts, grievance procedures, due process, and so on) which are available to the person who is treated unjustly at work. These two forces have combined to change the entire emphasis of discipline. The law which governs employees in the modern organization has little to do with putting down rebellions against property rights, squelching impertinence, or getting an eye for an eye.

> Modern discipline aims almost wholly at bringing people in the organization into line with the "law of the situation," which is created both by the organization and its surroundings.

A CODE FOR MANAGEMENT DISCIPLINE

The skills of chewing out a subordinate take on an entirely different coloration under this new code of discipline than those which existed in the smaller, more personally-owned firm of the past century, and extend into this in many places. In brief, this code of management discipline (which governs reprimand procedures) goes something as follows:

1. Discipline implies rules, not personal desires. Conformity in the directives of immediate superiors is, in part, a requirement of discipline. They are not the entire aspect of discipline, nor are all directives consistent with good discipline. Gordon Rattray Taylor has set up a requirement for leadership that the legitimacy of the leader must be acknowledged by the governed. This means the leader must clearly show a right to be in charge. The old expression "rule of law, not rule of men" is another way of putting it. Mary Parket Follet expressed it as being the law of the situation. The rules, under this concept, are not arbitrarily designed to please the boss, but are patently required for the organization to get where it wishes to go.

2. Discipline implies correction of error in a situation. The manager who objects to what is proposed or has been done or said, assumes the responsibility to propose, and perhaps execute, something else. Carping and criticizing for purposes of destroying the other's initiatives, or simply calling people wrong, places the manager in the position of spectator, rather than active participant in the game. Here's how one large company president put it:

> With my major officers, I know that their decisions are really choices among several alternatives they have considered. For me to impose my choice in preference to theirs also means that I'm assuring personal responsibility for the skill with which the decision is executed. I'd be foolish to do that. I therefore limit myself to asking pointed questions which assure me that all alternatives have been considered. Once that's done, I step back and let them go ahead with their own decisions.

3. The best discipline is situational authority. The manager who steps into a situation with an authoritative manner and directs changes with added comments on the qualification of the person who is doing the job, in effect relieves that person of his or her post—temporarily or permanently. On the other hand where the boss is merely suggesting, and the suggestion can be and has been upon occasion, rejected by the subordinate, the discipline is healthy and sound for the organization. For example, the comments of subordinates on superior's work will often be in this category, since its tenor is normally designed to avoid attacks upon the person, and is limited to the presentation of special knowledge and insights into the demands of the situation.

4. Discipline shouldn't damage delegation. When the manager "chews out" the subordinate in a manner that indicates an intent to substitute the bosses' judgment wholly for that of the subordinate, the cause can usually be traced to some personal pique. Either the offender was impudent or impertinent ("he's insubordinate"), or it's an ego-protection device for the whip-wielder. He sees the offender as a personal threat to him, or he feels insecure as a result of the acts of such people, and attacks them from the vantage point of his position of authority.

> Take the case of the personnel manager who made it a habit of walking around the plant and reporting any violations of regulations to the president. This was inevitably done by listing names of employees and their supervisors, as well as making caustic suggestions for action. The president, while not desiring to

have regulations flouted, advised the personnel manager to "report bad situations to supervision involved, and avoid personalizing your approach."

The emphasis in sound discipline must be on *what's wrong*, rather than *"who's to blame."*

5. Discipline must entail equity. Even the youngest child reacts unfavorably to anything which seems to smack of injustice. Favoritism, unequal application of the rules and discriminatory treatment, have immense capacities for arousing rebellion. People have gone to the barricades and have laid their lives on the line to prevent injustice, and will undoubtedly go to great extremes to prevent it again. To the average employee, fairness means the same thing as consistency.

6. The discipline of system and method is least objectionable. In circumstances where uniformity and conformity are desired, the best control over such behavior is to establish a uniform procedure and to explain it. This means that people govern their behavior to fit the procedure and, knowing that others have accepted the procedure, will probably not find it onerous.

> In one sales organization, each month over half the expense accounts submitted were rejected and returned for corrections or further information by the controller. Sizing up the situation, the sales manager printed up a new batch of expense forms, with detailed instructions for their completion on the bottom. Rejections fell sharply and the beginning of a feud was squelched. Nobody objected to following the procedure. They objected keenly to the personalized rejections without standards explained to them in advance.

Reducing order-giving to mean "following a set pattern of behavior," as contrasted with the requirements of "ask the boss what to do," has numerous advantages in maintaining discpline.

- It alleviates the possibility of personal affront to the boss because "orders" weren't "obeyed."
- It eliminates the possibilities which constantly exist of routine direction being full of pique or innuendo that creates resistance.

- It helps remove some of the emotional difficulties which grow out of one person's resentment of another who has power over him or her.

This doesn't mean that personal contact between the subordinate and boss is always undesirable. On the contrary. Such contacts are to be sought after. They are most effective, however, when they are within the framework of coaching, teaching, giving assurance, reacting to question, commending good performance, or establishing personal rapport, which indicates the regard of one person for the other.

7. Discipline should never rob a person of his or her dignity. Most arbitration cases over discipline are based on inequity or loss of self esteem on the part of the employee because of the manner in which the disciplinary action was taken. The famous instance of President Truman removing General MacArthur from his post aroused a national emotional binge simply because "of the way it was done." Even those who felt that MacArthur might have been insubordinate to his commander-in-chief were aroused at the indignity of the method of his removal. This indignity lay in the stature of the man, his past contributions and his sincerity in his desire to serve his country. The lessons for managers are clear. No single defect or act merits disciplinary action which leaves the person no dignified way of retreating to a position where his or her status and humanity are preserved. Some commonly held rules that every subordinate believes to be his or her due include:

- The right to privacy when being reprimanded.
- Freedom from "entrapment" in which a situation is deliberately rigged to cause a person to do something that invites discipline.
- The making of an example of an otherwise innocent and one-time offender, while flagrant violators are, by chance, allowed free with lesser penalties.
- The varying of the intensity of rules enforcement. Where violations of rules have been condoned, bad effects upon morale will follow a sudden and arbitrary tightening of these rules, without notice.

- Attacks upon someone's personal worth for specific offenses. Where we make an error, we concede the right of the boss to invite attention to these mistakes and direct us "not to do it again" or even to punish us, but we reject generalized complaints and suggestions about an over-all lack of adequacy or worth.
- Inconsistency of treatment, from time to time, or among persons. Consistency may be the hobgoblin of small minds, but in terms of discipline most of us are small.
- Comments about performance, that are only forthcoming when things go wrong, and never when good work is done. Recognition, as we've seen earlier, should cover both good and bad performance.

WHEN TO REPRIMAND

As in many of the arts, timing becomes of paramount importance in reprimanding a subordinate. Timing is probably one of the "skill" areas of management which only experience can develop; the artful manager studies the matter of timing and notes which sequence of reprimands has the most effect in achieving the best results.

> Take the case of the research manager who went to his management with an idea for a research project that would be both pioneering and daring in its nature, and very costly. With some misgivings, the approval was given to proceed. After spending more than twice his estimated budget, the research manager was asked for a progress report. At this point he confessed that he had reached a dead end, and suggested that the project be abandoned. Management very wisely agreed, without a word of protest or the demand for explanations of his action. The man was being sufficiently wracked by his own professional pride; added reprimand or censure at that time would have been very damaging, and might have caused the man to leave. Since he was basically a sound man, they allowed the matter to be quietly dropped. A year later, under his direction, an extremely profitable project paid off more than enough to cover the original losses on the wrongly selected project.

There are numerous instances when reprimands are best delayed or withheld completely. Good managers who are aware of the standards of performance by which their jobs are measured often punish themselves more severely than any outsider could do. In some cases, there may be a need for undisciplining.

> Fred G. was general manager of a consumer product division of a large company which was offered a chance to market a new product. Under the pressure of day-to-day business, an incomplete investigation resulted in the offer being declined, with the further result that the supplier took his product to a competitor, who made a great success of it. The chagrin and remorse of the first manager was so great that his president made a special trip to his home to assure him that nobody held this lapse against him, and to ask him to get on with doing the continued good job with the present line that he had been doing in the past.

Often it's the mistake of omission about which we punish ourselves most, and for which managerial discipline and reprimand are least needed. These can be used as occasions for coaching and teaching, but to "nag" is nothing more than pointing out inadequacies of the past about which the person can do nothing.

Generally, however, the timing of reprimands becomes one of deciding whether to collect several examples and do it for all of them, or to make an immediate reprisal. Usually the gathering of evidence is designed to make a more general case to prove some over-all deficiencies. This is often done when the person is being fired, and the specific incidents are collected and noted as evidence of an overall inadequacy which is large enough to require release. They may, of course, be accumulated for other purposes; for example, to convince an employee to drastically revise his or her behavior or attitude when the reporting of a single incident wouldn't have that effect.

> In a large southern insurance company, one of the better young sales managers had let success go to his head and was letting his performance slide. He often stayed home after heavy weekends, and was overly friendly with several female employees. The general manager in charge collected a number of specific incidents over six months and finally confronted him with these facts, plus some verbatim comments that

outsiders had made to him about the salesman's high living and apparent loss of his old abilities. Confronted with this array of facts, the young man was appalled and promptly turned over a new leaf.

In other instances, it's valuable to take each specific incident and make the reprimand immediately. As every parent knows, an immediate swat is more effective than the vague threat of "wait 'til Dad (or Mom) gets home." Distance and the possibility of future reprisals have a diminished effect upon a person's behavior. This is especially true with the new employee, and most especially with the young employee on his or her first job.

> One executive found that a new staff manager was habitually late in getting to work, and seemed happily oblivious to broad suggestions that everyone in *this* office works eight hours a day. After several such days, the boss confronted him one morning coming in fifteen minutes late, and ordered him quietly to go home for a week without pay. After a week, he came back and was a model employee.

Very often the timing of the disciplinary action can be made on the spot and effective immediately, and inevitably the result will be a serious rethinking of the situation by the employee.

THE SEVEN DEADLY SINS OF REPRIMANDING

There are some serious errors which a manager can make in reprimanding.

1. Failing to get facts. Be sure you have all the facts before leaping. Don't accept hearsay evidence or go on general impressions.

2. Acting while angry. Don't act while you've lost your temper. Be calm in your own mind, and as objective as possible in making a decision to reprimand. Ask yourself, "Is it possibly my fault that the error or violation occurred?"

3. Being unclear about the offense. Let the person know the general charge and the specific details of the defense. Don't allude to general complaints or refuse to give details.

4. Not getting the other person's side of the story. Always let the persons have their full say about what happened and their reason why they did what they did. There may be mitigating circumstances, conflicting orders or even orders you gave unclearly which were at fault.

5. Backing down when you are right. Compromise and understanding are virtues, but once you've decided and announced your decision, it is a mistake to relent. It merely indicates you were wrong in your first decision, and you'll lose the effect of your reprimand.

6. Failing to keep records. Disciplinary reprimands should always be recorded in the the personnel folder of the person. This becomes part of the work history of the person, and provides evidence in the event of further disciplinary requirements. In many cases, people who were known to be unsatisfactory employees over the years have been reinstated after discharge because the company could produce no evidence that the person had ever been told of his shortcomings.

7. Harboring a grudge. Once the reprimand has been administered and any sanctions or punishments administered, don't carry a hostile attitude forever after. The person required discipline and received it. Assume now that they are starting with a clean slate and let them know that you consider it a thing of the past.

REPRIMANDING WITHOUT LOSING THE TARGET'S REGARD

We've seen that it's a mistake to reprimand an employee in front of colleagues. This doesn't mean, either, that simply because it's private (and more personal) that anything goes in a reprimand.

Perhaps the most effective guide to maintaining the regard of the individual is to *know* the person you're dealing with. A raw beginner who is "just a kid" probably has a different image of what his or her relationship with the boss should be like from the old and experienced hand who is used to being treated with some respect.

> The key to effective reprimand is to fit the reprimand to the person's own self-image.

Every person has self perceptions which may or may not be accurate, but which he or she obviously likes. The wise supervisor knows his or her people, including how they see themselves. Let's see how this works in practice.

Harry B. is a supervisor of mechanical departments and is generally a responsible, mature person. He takes his work seriously and is most conscientious in his planning and the quality of the work under him. He takes himself somewhat seriously and brings an air of importance to the things he does. Yet he failed to perform adequately when it came to installing a new system of labor control, and the plant manager wanted to let him know that he was dissatisfied. He called Harry's secretary and arranged an appointment for two days ahead. He arranged a private meeting, and collected all of the facts and data carefully. When explaining his dissatisfaction over progress to date, he was straightforward but serious. No fireworks, no ranting or raving. He gave Harry ample opportunity to explain and talk things over. After securing agreement from Harry to give the thing a more vigorous try (and agreeing to do certain things which would help), the two shook hands upon parting.

There was no doubt in Harry's mind that he'd been hauled over the coals by the boss. Yet, since the boss treated him and the situation with the same seriousness with which Harry would have treated a lapse by a subordinate, no bad effects occurred. The system was installed in due course, without delay.

Another case was that of Charley B., an energetic young industrial engineer. Charley was bright, able, and enthusiastic. He had a bright manner of talking, and was witty in his responses. He also enjoyed a personal and informal relationship with fellow workers and with line managers. Charley's boss, Stella, was only a year or two older than Charley and knew him very well. When Charley slipped up on a job, Stella's call went this way:

"Hello Charley, this is Stell."

"Oh, hi, what's up?"

"Listen buddy, when are you gonna get on the ball?"

"Which one?"

"The Project Ten ball, that's which one!"

"Oh, that one."

"Yeah, that one. Look, buddy, if you don't have something to show me on that one by the end of this week, it's going to be you and me going around and around this building, and you know who'll be up front."

"I can imagine."

"What happened anyhow? The New York office is raising hell with me about this job."

"I kinda let 'er slip, I guess. How about something by Friday?"

"Could you?"

"Sure, anything for Superleader."

"Well, Superleader counts that as a promise, pal. If you don't have something by Friday, you'll be on the first rocket to the moon. This is hot, so put it up on your list of things not to goof off on."

As a result, the project was pulled out and Charley gave it some expert and rapid attention. In fact, he worked several evenings, and by Friday it was done. Because the reprimand was consistent with Charley's self-image, he hardly took it as a reprimand.

One of the greatest limitations in this technique is that it demands some perception on the part of the superior; a perception of how the subordinate sees him- or herself. That this perception isn't always accurate has been shown in many studies. Dr. Lee Danielson has shown, for example, that engineering managers tend to see their subordinate engineers as *emotional* people, whereas few engineers see themselves this way. Danielson suggests that this may be due to a lack of observation skills on the part of the supervisors, and also the fact that, because so many of their contacts with their subordinates are emotion-laden, they draw a distorted image. Yet even having imperfect images, and using them to shape the form and style of reprimand, is better than ignoring this important facet of discipline. The stuffy individual would resent a flippant approach to reprimanding, as much as the more easy going one would be repelled by any attempt to "act like a big shot" over a lapse. The important point is in the result achieved, rather than in the method used. Asking the man or woman to change their behavior with regard to their job is one thing. Asking them to simultaneously change their personalities and ways of adjusting to situations is another.

By fitting the method of reprimand to the self-image, the person frequently doesn't even see it as a reprimand in the conventional sense of the word. He or she stands corrected, and knows that he or she has failed to please, but doesn't feel that his or her integrity as a person has been violated. The range of such images is perhaps limitless. People see themselves as crisp administrators, hail-fellows, ivy-leaguers, egg heads, dedicated scientists, conservators of the business, weaklings, and thousands of other roles. Fitting the method to the perceived role the person plays, and making the reprimand method acceptable for the person in his or her role, is one of the tested ways of accomplishing the purposes of the reprimand without losing the subordinate's regard.

DISCIPLINE WITHOUT LOSS OF DIGNITY TO THE SUBORDINATE

Discipline problems are seldom ever created by acts or lapses of the moment, but instead occur over a length of time, and are created by the leader in the selection of subordinates. This is further accentuated by training. It is further a product of the organization of work and the ampleness of planning the work to be done. Where these things—selection, training, organization, and planning—are skillfully done, they minimize the necessity for conventional chewing-out forms of discipline. Since there is understanding from the first as to what the situation demands of the member, there's far less incidence of situations which call for a reprimand.

There are a variety of ways in which an employee receives dignity from a superior. The first is probably a simple cordiality in casual contacts. This cordiality often indicates a willingness to be friendly and helpful to the subordinate, without going so far as to indicate total dependence. The second major way in which people obtain dignity in their position as subordinates is through having superiors who help them succeed. By paying careful attention to their interests and helping them to accomplish them somewhat beyond what the employee might expect accords dignity to subordinates. On the other hand, arousing expectations of assistance by a superior, then not producing such assistance results in lost dignity for the subordinate.

This "set" or approach to management—the boss being the helper of the subordinate—has many concrete things to commend it in terms of results achieved. Perhaps the best practical way of doing it is to periodically sit down with the subordinate and jointly work out the objectives of the job. Each contributes what he or she sees as possible achievements during the period ahead, and they have a common ground upon which performance evaluation can be made, other than the subjective opinion of the superior. Yet such objective setting requires some additional steps from the boss.

- It requires that, at the end of the specified period, he or she sit down again and review with the employee the actual accomplishments against the goals established.
- It requires that the boss ask himself or herself privately, "What can I do, do differently, or refrain from doing, that would help this person accomplish these goals?"

The major advantage of this system of mutual goal-setting, between boss and subordinate, is that it imposes a system of self-discipline upon each subordinate, and a means of measuring performance against the agreed upon goals.

In companies where this system has been tried on a large scale—General Electric, General Mills, Michigan Bell Telephone, and Merck and Company—the effects have been highly satisfactory. As an executive from one of these firms put it:

> I sit down with the boss annually and we work out my program for the year in every area of my activity—including some personal development for me. Throughout the year, I have a ready reference on how well I'm doing against what my boss expects of me. At the end of the year, we sit down again and work out new goals, and review how well I did in the past year. Yet he doesn't have to sit in judgment on my performance, because I can do that for myself. We're working from the same standards, you see ... we agreed on them in advance. If I muff a job that I agreed to do, I don't have to wait for my performance review to learn about it. I have it in front of me constantly throughout the year.

THE DECLINE OF THE CHEWING-OUT

Although there will undoubtedly always be a certain amount of reprimanding and bawling-out of subordinates as long as one person works for another, as a general means of management, it's on the decline. This is only in part because we've become more civilized and considerate. The principal reason is that new amenities that work better in getting people to excel in their work have proven more effective. More rational organization of work, more participation and the breaking down of class and status systems carried into the work place from the outside, make temper tantrums less and less acceptable. In the light of this trend, it behooves the manager who uses rage and personal tyranny, as a system of motivating others into action, to have a serious look at himself and his techniques of management.

INDEX

A

Abilities, above-average, 129
Achievement motivation, 79
Action:
　business, dynamic basis, 65
　directing, 188
　dynamic concept, 60
　immediate, 188
　individual, 187-189
　manager, 36
　taking, 22, 23-24
Action plan, 30
Activity trap:
　antidote, 22-24
　　action, 22, 23-24
　　feedback, 22, 24
　　goals and plans, 22, 23
　　management cycle, 22
　　review, 22, 24
　falling into, 18
　habit, 18
　procedure, 19
　profession, 19
　religion, 20
　terrible effects, 20-22
　　misfits, 22
　　new affirmative action resisted, 21
　　no concern for goals, 21
　　not doing what boss wishes, 20
　　people's capacity shrinks, 21
　　performance pygmies, 20
　tradition, 19-20
Administrative assistant, 169-173
Administrators:
　follow procedures, 28
　not passive, 30-31
Affirmative action, resistance, 21

Aggressiveness:
　good reputation, desire, 201-204
　　appraisal procedure, 204
　　candidacy for higher jobs, 201
　　employee opinion, 203
　　feeling of infallibility, 202
　　intolerance of opposition, 202
　　peers, 204
　　realization of value, 201
　　sensitivity training, 203
　　techniques, 203
　　tricks to feed ego, 203
　mastery, desire, 198-201
　　desire to excel, 198
　　exceed best competitors, 199
　　excessive, cure, 200-201
　　maliciousness, 199
　　self-development habit, 198
　　temper tantrums, 199-200
　over, 197
　sought, 197
　wealth, desire, 204-207
　　dreams of youth achieved, 205
　　estate planning, 205, 206
　　expense account, 205, 206
　　family budget, 205
　　financial woes, 206
　　living standards, 205
　　long-range plan, 206
　　newsletter, 206
　　spending exceeding income, 205-207
　　too much, 206-207
Alliances, 240
Allies, 241
Appearances, 240
Appraisal procedure, 204
Assignments, 45
Assistant, administrative, 169-173

281

Assumptions, 218
Attack, direct, 81
Attitude, 130

B

Behavior modification:
  desired behavior in mind, 123
  get participation, 123
  reason for better habits, 120-121
  reinforcement, 123
  replace bad habit, 119-120
  set good example, 122
  small, successive steps, 123
  start new employee right, 120
  team building, 122
  try job yourself, 121
  watch work pattern, 118-119
  when progress stops, 124
  work habit, 117-118
Boredom, 56
Bottlenecks, 69
Brainstorming, 134
Budget, family, 205
Business schools, 216-217

C

Callousness to defeats, 78
Capacity, shrinking, 21
Capital investment, 52-53
Chance, 211 (see also luck)
Change:
  decision, 153
  make carefully, 153
  necessary, 57-58
  tastes, 214
Civic activities, 114
Cliques:
  catalog segments, 180-181
  four subdivisions, 181
  planning facilities, 184
  recognize existence, 179
  study operating techniques, 181-182
  team building, 179-180
  unhealthy competition, 147
  working through leaders, 183
Coaching, 45, 114 (see also Team)

Commitment, 73-74
Committees:
  economics, 192-193
  get participation, 186
  keeping under control, 191-192
  management, 192-195
  morgues for foolish ideas, 187
  organization chart, 191-192
  pack more weight, 186-187
  policy, 190
  principles of group effectiveness, 193
  problem solving, 190
  repositories for destructive criticism, 187
  test, 192
  tight procedures, 194
  topics, 195
  training, 190-191
  train members, 186
  uniformity of direction, 186
  weighing contributions, 193
  when, 185-187
  when individual action is best, 187
    directing action, 188
    immediate action, 188-189
    innovation, 188
  who, 189-191
Communication, 234-235 (see also Secrets)
Community, 74-75
Community activities, 114
Company:
  growth, 31, 35-36
  leading, 216
Compensation, 87
Competition:
  aim, 142
  basis, 141-143
  between small groups, 143
  brings out "will-do" factors, 45
  business and community, 140
  definition, 237
  exceed best efforts, 199
  fear of failure, 144
  hope of winning, 144
  human resource development, 142
  immediate group, 143
  in realm of ideas, 126
  instill desire to win, 147-149
    ask for extra effort, 148-149
    benefits of winning, 148

Index

Competition (cont'd.)
  incentive to win, 148
  let people know, 148
  interesting, 143-144
  internal, 143
  maturity, 238
  modern business, 140-141
  more personalized, 142
  new competition, 140
  product development, 141
  products, 214
  recognition, 144-145
  strategic management, 142
  technology and engineering, 141
  unhealthy, 145-147
    cliques, 147
    line and staff, 147
    partners at work, 146-147
  what it does, 140-141
  why, 143-144
  why change is necessary, 58
Conditions, outside, 70-71, 74
Confidence, 157
Confidences (*see* Secrets)
Conflicts of motives, 83-84
Conformity, 55, 240
Connections, trade, 214
Control, 59, 62-65
Corporate image, 75
Cost accountant, 112-113
Costs, 53, 57-58, 68-69
Counseling, 114
Courses, 114
Criticism, destructive, 187

D

Damage, Activity Trap, 20-22
Decision-making:
  cycle, 94
  familiar ground, 94-96
  fear, 101-102
    clinging to status quo, 102
    doesn't know own authority, 101
    insecurity, 101
    lack of clear-cut goal, 101
    strange ground, 101
  force and actions, 98-99
  identify hard facts, 97

Decision-making (cont'd.)
  listening to others, 102-104
  make areas clear, 166-168
  momentous decisions, 96-99
  not looking back, 99-101
  pure reasoning, 97
  rational aspects, 93
  theory covering subject at hand, 97-98
  what's worked in past, 97
  when to change decision, 104-106
Decisiveness, 78
Defeats, callousness, 78
Defensiveness, 86-87
Democratic leadership, 135-137
Dependent people, 56
Desire to excel, 41, 46-47
Details, 262-263
Development, research and, 53
Discipline:
  code, 268-272
  decline of chewing-out, 279-280
  mutual goal-setting, 279
  no loss of dignity, 278-279
  reprimand, 272-278
    errors, 274-275
    not losing target's regard, 275-278
    when, 272-274
Drifters, 17, 18-20
Drive, inner, 41-42
Dropping lines, 35
Dynamics, management, 58-61

E

Earthiness, 80
Egocentrism, 87
Employee opinion, survey, 203
Energy, high levels, 79
Engineer, 111-112, 141
Environmental obstacles, 82-83
Estate-planning, 205, 206
Ethical values, 90
Example, 122
Exception principle, 59
Executive time, 174-175
Expense accounts, 205, 206
Experience, 48
Experimentation, 55
Expert, 103

F

Face-saving, 211
Facilities, physical, 184
Falsehood, 261-262
Feedback results, 22, 24
Fighting:
  consolidate captured ground, 241-242
  express abhorence, 238
  gather allies, 241
  never lose temper, 238-239
  perpetuating rules, 241
  petulance and impatience, 238
  rules of game, 237-242
  to win, not to kill, 241
  winning is what counts, 239-241 (*see also* Winning)
Financial problems, 207
Flexibility, 109, 158 (*see also* Rigidity)
Frustration, tolerance for, 43
Future, predicting, 216-217

G

Goal:
  conversion into action plan, 30
  obstacles, 77-91 (*see also* Obstacles)
  realistic, attainable, 48
  setting, 30, 73-74, 279
  start with, 22, 23, 30
  strategic, 71-72
  strong orientation, 78
  substitute, 81-82
  unfreeze rigid behavior, 116
Goal-setting skills, 263
Government actions, 36
Group effectiveness, 193-194
Growth:
  company goal, 35-36
  necessary, 53
  patterns, 31

H

Habit, 18, 119-120, 120-121 (*see also* Behavior modification)
Hard work, 239
Hostile forces, 103

Human resources, 142, 218
Human values, 90

I

IBM, 31
Ideas:
  all levels in organization, 126
  creator, 30
  competition, 126
  democratic leadership, 135-137
  emphasis upon, 126
  foolish, 187
  learn to listen, 130-132
  participative management, 127-130 (*see also* Participative management)
  springing into action, 132-135
  values of society, 126
Image:
  corporate, 75
  what could be, 30
Improvement areas:
  bottlenecks, 69
  commitment by goal-setting, 73-74
  community, 74-75
  corporate image, 75
  costs, 68-69
  drifting in wrong direction, 70
  inputs and outputs, 72-73
  job done in same old way, 71
  Management by Objectives, 73
  outside conditions changed, 70-71
  strategic goals, 71-72
  taking too much time, 69-70
Improvers, 264
Inbred organization, 56
Incentives, 128, 148
Infallibility, feeling of, 202
Information, sift and screen, 261 (*see also* Secrets)
Initiative:
  attainable goals, 48
  based on experience, 48
  competition, 45
  conscious planning, 48
  definition, 39
  directed energy, 42
  domination by one person, 47
  each person responsible, 47

Index

Initiative *(cont'd.)*
  eye toward improvement, 41
  get things corrected, 43
  good of overall organization, 48
  good user of time, 43
  high tolerance for frustration, 43
  identifying people with, 45
  immediate action program, 43
  inner drive, 41
  in organization, 47
  instill desire to excel, 41, 46-47
  in subordinates, 46
  intelligent action, 41, 47-49
  job assignments, 45
  learn in tough situations, 45
  lowest level where decision can be made, 47
  manager coaches and guides, 45
  movement toward objective, 48
  old relationships, 43
  orderly plan, 48
  patience, 43
  pick important things, 41, 42-43
  pre-planned procedures, 48
  profit-mindedness, 43
  realistic goal, 48
  recognition for good work, 44
  restlessness, 41
  ruthlessness, 43
  "scale barrier," 41
  see results of performance, 45
  singleness of purpose, 44
  spot trend requiring action, 43
  systematic coaching, 45
  thick hide, 45
  tough-mindedness, 43
  tough problems to solve, 45
  variety of properties and skills, 39-40
  vigorous, positive approaches, 41
  "will-do" factors, 45
  willing to pay price, 45
Inner drive, 41-42
Innovation, 61-65, 188
Inputs, 72
Inspections:
  case for leader being seen, 256-257
  check out facts, 249
  detect cover-ups, 253-256
    advance information, 255-256
    compare, 254-255

Inspections *(cont'd.)*
  talk to people, 254
  discrepancies, 249
  don't generalize, 252-253
  don't undercut management, 251-252
  easily controllable things, 248-249
  enhance local management, 252
  ethics, 251-253
  find fault privately, 252
  let local people explain, 253
  people who know, 247-248
  showmanship, 250-251
  what lies beneath surface, 249
  what to look for, 247-249
Institutional values, 90-91
Integrity, 235-236
Intelligent action, 41, 47-49
Investment, new capital, 52-53

J

Job enlargement, 169
Job rotation, 113-114

K

Know-how, 213-214

L

Leadership:
  democratic, 135-137
  informal, 182-183
  integrity and secrecy, 235-236
Life in Crystal Palace, 57
Listening to others, 102-104, 130-132
Literature, 216
Living standards, 205
Location, trends, 214
Luck:
  concept, 211
  control, 213
  face-saving device, 211
  factor in success, 211
  helping your windfall, 219-221
  increase chances, 212
  keep abreast of latest trends, 213-215
  leadership, 221-222

Luck *(cont'd.)*
  persuasive argument for, 212
  plan for unexpected, 217-219
  predict hot items, 216-217

M

Management:
  dynamics, 58-61
  highest level, 29
  meetings, 216
  not passive, 28-36
  participative, 127-130
  strategic, 142
Management by Objectives, 73
Management cycle, 22-24
Managers:
  goal oriented, 31
  good, 28
  make things happen, 28
Manufacturing boss, 111
Markets, 55
Mastery, desire, 198-201
Measuring methods, 264
Meetings, 216
Memory, 80
Mental image, 30
Methods, new, 55, 71, 133
Missions, 72
Motives, conflicts, 83-84

O

Objective:
  more ambitious, 31
  point toward, 30
Obstacles:
  adjusting, 81-84
    conflicts of motives, 83-84
    direct attack, 81
    environment, 82-83
    substitute goals, 81-82
    trial and error, 82
  ends versus means, 88-91
  less satisfactory adjustments, 84-88
    compensation, 87
    defensiveness, 86-87
    egocentrism, 87

Obstacles *(cont'd.)*
    rationalization, 87-88
    withdrawal, 84-86
  qualities of busters, 78-80
    callousness to defeats, 78
    clear picture of reality, 80
    decisiveness, 78
    good memory skills, 80
    high energy levels, 79
    striving for perfection, 79-80
    strong goal orientation, 78
    using people well, 80
  values, 90-91
    ethical, 90
    human, 90
    institutional, 90-91
Opinion, sift and screen, 261
Opinion surveys, 203
Opposition, tolerance of, 202
Organization:
  areas for improvement, 72 (*see also* Improvement, areas)
  at rest, 53-54
  ideas at all levels, 126
  relate it to society, 264-265
Organization chart, committee, 191
Organization skills, 263-264
Ostracism, 181
Outmoded processes or products, 35
Outputs, 72
Overview, 262-263

P

Paperwork, 29
Participation, 123
Participative management:
  above-average abilities, 129
  better team players, 128-129
  growth in management, 129
  incentives, 128
  let off pressures, 129
  personal satisfaction, 128
Passive people, 56
Patience, 43, 238
Peers, 204
People, using well, 80
Perfection, striving, 79-80
Performance:
  judging, 157

Index

Performance *(cont'd.)*
  look good, 240
  rating, 159
  rewards, 55
Personal inspection, 245-257 (*see also* Inspections)
Personal staff:
  administrative assistant, 169-173
  clear decision-areas, 166-168
  close personal contact, 165
  hand-picked, 164-165
  informed, 165
  know what they're doing, 165
  secretary, 168
  they adapt to you, 165-166
  thing staff does, 166
Petulance, 238
Physical facilities, 184
Plans:
  for unexpected, 217-219
  human resources, 218
  orderly, 48
  start with, 22, 23
Policy committees, 190
Pressure, 48, 129
Priorities, 42-43
Problem-solving, 29
Problem-solving committees, 190
Procedure:
  activity becomes, 19
  pre-planned, 48
  tight, 194
Processes, outmoded, 35, 71
Product development, 141
Productivity per worker, 52
Product marketing, 55
Products:
  competitive, 214
  outmoded, 35
Profession, activity becomes, 19
Profit, obsessed with, 56
Psychological counseling, 114-115
Public opinion, 36
Punishments, 159

R

Rationalization, 87-88
Reality, clear picture, 80
Recognition, 44, 144-145
Reinforcement, 122
Reprimand, 272-278
Reputation, 201-204
Research, 53
Resistance to affirmative action, 21
Results, 28
Review, 22, 24, 59
Rewards, 55, 152, 159
Rigidity:
  civic and community activities, 114
  coaching and counseling, 114
  corrective action, 113-115
  cost accountant, 112-113
  courses and seminars, 114
  engineer, 111-112
  goals, 116
  job rotation, 113-114
  manufacturing boss, 111
  psychological counseling, 114-115
  salesman, 112
  staff type, 113
  surround them, 115
Rotation, job, 113-114
Routines, 17

S

Salesman, 112
Scale barrier, 41
Secretary, 168
Secrets:
  bad-news-for-you type, 232
  enjoined, 224-226
  give to get, 229-231
  hardest to keep, 231-232
  hurray-for-me type, 232
  I-told-you-so type, 232
  judicious handling, 226-229
  leadership, 235-236
  small talk, 232-234
  vs. good communication, 234-235
Secular stagnation, 54
Seminars, 114
Sensitivity training, 203
Sentimental attachments, 35, 80
Simplification, 259-265
Skills, 28, 198, 263-264
Small talk, 232-234
Society:
  relating organization to, 264

Society *(cont'd.)*
  values, 126
Specialists, 158-159
Staff:
  personal, 163-175 (*see also* Personal staff)
  rigid type, 113
Stagnation, identifying, 54-57
Standard makers, 264
Standards, high, 157
Stanford's studies, 31, 35, 54
Steps, break change into, 123
Strategic goals, 71-72
Subordinates:
  become coaches, 161-162
  boss-subordinate relations, 159-161
  how to use, 163-175 (*see also* Personal staff)
Substitute goals, 81-82

T

Talents, enlist, 30
Tastes, changes in, 214
Team:
  building, 122
  coaching, 156-161
    boss-subordinate relations, 159-161
    build flexibility, 158
    diverse specialists, 158-159
    high standards, 157
    judging performance, 157
    know each person, 156-157
    performance, not traits, 159
    rewards and punishments, 159
    show confidence, 157-158
    taking long view, 158
  picking and training players, 154-156
  subordinate managers, 161-162
  systematic coaching, 152-153
    condition group, 153
    deal one-on-one, 152
    make changes carefully, 153
    organizing work, 152
    physical environment, 152
    reward, 152
    show interest, 153
  train managers in building, 179

Team players, better, 128-129
Technology, 141
Temper, never lose, 238-239
Temper tantrums, 199, 200
Time, 43, 69-70, 174-175
Tools, 28
Topics, committees, 195
Tough-mindedness, 41, 43-46
Trade association meetings, 216
Tradition, activity trap, 19-20
Training, 154, 179, 186
Training committees, 190-191
Trends, 55, 72
Trial and error, 82

U

Unexpected, planning for, 217-219
University business schools, 216-217

V

Value systems, 90-91, 126, 239
Variables, 36-37
Veto power, 59
Viewpoint, breadth, 263-264
Vision, 30

W

Wealth, desire, 204-207
Withdrawal, 84-86
Worker, definition, 126
Winning:
  don't relax when, 241
  eye on main chance, 240
  hard work, 239
  is what counts, 239-241
  look conformist, 240
  look good in performance, 240
  strong alliances, 240
  think maverick, 240
  value systems, 239
Work habits (*see* Behavior modification)